Hinterland Remixed

Hinterland Remixed

Media, Memory, and the Canadian 1970s

Andrew Burke

McGill-Queen's University Press
Montreal & Kingston • London • Chicago

© McGill-Queen's University Press 2019

ISBN 978-0-7735-5858-8 (cloth)
ISBN 978-0-7735-5859-5 (paper)
ISBN 978-0-7735-5971-4 (ePDF)
ISBN 978-0-7735-5972-1 (ePUB)

Legal deposit third quarter 2019
Bibliothèque nationale du Québec

Printed in Canada on acid-free paper that is 100% ancient forest free (100% post-consumer recycled), processed chlorine free

This book has been published with the help of a grant from the Canadian Federation for the Humanities and Social Sciences, through the Awards to Scholarly Publications Program, using funds provided by the Social Sciences and Humanities Research Council of Canada.

Funded by the Government of Canada   Financé par le gouvernement du Canada   Canada Council for the Arts   Conseil des arts du Canada

We acknowledge the support of the Canada Council for the Arts.
Nous remercions le Conseil des arts du Canada de son soutien.

Library and Archives Canada Cataloguing in Publication
Title: Hinterland remixed : media, memory, and the Canadian 1970s / Andrew Burke.
Names: Burke, Andrew, 1972- author.
Description: Includes bibliographical references and index.
Identifiers: Canadiana (print) 20190145862 | Canadiana (ebook) 20190145986 | ISBN 9780773558595 (paper) | ISBN 9780773558588 (coth) | ISBN 9780773559714 (ePDF) | ISBN 9780773559721 (ePUB)
Subjects: LCSH: Popular culture—Canada. | LCSH: Arts—Canada. | LCSH: Collective memory—Canada.
Classification: LCC FC95.4 .B87 2019 | DDC 306.0971/09047—dc23

Contents

Figures *vii*
Acknowledgments *ix*

Introduction:
The Past Inside the Present *3*

1   Nation, Nature, and Nostalgia:
    Hinterland Who's Who *21*

2   "A record of the last wilderness on earth":
    La Région Centrale, Landscape, and
    the Long '70s *53*

3   "SCTV now begins its programming day":
    Television, Satire, and the Archive *85*

4   Memory, Magnetic Tape, and *Death by
    Popcorn* *115*

5   Remediating the Long '70s *146*

    Coda: Sorting through the Wreckage of the
    Twentieth Century *176*

Notes *187*
Bibliography *217*
Index *233*

Figures

1.1 "Herring Gull." Video still from *Hinterland Who's Who* (1966). *31*

1.2 Film still from Shawna Dempsey and Lorri Millan's *Lesbian National Parks and Services Presents: Endangered Species* (2009). Courtesy of Shawna Dempsey, Lorri Millan, and Videopool. *45*

2.1 Production still from Michael Snow's *La Région Centrale* (1971), 16mm film, 190 minutes, colour, sound. Photo by Joyce Wieland. Courtesy of Michael Snow. *57*

2.2 Film still from Michael Snow's *La Région Centrale* (1971), 16mm film, 190 minutes, colour, sound. Courtesy of Michael Snow. *73*

2.3 "The poor image." Parks Canada vignette for Kluane National Park and Reserve. *77*

3.1 Film still from Brett Bell's *Sign-Off* (2010). Courtesy of Brett Bell. *97*

3.2 Video still from SCTV's high school quiz show, *High Q* (1978). *101*

4.1 Film still from L'Atelier national du Manitoba's *Death by Popcorn: The Tragedy of the Winnipeg Jets* (2005). Courtesy of L'Atelier national du Manitoba and Winnipeg Film Group. *125*

4.2 Burton Cummings in film still from L'Atelier national du Manitoba's *Death by Popcorn: The Tragedy of the Winnipeg Jets* (2005). Courtesy of L'Atelier national du Manitoba and Winnipeg Film Group. *138*

4.3 "Winnipeg is losers." Film still from L'Atelier national du Manitoba's *Death by Popcorn: The Tragedy of the Winnipeg Jets* (2005). Courtesy of L'Atelier national du Manitoba and Winnipeg Film Group. *142*

4.4 Film still of Sylvain Séguin in L'Atelier national du Manitoba's *Death by Popcorn: The Tragedy of the Winnipeg Jets* (2005). Courtesy of L'Atelier national du Manitoba and Winnipeg Film Group. *144*

5.1 Installation view of Geronimo Inutiq's ARCTICNOISE (2015). Photo by Henri Robideau. Courtesy of grunt gallery, Vtape, and Igloolik Isuma Productions. *150*

5.2 Film still from Caroline Monnet's *Mobilize* (2015). *166*

C.1 Film still from Mike Rollo's *Farewell Transmission* (2017). Courtesy of Mike Rollo. *180*

C.2 Film still from Amanda Dawn Christie's *Spectres of Shortwave* (2017). Courtesy of Amanda Dawn Christie. *183*

Acknowledgments

Hinterland Remixed came together over a number of years and benefited enormously from the encouragement and support of friends, family, and colleagues. Although the project is quite clearly a product of my own passions and preoccupations, my energies have been sustained every step along the way by those who have both inspired and indulged them. My thanks go to all those who helped me to believe that this project was worth pursuing and that its questions were worth investigating.

I am fortunate to have had the institutional support of the University of Winnipeg during the writing of *Hinterland Remixed*. Financial support from the Research Office kick-started the project and then allowed me to present early versions of several chapters at conferences as the project developed. Furthermore, the University of Winnipeg has offered a rich and vibrant atmosphere for my research, and my colleagues in the Department of English deserve thanks for their support of *Hinterland Remixed* as it developed from a disparate set of ideas to a full-fledged research focus. Special thanks to Catherine Hunter, the late Alden Turner, and Brandon Christopher, all of whom, during their time as department chair, were unwavering in their support of my research, no matter the twists and turns it took.

Over the years, I had the opportunity to discuss aspects of *Hinterland Remixed* with colleagues near and far. I am grateful for their comments and suggestions, as well as their more general collegiality, friendship, and support: Janine Marchessault, Will Straw, Jennifer VanderBurgh, Marcie Frank, Ian Balfour, Zoë Druick, Liz Czach, Mike Baker, Darrell Varga, Aimée Mitchell, Brenda Austin-Smith, George Toles, Karen Lury, Amy Holdsworth, and Malini Guha. I am also lucky to have friends who have shared ideas, memories, and insights with me over the years that have helped me to think through the material I discuss in *Hinterland Remixed*: Christine Kim, Yusuf Varachia, James Hanley, Naomi Hamer, Zbigniew Izydorczyk, Jo-Anne Balcaen, Todd Munro, Karim Vickery, Michael Davidge, Jane MacPherson, Jef Ekins, Doug Bond, Rodrigo Beilfuss, Chandravani Sathiyamurthi, Cheryl Cowdy, Elicia Clements, Robert Stacey, Lukas Neville, Indra Kalinovich, Elise Watchorn, Justin Lee, Vanja Polić, Tomislav Jurkovic, Alan Filewod, Linda Warley, Karis Shearer, Erin Moure, Nelson Chan, Russ Cochrane, Daegan Fryklind, and David Cuthbert.

One of the best parts of writing *Hinterland Remixed* has been meeting and even getting to know some of the artists and filmmakers whose work I admire greatly: Matthew Rankin, Walter Forsberg, Mike Maryniuk, Michael Snow, Amanda Dawn Christie, Brett Bell, Mike Rollo, Shawna Dempsey, Lorri Millan, Tim Dallett, and Adam Kelly. Their generosity in supplying images and answering queries has been extraordinary. Monica Lowe of the Winnipeg Film Group has been an absolute star, helping me with image permissions and putting me in contact with artists and filmmakers. Immense thanks go as well to Dave Barber, the senior programmer at the Winnipeg Film Group's Cinematheque, whose work in bringing independent and experimental cinema to the city is legendary. Seeing the films I discuss in *Hinterland Remixed* at the Cinematheque alongside enthusiastic and engaged audiences has been absolutely essential to the project.

As a book examining residual media of the 1970s, *Hinterland Remixed* relies heavily on the work of librarians and archivists. I am lucky that the University of Winnipeg Library has a strong collection of material related to the subject and that I have colleagues in the library who took an interest in the project. My thanks go to dean of the library Gabrielle Prefontaine, university archivist and digital curator Brett Lougheed, and scholarly communications and copyright librarian Brianne Selman. I also thank archives manager Dan Pon of grunt gallery and the archivists at the National Film Board of Canada.

I presented portions of *Hinterland Remixed* at various conferences hosted by the Film Studies Association of Canada, the Society for Cinema and Media Studies, the Modern Languages Association, and the journal *Screen*. I thank the organizers, my fellow panelists, and the audiences at these conferences for their questions and comments about the work. I also had opportunities to deliver more substantial excerpts from the project as keynotes, invited talks, or panel presentations. Special thanks to those who extended these invitations: Brett Lougheed of the University of Winnipeg Archives, Greg Bak of the Archival Studies program at the University of Manitoba, Katelyn Dykstra of the University of Manitoba's Graduate Student Association of English, Film, and Theatre Students, and Vanja Polić of the Croatian-Canadian Academic Society.

An earlier version of chapter 4 was published in Zoë Druick and Gerda Cammaer's edited collection *Cinephemera: Archives, Ephemeral Cinema, and New Screen Histories in Canada* (Montreal and Kingston: McGill-Queen's University Press, 2014).

Working with McGill-Queen's University Press has been a terrific experience. I am immensely grateful to Jonathan Crago, whose sharp editorial eye could see a complete book in what I had written when I could see only a number of individual chapters all pulling in slightly different directions. His intelligence, patience, and good humour made it possible for me to find the ideal shape and form for *Hinterland Remixed*. Thanks as well to Kathleen Fraser and Finn Purcell at the press for their work in seeing *Hinterland Remixed* into print. I thank the two anonymous reviewers of the manuscript for their generous and insightful comments. I am also grateful to Robert Lewis, whose work in copy editing the final manuscript brought a new level of clarity to its argument.

My own memories of the 1970s are tied to my childhood, especially the experience of going to films and watching television with my family. I am indebted to my mother, Sandra Burke, and my late father, Allan Burke, for allowing me to watch my fair share of television when growing up and grateful to my sister, Teresa Huskilson, for watching alongside me. My mother-in-law, Adrienne Rifkind, is a fellow cinephile with a deep knowledge of film and television history, and I am thankful for her interest in my work and ongoing encouragement.

Finally, my deepest gratitude goes to Candida Rifkind, without whose love, support, and encouragement I would never have been able to embark on a project like *Hinterland Remixed*, let alone complete it. Her intelligence came to my aid when I needed to work through complex ideas, and her empathy was imperative in those moments when my confidence in the project wavered. Alongside our cats, Coco and Yuki, she has been there from start to finish, making this work possible and worthwhile.

**Hinterland
Remixed**

Introduction: The Past Inside the Present

As the 1970s recede further into the past, it may feel as though we have left the decade behind. *Hinterland Remixed* proposes that the opposite is true: the remainders and residues of the 1970s are all around us and exert a subtle yet substantial influence on the present, shaping how and what we think of the world today. In Canada the 1970s are in many ways a decade lost to cultural history, with the events of 1967 – Canada's Centennial and Montreal's hosting of Expo 67 – neatly serving as the gravitational centre for any account of modern Canada. There is no disputing that these state-fuelled spectacles of modernity, these performative displays of Canada's maturity and independence designed for both domestic and international audiences, are landmark moments in the formation and consolidation of Canadian culture and identity. Nevertheless, *Hinterland Remixed* resists this focus on 1967, and on the 1960s more generally, as the precise moment when nation and culture coalesced into a coherent contemporary form. It turns instead to the 1970s – and even proposes a long '70s that swallows and subsumes bits of the decades that lay on either side – in order to argue that this decade, with all its extended, messy weirdness, in many ways better captures the contradictions and complexities of contemporary Canadian life.

The focus of *Hinterland Remixed* is the conjunction of memory and media. What remains of the 1970s today are its traces, transported into the present via obsolete media formats: 16-millimetre film, video, and analog photography. The work of interpretation is therefore the work of extrapolation – the effort to project from the bits and pieces that have survived and still circulate a larger sense of what the decade was like, what it was about, and how it might be remembered. The guiding principle of this book is that a fuller sense of any national cultural formation can be gleaned from experiments rather than exemplars. As a consequence, *Hinterland Remixed* most often opts for the incidental rather than the monumental, the idiosyncratic rather than the blandly representative. Although there is no doubt that Michael Snow's *La Région Centrale* (1971) and SCTV (1976–84) – the subjects of chapters 2 and 3 of this study respectively – are crucially important works in their respective domains of experimental film and popular television, this centrality, or even canonicity, is not what is of interest here. *Hinterland Remixed* looks at these works awry, less concerned with their exceptionality than with their embeddedness – the ways that their unexpected connections to a wide array of other cultural forms and phenomena of the period make them ideal objects for an investigation into both the decade itself and its ongoing influence and impact. In so doing, this study follows the example of Walter Benjamin. It picks among the remainders of an earlier era to find those fragments whose sparks illuminate both past and present.[1] It returns to the products of the period to remember and reassemble what Raymond Williams would call its "structure of feeling," but *Hinterland Remixed* also looks at works by contemporary artists who remediate older material in the effort to both remember and re-examine the decade.[2] At the heart of this study is the understanding that the landscape of the 1970s – actual, cultural, cinematic, and televisual – is now perceptible only through its traces. Yet I also recognize that the contemporary landscape is nothing more than the accumulated traces of past ones. The "present" names, for each sequential fleeting instance, the configuration of residues that surround us.

As much as the aims and ambitions of *Hinterland Remixed* reside in my desire to revisit an overshadowed decade in order to reveal its impact and importance, I must confess that the initial catalyst for this project was simply a fascination with the look and feel of the work from the period. The grain of film images and the texture of video footage, whatever the digital capacity to replicate these things, are signs of their pastness, indexically linking them to the era of their production. The same can be said of audio, which conveys through its tone, colour, and texture all kinds of information about place and period beyond its ostensible content. As I argue throughout, even though the substance of sound and images might speak to specific historical circumstances and ground them in their age, it is evident that their grain, tone, and texture likewise evoke their period, metonymically binding them to their moment. Admittedly, there is also clearly an affective dimension to this link between the feel of an image and the feeling it catalyzes, especially when the period in question is recent enough to be the stuff of personal memory. But rather than disavowing the biographical and fetishistic aspect of all this, I embrace and complicate it. The image's surface quality, its particular tone and saturation, and the signs of its decay and deterioration combine to lend it a curious force and power. Film and video transport content from the past to the present, but their form constitutes a kind of content as well, condensing into the grain and texture of the image and soundtrack the larger infrastructure of media systems and modes of cultural production that structure and define their period. Furthermore, the signs of that passage through time – the damage and wear – tell a story as well, whether about its careful preservation or about it miraculous survival. My attention throughout *Hinterland Remixed* to the textural, almost tactile, dimension of the image and soundtrack is, at once, an affective response to the markers of period and an analytical strategy grounded in the belief that the quality and condition of the image and the soundtrack can be as compelling as their content.

Throughout the process of writing this book, there was one particular phrase that echoed in my head: "the past inside the present." The phrase, drawn from a track by the Scottish electronic music duo Boards of Canada, speaks to the affective charge that animates the relationship between analogue media and cultural memory. The members of Boards of Canada, brothers Michael Sandison and Marcus Eoin, spent part of their childhood in Calgary. During their time in Canada, they were, as most Canadian kids of the period would have been, exposed to the synthesizer-rich, and often boldly experimental, soundtracks of National Film Board (NFB) productions of the 1970s and early 1980s. In their work, most notably on their debut full-length album, *Music Has the Right to Children* (1998), Boards of Canada drew extensively on their memories of classroom screenings and television broadcasts of NFB films, crafting a sound-world that is both soothing and sinister. The band's signature decelerated mid-tempo beats and use of warm, analogue electronics combine with samples sourced from educational films and children's programming to produce an altogether unsettling listening experience. The music simultaneously evokes the lost plenitude of a 1970s childhood and the sense that something altogether more menacing lurks behind it.

On their follow-up album, *Geogaddi* (2002), Boards of Canada pushed further into the ways that the present is haunted by the unresolved tensions of the past and the unactualized ambitions it harboured. The album opens with the ambient drones of "Ready Let's Go," which are punctuated by a sluggish series of tones vaguely reminiscent of a 1970s-era television station identification. But the actual content of the track seems less important than its sonic texture: it sounds as though it is being played on a malfunctioning, or perhaps just poorly manufactured, domestic cassette player of the sort that was everywhere in the late 1970s and early 1980s. The sound is dampened and compressed, and it feels like the tape is running just a bit too slowly, causing shifts in pitch and a slight unevenness of tempo. The power of "Ready Let's Go" is that it calls attention to the ways that sound and memory are mediated. It foregrounds the presence of the playback medium – as Adam Harper puts it, "We're listening to the listening device" – and reminds listeners that technology makes their experience possible at the same time that it stands between them and the music itself.[3] Furthermore, it also evokes a whole scene of listening: the wow and flutter of the tape elicit memories of the analogue era, and the poor audio quality is suggestive of the tape-to-tape copying that flourished in the era before digital. The track clocks in at just under a minute, yet it manages to establish a whole set of connections between media, memory, and modern life.

If "Ready Let's Go" serves as the album's prologue, the subsequent track, "Music Is Math," fully establishes its themes and temper. The title itself feels as though it could be that of a 1970s school textbook, reflective of a pedagogy grounded in the certainties of science and a commitment to rationality, even when it comes to the teaching of the creative arts. The warm drones of "Ready Let's Go" are replaced with steadier tones, the melody unfolding slowly over the course of its opening thirty seconds. The minimal beat kicks in abruptly once the full melody has been introduced. It is more a metronomic pulse than anything else. And just before the 60-second mark, a sampled voice – slightly slowed-down, drawing out each syllable, and unidentifiable as either male or female – says, "The past inside the present." The precise tone of the voice and the manner of the message's delivery make it feel simultaneously peculiar and profound. After a brief moment of stasis, when the song's basic elements hang in the air, a big beat kicks in, and the track takes shape as one of the band's signature tunes, a kind of haunted analogue reverie. The sample itself is repeated a handful of times throughout the remainder of the track, yet these echoes never fully replicate the force and impact of its initial appearance.

The phrase itself is suggestive of haunting – the ways that the past unsettles the present, nestled inside it in a manner that is not always noticed but nevertheless frequently felt and experienced. In the years following *Geogaddi*'s release, critics kept returning to this track, drawn in by its spectral power or even occult force. In an effort to account for its uncanny resonances and linking it to a whole series of other sonic spectral transmissions that appeared in the following years, critics such as Mark Fisher and Simon Reynolds appealed to Jacques Derrida's notion of "hauntology." Derrida coined the term in *Specters of Marx* (1994) in an effort to account for how, even in the wake of the collapse of the Soviet Union, there remained a way that the present remained unsettled. For Derrida, the ghost of Karl Marx continued to haunt Europe (and the rest of the world as well) in the sense of being both absent and present. Even though it appeared that events had consigned his ideas to the dustbin of history, the desire represented by Marx persisted despite his apparent demise.[4] In musical terms, hauntology manifested itself in a return to the analogue technology of an earlier period, namely the modular synthesizers and other electronics that, in the 1970s and early 1980s, metonymically represented the boundless possibilities of the future. However, in addition to these possibilities, the movement seemed to be equally about memory – not simply about reminiscences of a 1970s childhood but also about memories of a future that was promised yet never came to pass.⁵

Hinterland Remixed picks up on this feeling of lost possibilities, looking both at works from the Canadian 1970s that archive them and at contemporary pieces, performances, and projects that dig into that archive to rediscover, remediate, and remix them. At this point, it seems essential to establish that this type of remembering amounts to more than mere nostalgia, as well as to distinguish soft forms of reminiscence from harder kinds of historical reckoning. Svetlana Boym's distinction between restorative nostalgia, the kind that wants to return to or recreate the past based on conservative desires to restore and maintain a lost past, and reflective nostalgia, the kind that fully understands that the past is past and was not perfect yet nevertheless takes pleasure in the act of memory, is crucial to understanding that nostalgia is not, simply because of the presence of emotion itself, corrupt or contaminated.⁶ *Hinterland Remixed* takes up questions of the affective force of memory, addressing the unexpectedly intense attachments that many people have to something like the *Hinterland Who's Who* (1963–78) series of public service announcements. These affective energies need not be understood as dissipative or enervating but, as Boym suggests, can be seen as ripe for sublimation into activity that cannot be reduced to simple conservative resentment.

Although it is one thing to establish that some forms of sentimental recollection of the past are not necessarily wholly compromised or complicit, it is important to make an even bolder case, one that does not concede memory and nostalgia to the right but instead stakes out a left nostalgia, or at least a politically progressive one. To do so is to understand memory as a resource that should not be given up or given away. As Fisher notes, "the 1970s were in many respects better than neoliberalism wants us to remember them," and the vilification of the decade needs to be both questioned and contested.⁷ There are clearly hazards to this approach, all of which are detailed by Walter Benjamin in "Left-Wing Melancholy" (1931) and reiterated by Wendy Brown nearly seventy years later in "Resisting Left Melancholy" (1999). *Hinterland Remixed* heeds these warnings yet takes solace from Benjamin's own method and practice, which, to steal a phrase from his essay on surrealism, is finely attuned to "the revolutionary energies that appear in the 'outmoded.'"[8] As Fredric Jameson explains, whatever the warnings of "Left-Wing Melancholy," Benjamin's attention to the residues of the past and his clear affection for the minor, incidental, superannuated, and deteriorated set out a mode and method of remembering that are at once deeply personal and provocatively political: "But if nostalgia as a political motivation is most frequently associated with Fascism, there is no reason why a nostalgia conscious of itself, a lucid and remorseless dissatisfaction with the present on the grounds of some remembered plenitude, cannot furnish as adequate a revolutionary stimulus as any other: the example of Benjamin is there to prove it."[9] *Hinterland Remixed* aspires to this lucidity and remorselessness throughout but does so in the recognition that the "remembered plenitude" of the past is always partial and problematic.

The past, to put it bluntly, was never perfect but defined by all kinds of inequities that haunt and cloud the remembered pleasures and possibilities that were only ever on offer for some. That is true everywhere, but in Canada it is especially important to recognize that many of the ambitions and desires of the past were contaminated in the first place, imagined as being the right and preserve of a select few rather than as belonging to the whole. For Indigenous people, racial minorities, the LGBTQ2 community, and other people and groups who faced exclusion and discrimination during the period, the past may not seem like the place to find the resources needed to reanimate the revolutionary energies that could radically transform the present. My study here fully registers this fact and recognizes that the past is more vexed and complicated for some than others. It seems important to establish from the outset that the return to the 1970s in *Hinterland Remixed* is not in any way an invitation to an uncritical celebration of the decade. I aim at quite the opposite: to show how the decade was deeply divided and contradictory, harbouring desires and ambitions for progress at the very same time that it held tight to fundamental exclusions and injustices. As Benjamin establishes absolutely, when it comes to cultural memory and its various returns to and remediations of the past, "There is no document of culture which is not at the same time a document of barbarism."[10]

Having already confessed to fetishism and nostalgia, albeit with certain caveats and qualifications, I acknowledge that *Hinterland Remixed* plays a little fast and loose with periodization as well. The focus of the study is the 1970s in Canada, but it understands the decade not as something that was neat and tidy, beginning promptly on 1 January 1970 and ending as the clock struck midnight on 31 December 1979. Instead, it understands "the 1970s," both in Canada specifically but elsewhere as well, to be something that slowly emerged over the course of the decade that preceded it and that only gradually disappeared in the decades that followed. Rather than a rigid historical approach that would restrict discussion to events that clearly happened in the decade, I adopt a method that starts with the assumption that "the 1970s" names a period and an attendant "structure of feeling" (to borrow Raymond Williams's concept once again) that commenced long before the decade actually began and persisted long after it officially ended.[11] This is, of course, a matter of framing. Nothing like "the 1970s" actually existed out there in nature or the world. It is a product of discourse, part of the necessary parcelization of the past that makes it possible to talk about cultural history, or history itself, at all. Likewise, Williams's evocative phrase "structure of feeling" offers a means to understand period and history by way of a moment's affective and sensorial integrity. As Ben Highmore argues, the usefulness of Williams's concept resides in both its flexibility and its suggestiveness – the ways that it opens up an understanding of history to all those everyday feelings and sensations that are usually left out of more formal, conventional studies of the past. For Highmore, "structure of feeling" gives "us access to the way feelings and tastes are an activity of 'worlding' that renders life as *this* life, and renders time as *this* time and not another."[12] Williams argues that "structure of feeling" offers something more capacious than either "world-view" or "ideology" in the way that it opens up to an understanding of the past "concerned with meanings and values as they are actually lived and felt."[13] Art plays a crucial role in preserving the structure of feeling of any specific historical moment and making it, or at least a partial sense of it, accessible once that moment has passed and everyday lived experience has been reshaped and transformed.[14] Although Williams points to the ways that Charles Dickens or Emily Brontë preserve the structure of feeling of the 1840s as his privileged example of this process, *Hinterland Remixed* works on the assumption that the audiovisual residues of the 1970s function in a similar way, preserving the decade's structure of feeling and making it accessible in some measure to those decades that have followed.[15]

Thinking in this flexible way about period, which understands that it is a proposition rather than a perception, opens up the possibility of tracking the flow and movement of cultural history. *Hinterland Remixed* asks how our understanding of the recent past would be different if it focused not on the glow of 1967 but on the afterglow of that momentous year: the fraught decade that followed. It also recognizes that the energies and anxieties that distinguished the decade – from the oil crisis and inflation to unemployment and acid rain – appeared and receded within an extended temporal frame. Of my first three chapters, two wrestle with television series that seem to emblematically represent the decade and distill something of its essence yet barely overlap: *Hinterland Who's Who* (1963–78) and SCTV (1976–84). The subject of my second chapter, Michael Snow's *La Région Centrale* (1971), offers a precise production date, which seems indisputably to confirm its status as a product of the 1970s, yet the film is best understood as a work that emerged from a 1960s milieu and is in dialogue with all kinds of experimental practices and popular forms produced in the decades that followed. The same temporal flexibility characterizes the final two chapters of the book, which focus on contemporary remediations of 1970s material. Geronimo Inutiq's multichannel work ARCTICNOISE (2015) wrestles with the legacy of Glenn Gould's radio documentary *The Idea of North* (1967), which forms part of the larger *Solitude Trilogy* (1967–77). L'Atelier national du Manitoba's collage film *Death by Popcorn: The Tragedy of the Winnipeg Jets* (2005) rummages through the audiovisual legacy of the city's beloved hockey team, from their formation in 1972 through to their departure from the city in 1996. I am not suggesting that the Canadian 1970s secretly lasted from 1963 to 1996, but I am proposing that a more elastic understanding of the period is key to understanding the ways that a decade emerges, unfolds, and persists. This more supple conception of the decade introduces the possibility of a long '70s in Canada, one that takes Centennial enthusiasms as a starting point and tracks what happened when the modern

Canada imagined in that exercise confronted the quotidian conditions and concerns of the period that followed, from fears of ecological catastrophe to worries about geopolitical antagonisms. If the Centennial marks a possible beginning for the long '70s, it had surely come to a close by the early 1980s, when the advent of neoliberalism and the political shift rightward, both in Canada and elsewhere, foreclosed on the final phase of the "social democratic consensus," to borrow a phrase from the British context, that defined the postwar period. Surely, by the summer of 1984, which saw both the cancellation of SCTV and the election of Prime Minister Brian Mulroney, it was all over. A new, and clearly different, set of social, cultural, political, and ideological conditions had established their dominance.

Throughout *Hinterland Remixed*, I make a series of connections between what might seem like fairly disparate cultural phenomena, whether it is thinking of Michael Snow's cinematic experiments alongside low-budget Canadian wilderness horror films or linking the *Hinterland Who's Who* theme to a classic Montreal disco track. Although at times this might seem like a kind of wilful eclecticism, I argue that such associations allow for a fuller understanding of culture as a heterogenous formation capable of generating vastly different kinds of reactions and responses to the world that are nevertheless bound together by the fact that they share a cultural moment. In "Periodizing the 60s" (1984), Jameson argues that his identification of the 1960s as a coherent object of study does not impose a uniformity or sameness on the people, products, or philosophies that fall within that frame: "the 'period' in question is understood not as some omnipresent and uniform shared style or way of thinking and acting, but rather as the sharing of an objective situation, to which a wide range of varied responses and creative innovations is then possible, but always within that situation's structural limits."[16] That, of course, is true of the 1970s as well, and my account here registers this heterogeneity at the same time as it bundles cultural objects together in an effort to see how they connect despite their differences in form, function, milieu, and media. Period is produced rather than simply perceived, and the 1970s that *Hinterland Remixed* proposes is one where the political complexities, anxieties, and uncertainties of the decade find expression in a multitude of ways that nevertheless can be read together.

Just as period represents an artificial frame imposed in the effort to make sense of the heterogeneous elements that fall within it, so too does nation. As much as I think considering *La Région Centrale* in a specifically Canadian context allows us to see the ways that it is embedded in a national cultural field and engaged with other works from the Canadian 1970s, this reading does not pre-empt other possibilities, including, for example, how it was clearly in dialogue with structuralist film experiments happening worldwide in the late 1960s and early 1970s. Furthermore, Canada itself is a heterogeneous thing. Needless to say, any attempt to grapple with the meaning and significance of the Canadian 1970s needs to begin with the recognition that it was not experienced and is not remembered in the same way by everyone everywhere. That is perhaps most obviously true of Quebec, where the events and circumstances that shaped the decade on a provincial level surely affect the content and the charge of cultural memory. And even though they are not my focus here, films such as Jean-Marc Vallée's *C.R.A.Z.Y.* (2005), the story of a queer kid obsessed with David Bowie that is set in 1970s suburban Montreal, and Luc Bourdon's *La part du diable* (2017), an archive film that assembles a portrait of the province from the Quiet Revolution to the 1980 independence referendum, suggest that Quebec, in its own specific way, remains unsettled by the 1970s and continues to sort through the decade's residues to figure out exactly what went on and how it might be remembered. So, although the extraordinariness of the decade in Quebec definitely invites a more specific study that zeros in on cultural memory and the Québécois 1970s, I think it is important to recognize that other provinces, even other communities, also demand this kind of closer analysis. As I have already stressed, how the decade was experienced and is remembered by Indigenous people merits much closer consideration, as does how the cultural memory of the decade has taken shape for those who arrived from Asia, Africa, or the West Indies before it began, while it was unfolding, or after it finished. Throughout *Hinterland Remixed*, I wrestle with how cultural memory itself can function as a means of dominance and exclusion, perpetuating racism and continuing the inequities and brutalities of settler colonialism. But I also examine the ways that memory is contested political terrain and how Indigenous artists, curators, and filmmakers especially have rightly refused to concede the terrain of the past to the dictates of dominant memory and have engaged in memory work as a political practice.

Hinterland Remixed is roughly designed as a book with two halves, the first focused on material from the 1970s and the second on material that remediates the 1970s. But, like the decade itself, it is a lot messier and more complicated than that. The opening three chapters survey the landscape – actual, cultural, cinematic, and televisual – of the 1970s, whereas the final two chapters and a brief coda concentrate on the contemporary remediation of the decade's remainders and residues. Yet, in practice, as much as this description might serve as a solid thumbnail of the book's arc and logic, the fact is that landscapes and residues mix, with each chapter ranging backward and forward in time to register the ways that the landscape of the 1970s is now perceptible only through its residues and the ways that the residues now form part of today's landscape. So, rather than imposing an artificial divide, *Hinterland Remixed* adopts a flexible approach that pursues ideas, associations, and connections across both time and space.

The opening chapter revisits the *Hinterland Who's Who* series of public service announcements that aired regularly on Canadian television from the mid-1960s until the late 1980s. Commissioned by the Canadian Wildlife Service and made by the NFB, this series of minute-long informational films about quintessentially Canadian animals – the earliest set from 1963 includes the beaver, moose, and loon – is perhaps the best example of the kind of public service filmmaking that flourished during this period. Practical in aim, pedagogical in ambition, and a bit soporific in execution, the *Hinterland* series was the product of a liberal democratic state and corresponding broadcast ecosystem that now seem resolutely part of the past. The chapter takes up how strange these clips seem today and uses this impression to consider whether cultural memory may serve as a bulwark against neoliberalism and the erosion of both film and television as public service terrains. But what is also remarkable about the *Hinterland* shorts is how fondly remembered they tend to be and how entrenched in collective national memory they are. This affection for them means that they have become the subject of both loving tribute and artistic reinvention. *Hinterland* homages, whether on television, in the gallery, or made by ordinary people and uploaded to YouTube, consolidate their place in the Canadian cultural imaginary.

Even though they were made to promote conservation, the *Hinterland Who's Who* films are strangely elegiac in tone, capturing the decade's anxieties about ecological catastrophe. They convey a sense of living, to reference the title of a 1970 Neil Young song, "after the gold rush," in an age when mother nature is in peril and emergency plans for an extraplanetary escape have already been implemented. I dive deeper into the decade's fears of environmental collapse in my second chapter, on Michael Snow's experimental landscape film *La Région Centrale*. Filmed in September 1970 with a camera mounted on a gyroscopic device planted in barren tundra just over a hundred kilometres north of Sept-Isles, Quebec, Snow's film provides a 180-minute, 360-degree view of this northern terrain. *La Région Centrale* is rightly identified as a landmark landscape film, with critics most often zeroing in on its formal rigour and conceptual inventiveness. Although I do not dispute these things, I turn instead to the way the film, whatever Snow's formalist, structuralist intentions, resonates with other aspects of 1970s culture. The film's vision of an abandoned or evacuated earth connects it to what is perhaps the dominant strain of 1970s sci-fi: the catastrophe film. Furthermore, *La Région Centrale*'s foray into the wilderness puts it in unexpected dialogue with the Canadian-made hinterland horror films of the decade. I propose these pop cultural connections not to shock or scandalize but to investigate the ways that terrain was top of mind in the Canadian 1970s and surely connected not only to ongoing fears of a polluted or poisoned earth but also to the history of settler colonialism and the clearing of the land of its Indigenous population to make way for the formation of the nation itself. Filmed in the wake of the moon landing, Snow's film evokes a kind of wonder about the new ways of seeing and the desire to stretch human perceptual capacity to its very limits, yet it also communicates real anxieties about the end of all things, with, as Snow himself put it, *La Région Centrale* serving as "a record of the last wilderness on earth."[17]

Chapter 3 turns from Snow's subarctic cinematic landscape to SCTV's televisual one. *La Région Centrale* is very much a film about the experience of watching, and the same is true, albeit in a slightly different way, of SCTV. In this chapter I argue that, in the absence of a comprehensive and truly accessible archive of the history of Canadian television, SCTV provides an invaluable snapshot of what television was like in the 1970s. The show's central conceit, that SCTV is a network that provides a full range of programming from the six o'clock news to high school quiz competitions to late night talk shows, means that its parodies have also served as a means of preservation. What SCTV archives is not simply the types of programs that populated 1970s television but also the experience of watching, with its flow punctuated by commercials, station identifications, public service announcements, promos for upcoming programs, and so on. These "paratelevisual" elements, as I term them, are rarely the subject of academic study but are a crucial part of television history, and SCTV provides an impetus to think more about their function and form. Furthermore, since the show was filmed in Toronto and Edmonton, and often on location, it captured the urban and suburban landscape of 1970s Canada in ways that make them feel as strange and unsettling as Snow's subarctic terrain. Media and memory converge in SCTV, and from the vantage point of the present, the show now serves as an archive of forms, a history of flow, and a record of landscape.

Shifting focus from preservation to salvage, my fourth chapter examines L'Atelier national du Manitoba's found-footage franchise autopsy *Death by Popcorn: The Tragedy of the Winnipeg Jets* (2005). Consisting in large part of video footage gleaned from tapes tossed in a dumpster outside the city's local CTV affiliate, *Death by Popcorn* reveals the connections between format and memory, showing how, in Winnipeg, hockey misery and civic self-laceration have been captured and conveyed in the low-resolution of the salvaged video image. Zeroing in on the distress caused the Jets' departure from the city in 1996, *Death by Popcorn* connects cultural memory and civic identity, trawling through the abandoned cassettes in an effort to understand the links between tapes and trauma. The chapter draws on recent work on the history of the videocassette to show how the poorness of the video image communicates Winnipeg's hurt and longing far more than any high-definition one could. I argue that *Death by Popcorn* is a film specifically about video-era Winnipeg, a periodization that recognizes the ways that format mediates memory and one that acknowledges the affective dimension of the audiovisual.

My final full-length chapter turns to work by contemporary Indigenous artists, curators, and filmmakers that remixes and remediates material from the Canadian 1970s. At the heart of the chapter is an analysis of Geronimo Inutiq's ARCTICNOISE (2015), a multichannel, audiovisual gallery installation that draws on and reworks Glenn Gould's radio documentary *The Idea of North* (1967). An Inuk DJ and artist, Inutiq challenges Gould's limited vision of the North, a place to which the famed pianist had never travelled, and exposes his ideas about it as the stuff of southern Canadian, settler colonial fantasy. The force of ARCTICNOISE derives from Inutiq's technical prowess. ARCTICNOISE is not a simple or straightforward repudiation of Gould's imagined North but takes shape instead as a complex meditation on the importance of voice and the power of remix to intervene in and transform the audiovisual archive of a people and a place. I argue that Inutiq is not alone in this desire to work with archival materials in the effort to transform understandings of the past and to project possible futures. Caroline Monnet's *Mobilize* (2015) draws on the NFB archives to create an exhilarating and dynamic portrait of Indigenous life in 1960s and 1970s Canada. Monnet's desire to make a film that, as she puts it, shows "Indigenous people kicking ass on-screen" points to the ways that – among the blatant misrepresentations that populate the archive, namely the abundance of images by predominantly white filmmakers that sentimentalize, demonize, or eulogize Indigenous life – there exist other images that can be extracted and remediated to present a very different portrait.[18]

Monnet's use of images from 1970s NFB films such as *Cesar's Bark Canoe* (1971) and *Cree Hunters of Mistassini* (1974) exploits the rich tones and vibrant colours of the era's film stock to craft a vision of Indigeneity that bridges tradition and modernity, wilderness and city. In its selective remediation of archival material, Paul Seesequasis's *Indigenous Archival Photo Project* shares with Monnet's film a desire to revisit and recirculate images that are evidence of Indigenous strength, power, community, and ingenuity. Drawing on the holdings of Library and Archives Canada as well as provincial archives and museum and university collections elsewhere, Seesequasis's project began online in 2015 and exemplifies the way that social media can be used as a catalyst for, and keeper of, cultural memory. Seesequasis's posts, whether on Twitter, Facebook, or Instagram, frequently result in the identification of those pictured and in reminiscences about specific people, places, and events. I argue that the participatory dimension of Seesequasis's project points to the way that the recirculation of archival images not only transforms understandings of the past but also nourishes the present in the way that it establishes the continuity of Indigenous struggle. Even though the *Indigenous Archival Photo Project* includes images stretching from the 1920s to the 1980s, I zero in on selected photos from the 1970s to show specifically how the remediation of images from this period, defined by the emergence of Red Power and a politicized militancy, puts them in explicit dialogue with the struggles of today, from the Standing Rock tribe's protest of the Dakota Access Pipeline to the popular opposition to the Kinder Morgan Pipeline, which stretches from Edmonton to the coast of British Columbia.

Having examined a whole series of residues, remainders, remixes, and remediations of the Canadian 1970s over its five chapters, *Hinterland Remixed* concludes with a brief coda that surveys the infrastructural ruins and technological wreckage of the decade. Now that the twentieth century is over and the transition from analogue to digital technologies is nearly complete, the question arises of what should happen to the broadcast and exhibition infrastructure, as well as the production equipment, that made such a world possible. A trio of recent artists takes up this question, focusing on the disappearance of the twentieth century – the decommissioning and demolition of the systems, nodes, and networks that, even though they may have dated to an earlier era, were nevertheless central to the production and transmission of the decade. Mike Rollo's *The Broken Altar* (2013) visits the abandoned and decaying drive-ins of the Prairies in an elegy to the culture of open-air cinema projection and the films that sustained it. His more recent *Farewell Transmission* (2017) documents the demolition of Regina's CBK-TV transmitter station, located in Watrous, Saskatchewan. Built in 1939, the station was operational throughout the 1970s. Rollo's images distort and distend, evoking a spectral presence, the ghosts of past transmissions bemoaning the fate of the building and the whole system that sustained them. Similarly, Amanda Dawn Christie's *Spectres of Shortwave* (2017) examines the 2012 shutdown of the Radio Canada International shortwave relay station on the Tantramar Marshes near Sackville, New Brunswick. Coupling images of the towers and surrounding landscape with the voices of local residents for whom the station was a loved landmark, Christie's film examines this loss and considers the ways that the local is bound to the national and the global. The coda comes to a close with a look at the work of the Artifact Institute, founded in 2007 by Tim Dallett and Adam Kelly, who, in a series of exhibitions and projects over the past decade, have assessed and catalogued the electronic remains of various arts and cultural organizations. The institute's work with the now surplus technological objects of the recent past points to another way that the 1970s still surround us, namely in the form of waste. Yet these melancholy objects, once the stuff of creation and production, still bear some kind of energy and are thus capable, even in their twilight, of serving as a sign and reminder of the desire they once catalyzed.

The central ambition of this study is to assess the place that the 1970s occupy in the national cultural imaginary in an effort to estrange the present. The return to the 1970s, whether by contemporary artists who work with its remainders or by a critic revisiting its landmarks and erratics, makes visible the ways that a progressivist notion of history, one that sees things only getting better and conditions improving, is both scam and sham. Not only does it ignore all those for whom the neoliberal present means exclusion and immiseration, but it also forecloses on the kind of utopian thinking that was everywhere in the 1970s and that, however compromised it was by blind spots and omissions, may serve as a resource in the present.

Although it might be an unexpected touchstone for a book about cultural memory and the Canadian 1970s, Charity Scribner's magisterial *Requiem for Communism* (2003), a study of how the everyday material remainders of the former Eastern Bloc have been taken up in film and the visual arts, sets out important ways of thinking about the connections between memory, moving images, and material culture. Drawing on Walter Benjamin's argument that, as she paraphrases, "real historical memory sustains emancipatory potentials that were once crushed," Scribner details the desire manifested in film, literature, and visual arts to "recollect ways of living and working that were imagined to be possible under the socialist alternative, but also to resuscitate the principle of hope that inspired much of the last century's social and cultural production."[19] *Hinterland Remixed* takes seriously this impulse within a different set of circumstances – the liberal democratic state rather than the socialist one; Canada rather than East Germany – in order to investigate both the possibilities and the hazards of national cultural memory. Moving images often facilitate the positive forms of recollection and resuscitation that Scribner names, yet they always run the risk of romanticizing the past or encouraging us to slip into a comfortable mode of reactionary yearning. As fraught as the exercise of remembering is, *Hinterland Remixed* argues that it a risk worth taking, not least because revisitation, remediation, and return provide the basic resources for imagining the future.

1
Nation, Nature, and Nostalgia: *Hinterland Who's Who*

For those who watched Canadian television in the 1960s, 1970s, and 1980s, the haunting flute melody that begins the *Hinterland Who's Who* public service announcements is instantly recognizable. Commissioned by the Canadian Wildlife Service and produced in conjunction with the National Film Board (NFB), the *Hinterland Who's Who* vignettes profiled a wide array of animals native to Canada, showing each of them in their natural habitat and providing some basic facts about the species and its behaviour through voiceover narration. This straightforward description of the formal features and pedagogical aims of the series, however, does not capture the allure of the clips themselves. The force and impact of these films derive primarily from their tone and texture. The somnambulistic cadence of the voiceover narration, the eerie stillness of the wilderness soundscapes, and the sparse randomness of the information provided about the featured animals are the defining features of the shorts and combine to produce an unusual televisual experience. Made between 1963 and 1977, but still airing regularly on Canadian television well into the 1980s, these shorts are both educational and political. They convey factual information about the natural world, and they communicate a very specific idea of Canada grounded in the imagined connection to that world. But they are also odd and evocative in ways that exceed both their pedagogical intent and ideological effect.

My aim in this opening chapter is to account in some small way for the affective force of the *Hinterland Who's Who* shorts and to register their impact on national cultural memory – the way that they bring the past into the present. Part of this desire is generational, even biographical, having to do with the formative experience of seeing these shorts innumerable times at an impressionable age. Yet I argue that the force and significance of the series extend beyond the personal and sentimental. These shorts connect in strange and interesting ways to the dominant national preoccupations of the era when they were made and, as a result, now function metonymically as symbols and mnemonic representatives of their historical moment. Because of the extended span of time over which they were made, they share a moment not only with Canada's Centennial in 1967 and the cultural enthusiasm of Expo 67 but also with the oil crisis and the economic malaise of the 1970s. They are perhaps the quintessential product of the long '70s that this book names and examines. They clearly belong to a set of federal government initiatives in the 1960s and 1970s to define Canada as a modern nation distinguished by its strong links to nature and the natural environment. But they are also the products of a culture increasingly alienated from nature and haunted by the spectre of environmental degradation. For those watching these shorts during the era when they were first broadcast, the experience of nature was increasingly mediated by television. This reality meant that the animals represented in the *Hinterland Who's Who* clips were as much a part of the televisual landscape as a natural one. The odd tone of the shorts is, I argue, a consequence of this predicament. *Hinterland Who's Who* is both educational and elegiac, a pinnacle of public service broadcasting that was haunted by its own imminent disappearance as the state-led initiatives of the 1960s and 1970s gave way to the neoliberalisms of the 1980s and 1990s that saw the dramatic reduction, if not total elimination, of this type of material from television screens. Today, *Hinterland Who's Who* preserves a landscape that has disappeared, a specific era of Canadian television that experimented with the possibilities of the pedagogical, producing work that, even while it delivered a series of basic facts about the selected animals, managed to be both bracing and bold.

The original *Hinterland Who's Who* series documented the distinctive natural landscape of Canada and focused on animals most readily associated with the nation, yet the 60-second clips also stood out distinctly in the televisual landscape of the period, differing dramatically in style and atmosphere from the regular programming that surrounded them. This stylistic and tonal oddness, a calm contemplativeness that is also strangely eerie and elegiac, is the main reason these vignettes are so powerful. It distinguished them when they first aired from the programs and advertisements that preceded and followed them. But it is also why they have stuck so resolutely in memory for those who experienced Canadian television in the era when they were in heavy rotation. So, as much as I look at the *Hinterland Who's Who* clips in the context of their original transmission, I also think about how they have been remade and remediated, as well as the place they occupy in national cultural memory. The mnemonic tenacity of *Hinterland Who's Who* has come, at least in part, from its susceptibility to parody. Over the years, it has invited spoof versions on television, in the gallery, and online. These unofficial extensions of the series ensured that *Hinterland Who's Who* remained in cultural circulation even after its run was complete, but they have also increased the cultural weight and significance of the series itself. With each reworking and remediation, the place of *Hinterland Who's Who* in Canadian cultural memory is further secured and consolidated.

The *Hinterland Who's Who* clips had largely disappeared from television by the mid to late 1980s and have only become readily available again quite recently. They were initially uploaded to YouTube by individual enthusiasts, who, after the introduction of the platform in 2005, scoured old VHS tapes not for the programs intentionally recorded but for these treasured bits in between. More recently, they have been posted on the website of the Canadian Wildlife Federation, and they received a formal release on a promotional DVD celebrating the fiftieth anniversary of the series in 2013. In the intervening years, these shorts, despite being unavailable, assumed a kind of talismanic status, a lost bit of Canadian television history beyond the scope of commercial reissue or official, subsidized digital-archival collection. They were the absent objects of cultural memory, preserved primarily in the minds of those who recalled and recollected them. I find this form of mnemonic preservation particularly interesting, not least for the way that it sustains the force of the thing remembered, even intensifies it, while the audiovisual object is officially out of circulation, stored on film reels and videotapes in archives that do not recognize their importance or that lack the funds to do anything with them.

While thinking more about this trajectory from televisual disappearance to digital return, I also claim that these films represent loss in a far more general way. This is not necessarily loss in terms of the endangerment, even extinction, of any of the species represented, although that is an analogy that I hope to develop a little, but loss in terms of the disappearance of a whole "structure of feeling" and way of life.[1] The continuing force of these vignettes fits with some forms of contemporary nostalgia for the long '70s, public service broadcasting, and the welfare state, or at least for a historical moment prior to the full implementation of neoliberalism. Broadly speaking, and perhaps operating most powerfully in the nooks and crannies of the online world, there is a melancholic fascination in today's culture with things that were produced in recent memory but seem to come from a different world altogether. This tendency is perhaps more pronounced elsewhere than in Canada. For perhaps obvious reasons, it is most recognizable in the former Eastern Bloc as the object-world of communism disappears and its media landscape recedes in memory as well.[2] But this phenomenon is not restricted to the former second world. The United Kingdom seems particularly susceptible to these kinds of feelings, especially among those on the left who hold onto the 1960s and 1970s as a reminder of a time before Thatcherism's accelerated transformation of the economy, the state, and society. There were, of course, those at the time who witnessed this transformation as it occurred and recognized that Thatcherism did not start punctually with her election in 1979 but named a tendency, a rightward drift, that was well underway in the years before. Stuart Hall, most notably, identifies Thatcherism as the conclusion to "The Great Moving Right Show" that was already well underway before she took office and accelerated the process.[3] What is striking about Hall's writing from the period is that it is in no way elegiac for a passing 1960s and 1970s and their structure of feeling even though it fully recognizes the catastrophe that Prime Minister Margaret Thatcher represented.

By the 2000s, Hall's clear-eyed skepticism about the postwar welfare state had largely disappeared, and the sounds, images, ideas, remainders, and remnants of welfare state socialism seemed once again to have renewed cultural purchase and, to some degree, to be the subject of nostalgia. As I argued in the introduction, this shift occurred first in relation to music, where critics Simon Reynolds and Mark Fisher have borrowed Jacques Derrida's term "hauntology" to characterize a varied selection of electronic music artists, the Scottish duo Boards of Canada among them, whose recordings, as Reynolds puts it, "explore a zone of British nostalgia linked to television programming from the sixties and seventies."[4] Ghost Box, a record label that specialized in electronic works that evoked an imagined 1970s somehow defined by both socialism and the supernatural, is central to Reynolds's and Fisher's speculations. The name of the label itself points to television as a haunted medium, but this focus on memory and media has a clear political dimension as well. If Derrida's notion of hauntology considers the uncanny persistence of Karl Marx's ideas even in the wake of communism's collapse in the Soviet Union, its redeployment by Reynolds and Fisher seeks to name and identify the ongoing subterranean or subliminal influence of the postwar consensus, or at least distorted memories of it, on contemporary cultural production. As Reynolds explains in relation to Ghost Box, "Running through a lot of the music, as well as the artwork and the conceptual framing of the project, are ideas of a lost utopianism: the post-welfare-state era of benevolent state planning and social engineering."[5] Neither Reynolds nor Fisher are bleary-eyed nostalgists pining for a lost 1970s, and although the bands on Ghost Box are fascinated with the tones, textures, and design of the period, neither are they. All do, however, recognize the ways that the past and its sonic, visual, and material remnants might serve as an archive of the unactualized, a repository of hopes and desires that may be of some use to the present. This is not uncritical nostalgia but the recognition that, for all its exclusions, limitations, and problems, the past might still be capable of sustaining a depleted present or rousing it into political action.[6]

The situation in Canada clearly differs from that of the United Kingdom for a variety of reasons. Even though the political ascendency of Prime Minister Justin Trudeau in 2015 clearly brought with it memories of 1960s Trudeaumania, as well as memories of the beleaguered Prime Minister Pierre Elliott Trudeau of the later 1970s and early 1980s, and even though there are surely some who harbour a deep historical hostility to Prime Minister Brian Mulroney, elected in 1984, such a scenario does not quite fully add up to the context of hauntology's emergence in the United Kingdom, bookended by the images and ideas of a munificent municipal socialism and the rise of the monstrous Thatcher, who would crush it all. Nevertheless, as I detailed in the introduction and explore throughout *Hinterland Remixed*, there are ways that the past ten or fifteen years have seen a return to the recent Canadian past in specifically televisual terms, from the rise of YouTube channels such as RetroNewfoundland, RétroMontréal, Retrontario, and RetroWinnipeg, which document the televisual ephemera of local stations and regional affiliates, to the Kickstarter-funded republication of the CBC's *Graphic Standards Manual* (1974), which details the work of Burton Kramer, whose "exploding pizza" logo is much beloved by contemporary graphic designers and amateur design enthusiasts.[7] Yet the *Hinterland Who's Who* shorts represent, I think, the privileged example of this return. These shorts are haunting not simply because they reproduce the call of the loon or because the narration is distinguished by an undercurrent of deep sorrow but also because, even after they disappeared from television, they remained in cultural memory, frequently as a kind of half-remembered experience of an era that was defined by a set of political possibilities and aspirations that have disappeared from the present. Their persistence constitutes a kind of nostalgia that is politically redeemable. It is not a nostalgia that is, as Svetlana Boym puts it, restorative, that aches for a return to or reconstruction of the past, but is a reflective nostalgia focused on the longing itself and what it might reveal about the limitations and occlusions of the political and cultural present. As Boym argues, one of the ways that reflective nostalgia differs from the restorative kind is that "it loves details, not symbols."[8] This preference characterizes the mnemonic and affective relationship to the *Hinterland* shorts: the fascination with and attachment to them is caught up in their, often idiosyncratic, formal details.

Perhaps the most distinctive of all the formal features of the *Hinterland* shorts is the woodwind melody that serves as its theme. Written by John Cacavas, and officially titled "Flute Poem #1," the

Hinterland theme is almost unbearably melancholic. This theme tune is what people tend to remember most distinctly about the series, and as a result, it now serves as a mnemonic cue that can trigger a whole range of memories not simply about the series but also about the scene and the situation of seeing them. I am especially interested in the varying scale and scope of the remembered viewing context that the shorts and their theme tune catalyze. Through a form of metonymical condensation, both the memory of 1970s living rooms and the geopolitical situation of the period as a whole are somehow bound up in the simple flute melody that identifies the series. Amy Holdsworth argues that these kinds of sensory and sensual details about specific contexts of viewing should not be left out of discussions of television and memory: "For me, for my memories, television is an integral part of that scene and network of senses and impressions that constitute an experience of living within a domestic space and within a particular society. Television, for me, is remembered as a sensual experience, and in particular is characterised by the memories of light."[9] Even though I surely would have seen the *Hinterland* shorts at various times of the day and throughout year, the flute melody itself always conjures up a memory-image of a crisp, clear Sunday morning in the fall, the sun struggling to lend the day any warmth, all seen through a picture window with a view of the outside that competes unsuccessfully with the television for my attention. Condensed into this scene, although not ostensibly present in the frame itself, is the sense of a late-1970s world that stretches far beyond the scene, its geopolitical antagonisms being felt, but not fully understood, by the kid watching the public service announcement and waiting for the regular programming to return. As Holdsworth explains, these kinds of memories "are not fully formed; they are fragments, not the 'flashbulbs' seen to characterise the experience of viewing media events but more like the flickers of the old analogue signal. These 'flickers' are not momentous, life-changing or memorialised (though they are undeniably tinged with nostalgia) but they are both informed by and provide a sense of the experiences and memories of viewing."[10] The *Hinterland* flute melody establishes the link between the metonymic and the mnemonic – the processes of condensation that make it possible to reconstruct from a flicker or fragment a whole viewing situation that includes both the intimate, affective sense of the domestic scene and the anxieties and apprehensions of the wider world beyond.

In a 1993 *New York Times* article, Douglas Coupland attempted to explain to a predominantly American readership the central place that the *Hinterland* shorts occupy in Canadian cultural memory: "A famous series of N.F.B. short films was called 'Hinterland Who's Who.' It had as its trademark the call of the loon, a sound that now evokes in many Canadians who watched this program a sense of primal patriotism infinitely greater than even the national anthem."[11] The sense that, for some at least, the mnemonic trigger is "primal" points not only to the ways that music and musical cues work in relationship to memory itself, and in some cases to ideas of the nation, but also to how the ordinary and the banal can in certain circumstances constitute an object of intense identificatory attachment and a catalyst for complex memories.[12] So even though the full historical and political circumstances that saw the emergence of hauntology as a useful theoretical concept in the United Kingdom do not quite exist in Canada in the same way, the benefit of its importation resides in its attention to the way that national affect is caught up in incidental and idiosyncratic things – examples of what Michael Billig has termed "banal nationalism."[13] These elements of the recent past, such as the *Hinterland Who's Who* shorts, retained a kind of spectral presence even when, maybe especially when, they fell out of circulation and existed only as memory. And they continue to haunt today because of the way that they, metonymically, conjure up a recent past whose contours now seem both alien and impossible.

But this sense of a primal attachment to the sound of the loon, for obvious reasons, cannot and should not be presented as a universal claim: not all Canadians, even those of my generational cohort, have the same affective relationship to these films. I want to say from the beginning that this is no effort to define Canadianness on the basis of whether one tears up when faced with grainy footage of beavers and is told a series of seemingly random facts about them. My much more modest claim is that these residues of the Canadian televisual past retain a weird power not simply due to the basic mechanics of nostalgia but also because they trigger a sense of the ways that the world has changed in the intervening decades. They speak to how certain political possibilities have disappeared as a result of the political, economic, and ideological transformations of the past thirty or forty years. Nestled within this modest claim is a larger claim about cultural memory and what I have no hesitation in calling the golden age of the public service announcement, that period from the mid-1960s until the late 1980s when the experience of television was punctuated by these productions that were neither commercial nor promotional but were driven by a very different set of social aims and ambitions. My argument is that these films are interesting and important and that they merit far more scholarly and cultural attention than they have hitherto garnered. Not only do they tell us much about a recent past that is increasingly difficult to remember in the wake of significant changes to the social, political, and ideological landscape, but they are also fascinating documents in and of themselves, a form of creative filmmaking and televisual production that, as much as the celebrated feature-length films or primetime productions of the same period, is marked by a late-modern adventurousness and formal audacity.

The Product of a Bureaucratic Ecosystem

Before going any further with these aesthetic and historical claims, I want to look at the series itself and detail the formal features that set it apart. The original set of four black-and-white *Hinterland Who's Who* 60-second shorts, featuring the beaver, moose, gannet, and loon, were produced in 1963 at the behest of the Canadian Wildlife Service, which recognized that television was a means through which it might fulfil its public education mandate.[14] It commissioned the National Film Board of Canada to make these shorts, but the NFB did not produce them in-house, choosing instead to contract an outside corporation, Motion Picture Centre Ltd of Toronto, to assemble the shorts out of material drawn from the NFB vaults as well as stock footage purchased from other suppliers.[15] As explained in a report from the late 1960s titled "Television Public Service Spots Good Business for Any Renewable Resource Agency," written by by Darrell Eagles, head of editorial and information for the Canadian Wildlife Service, the beaver, loon, gannet, and moose were chosen, at least in part, for pragmatic reasons. As Eagles notes, these "four species were well represented in the Film

Board's stock-shot library."[16] This initial set of public service announcements proved popular enough that in 1966 the Canadian Wildlife Service commissioned four more 60-second spots (red fox, caribou, Canada goose, and herring gull), this time in colour, as well as having colour versions produced of the original quartet of shorts.

Subsequent sets of shorts were produced in 1968–69 (mallard duck, ruffed grouse, chipmunk, and bighorn sheep), in 1969–70 (peregrine falcon, cougar, black duck, and woodchuck), in 1971–72 (blue jay, robin, grizzly, and wolf), in 1973–74 (snowy owl, polar bear, muskox, ptarmigan, bison, killdeer, trumpeter swan, and canvasback duck), and in 1976–77 (whooping crane, greater snow goose, raccoon, and black bear). In total, thirty-two *Hinterland Who's Who* colour shorts were made between 1966 and 1977, all of which had corresponding French versions issued under the series title *Merveilles de la faune*.[17] They are a powerful collection of short films, not least for the way they distill and condense ideas of nation, nature, modernity, and modern life. Inasmuch as they take the natural environment – the wilds and wildlife of Canada – as their ostensible subject, they are also about, in a very powerful way, the urbanization and industrialization of Canada and the impacts of the accelerated modernization of the postwar period on the identity of the nation and on the psychic makeup of its citizens. They are a specifically Canadian representation of, and reaction to, political and economic transformations that were occurring worldwide at the time. As a result, they provide insight into national circumstances but also represent part of the global picture. The *Hinterland Who's Who* shorts depict the experience of modernity and modernization and visually represent a world increasingly defined by the transformation of the natural environment (see figure 1.1).

There is a formal consistency to the *Hinterland Who's Who* shorts, from the earliest black-and-white series made in 1963 to the final set from 1977. It is particularly astonishing that the formal features of the *Hinterland* films were so firmly established from the very beginning. This consistency and continuity played a significant role in the success of the series during its initial run and contributed immensely to the mnemonic tenacity of the series in the years of its absence. The formulaic breeds familiarity, and even from watching just a handful

1.1. "Herring Gull," *Hinterland Who's Who* (1966). Each *Hinterland Who's Who* short has a formulaic structure.

of the spots, it is possible to compile a list of *Hinterland*'s defining characteristics and some of their affective consequences:

- Each film begins with John Cacavas's rustic flute melody.
- The series title appears as the flute melody draws to a close, followed by on-screen text that provides the name of the featured animal.
- The featured animal is pictured in its natural habitat.
- The musical soundtrack is replaced by ambient noises of landscape and animal activity.
- The closely mic'd and powerfully voiced narration begins, hovering somewhere between objective dispassion and mild melancholia.
- The narration conveys a series of facts but also frequently constructs a kind of scientific narrative about the animal, structured around annual activity or larger lifecycles.
- Periods of prolonged silence punctuate the narration, inviting contemplation of the animal represented.
- Cuts or dissolves transition between different seasons or stages of animal life.
- The viewer is invited to contact the Canadian Wildlife Service in Ottawa for more information on the featured animal.
- The logo for the Canadian Wildlife Service of Environment Canada appears on-screen and is followed, in later years at least, by the wordmark for the Government of Canada.

These are the formal features that distinguish the *Hinterland Who's Who* shorts, yet the power and force of the series reside in the tone and atmosphere that the combination and repetition of these formal details generate. All of the shorts bear this out, I think, but I want to look closely at the spot for the beaver to investigate the mechanics of affect and to think about how the shorts represent the natural world and its animal inhabitants.

The spot for the beaver, not surprisingly given the animal's iconic status in mythologies of the Canadian nation, is one of the original four *Hinterland Who's Who* clips. There are several differences between the original black-and-white version from 1963 and the colour one from 1966. Both versions feature the beaver swimming, diving, and gathering wood to build a dam, but they use different film clips to do so. The voiceover commentary is largely the same in each clip, as the announcer provides a short history of the beaver's significance to Canada and provides details of the species' narrow escape from extinction and its managed reintroduction into the Canadian wild. The narration for both the 1963 and 1966 versions begins, "There was a time when Beaver lodges like this one and the busy beavers that built them had almost disappeared from Canada because of overtrapping. But the beaver, who will always be associated with Canada's early days, has been reintroduced into many areas and has made a successful comeback. [pause] The beaver builds dams because he has to store his winter's food in water deep enough not to freeze. [pause] With all the woodcutting that the beaver has to do[,] it's fortunate that his incisor teeth never stop growing."[18] Although the clip acknowledges the catastrophic impact of the fur trade on the beaver population, it effectively relegates this damage to the past and stresses more recent successes made possible by human and state intervention, including the work of the Canadian Wildlife Service itself. It would be too crass to refer to the clip, or the series as a whole, simply as a vehicle for an ideology of social welfare state interventionism, but it is important to recognize how it assumes government-led environmental protectionism to be both modern and desirable. Furthermore, albeit perhaps in a somewhat oblique fashion, the beaver's stockpiling of resources for the winter ahead constitutes an analogy for the federal stewardship of the natural environment itself.[19]

The colour version of the beaver clip neatly excises the most playful part of the original. In the black-and-white version, over images of a beaver on land attending to its coat, the narrator explains, "This fellow is not itchy; he's really grooming himself, redistributing the oil that keeps his fur waterproof."[20] The striking thing here is the way that the voiceover sentimentalizes the beaver's activity, casting it as a "fellow" and, in a comic manner, as cartoonishly feline, even as the narration delivers a rigorously scientific explanation for the behaviour. This tendency to domesticate and sentimentalize is a hallmark of the wildlife film from its earliest days, but it is particularly acute in the postwar period, due in part to the impact of Disney's *True-Life Adventures* (c. 1948–60), which often featured similar voiceover narration that emphasized the cartoonish and the cute. This lightness also translated to television, where popular wildlife programs such as *Mutual of Omaha's Wild Kingdom* (1963–88; revived in 2002) often juxtaposed the comedic and sentimental with scenes of peril or threat.[21] The excision of the cartoonish description of the beaver from the 1966 version set the tone for the remainder of the series, which eschews lightheartedness and maintains a seriousness that is at once scientific and bureaucratic. The *Hinterland Who's Who* films feel like the creation of a government agency tasked with the production of informational and pedagogical content that turned out to be, almost inadvertently, entertaining.

The series title itself is slightly unusual and was chosen from a lengthy list of competitors. A 1963 document from the NFB archives, assembled by the Canadian Wildlife Service's Dave Smith and labelled "Suggested Titles – Canadian Wildlife Service," lists over thirty other suggested titles for the series. These include ones that reference the format of the public service announcement (*A Nature Minute* and *One Minute With ...*), ones that imagine the series as a kind of scientific survey or bureaucratic count (*Backwoods Census '63, Nature List '63, Wildlife Roll Call '63, Wildlife Census, Wildlife Parade, Animals We Know,* and *Roll Call of the Wild*), and ones that play on ideas of nation and citizenship (*Untamed Residents, Natives of Canada, Canada's Free Citizens, Backwoods Citizens, Citizens of Nature,* and *Citizens of the Wild*).[22] Although these titles playing on the notion of citizenship would ultimately be jettisoned in favour of the somewhat more obscure *Hinterland Who's Who*, they are important in that they tie the series to what Zoë Druick calls "one of the most important discourses" of the NFB's dominant mode of "government realism."[23] The pedagogical aim of the series, to teach viewers something about animal species native to Canada, is inextricably intertwined with the idea that such knowledge will make them better citizens. Imagining the animals represented in the clips to be Canadian citizens as well is a conceit that emphasizes the conservationist role of government. The clips are products of the social democratic welfare state in two senses: they aim to make better citizens of the viewer, and they are meant to protect and preserve the animal species they represent by means of this popular pedagogy.

In the original debates, by far the greatest number of contending titles are variants of the one that was eventually chosen: *Who's Who in* the Backwoods, Canada's Backwoods Who's Who, Who's Who in the Back Country, Who's Who in the Hinterland, Wildlife Who's Who, Canadian Wildlife Who's Who, and Who's Who of the Wild.[24] Why "who's who"? The phrase itself is neatly onomatopoetic, evoking the call of the owl in a way that instantly aligns the series with nature and the wild as well as with owlish wisdom and learning. Yet the ultimate referent, perhaps surprisingly, is governmental rather than environmental.

First published in London in 1849, *Who's Who* is an annually updated reference publication that is comprised of biographical sketches of important social, cultural, and political figures. The first edition of *Canadian Who's Who* appeared in 1911 and has been updated on a regular basis since then. The function of these publications is tied up with ideas of social status and hierarchy, especially as they relate to the operations of government; they are a go-to source for information on people who are of sufficient enough importance that you need to know a little about them if you yourself are going to succeed.[25] The idea of a *Hinterland Who's Who* brings together the bureaucratic and the biological: the joke that structures the series title is that these animals are the ones with accrued Canadian cultural capital, the ones you need to know in order to fulfil your duties as a Canadian. Such a joke, I like to think, could have come only from within government and could have been realized only in films produced by an affiliated government agency. The hothouse atmosphere of bureaucratic intrigue and interagency infighting manifests itself in the title, which takes the form of a wry commentary on public service filmmaking.

Seen in this way, one concrete companion to the *Hinterland Who's Who* films is Donald Brittain's acerbic satire of the federal government's idiocies and inefficiencies, *Paperland: The Bureaucrat Observed* (1979). Brittain's film, produced of course by the NFB, perhaps counts as the first remediation of the *Hinterland* series. The film begins with a long shot of a bureaucrat skating down Ottawa's Rideau Canal dressed in a trenchcoat and toting a briefcase. The voiceover adopts a mock-authoritative tone that parodies the nature documentary in the way that it classifies its subject and situates it in its natural habitat: "Here he comes now, trying to act like a normal human being. But he is that most despised of human creatures. His activities have brought down upon his shoulders the scorn and outrage of history's multitudes.

He is *homo bureaucratus*, the bureaucrat. And he lives in a land of paper." So whereas the *Hinterland* films imagine nature in terms of a social structure, Brittain's film sees the bureaucrat as a species in nature, albeit a despised one. Yet, for all its barbed wit, *Paperland* is more celebratory than corrosive, using satire to support rather than slander bureaucracy. Both the bureaucrat's *Paperland* and the "who's who" *Hinterland* are public territories, the exact topography of which is becoming harder and harder to remember today as the neoliberal assault on both the public service and the environment escalates and intensifies.

One of the things that makes Brittain's film and the *Hinterland* series feel so odd today is that their immediate context, the late period of the social democratic welfare state, suffuses their very form and structure. As a consequence, their distinctive formal features, especially those of the *Hinterland* series, now stand in for an entire historical period and its attendant structure of feeling. It may seem risky or reckless to hang so much on a mere flute melody, yet there is an increasing recognition in both film and memory studies that "residual media," to invoke the title of Charles Acland's influential edited collection of 2007, and ephemeral forms are vehicles that transport the past into the present. In so doing, they bring along with them energies and ambitions that may have defined their own historical moment but are increasingly invisible or even unimaginable to us today. These items, sounds, and images are uncanny because they are not fully at home in the present moment and constitute a challenge to the certainties of the contemporary. They haunt and unsettle precisely because they are shadows, not simply of the past but also of a future that never came to be.

The Paratelevisual

Even though the general set of ideas about history, memory, and residuality on which I draw throughout *Hinterland Remixed* could be applied to just about any stray piece of the past that has survived into the present, I argue that the public service announcement is a privileged vehicle for this kind of uncanny transportation. This fact has something to do with the role they played on television in the first place. They were not, strictly speaking, part of the structured flow of televisual content, from the cartoons, game shows, and soap operas that populated morning and afternoon schedules to the newscasts and reruns of the supper hour to the sitcoms and dramas that ruled primetime. They also differed from what many would call the real content of television – the advertising that underwrites and dominates commercial broadcasting – even if they often shared with advertising a length of 30 or 60 seconds. They fell into the intervals and interstices between these two types of televisual content, themselves occupying a kind of hinterland beyond both advertising and programming, a wild space defined ironically by its public mandate and pedagogical aspirations.

We need a term for this other kind of television content, not simply public service announcements but also the station identifications, test cards, colour bars, promotional bumpers, interval junctions, tests of the emergency broadcast system, and closedowns of the broadcast day. The term I have settled on is the "paratelevisual," adapted from Gerard Genette's concept of the paratextual, which names all those parts of a book that are not the text proper: the cover, the title page, the colophon and copyright information, the dedication, the appendices, the index, and even the note on the type font in our designed-obsessed age. Borrowing from Jorge Luis Borges, Genette argues that the paratext is a "*threshold*" that occupies the border and the boundary between the book and the world.[26] The paratelevisual refers to those things that likewise form part of the infrastructure of television but, sitting on the threshold between the world of television and the world itself, are not usually considered to be its true content.[27] For Genette, the paratextual is secondary and subordinate yet remains central and integral. The paratelevisual, I argue, occupies this same territory. It is not by any means the main stuff of television, yet it forms an integral part of television, which would be inconceivable without it.

The paratelevisual should also be understood in relation to Jeffrey Sconce's concept of the paracinematic. For Sconce, the paracinematic names those subgeneric productions that have traditionally been beyond the pale of critical respectability but are frequently subject to enthusiast celebration and scholarly recuperation. He lists Japanese monster movies, beach-party musicals, and juvenile delinquency documentaries as key examples of the paracinematic but suggests that government hygiene films fall into the category as well.[28] And this precedent, I think, is enough to make the leap from the paracinematic to the paratelevisual – to understand genre films and government productions as cohabitants in a hinterland beyond critical attention and approbation that entertain, compel, and unsettle. The special bonus of "the paratelevisual" as a term lies in its proximity to the paranormal and the hauntological. As the content beyond content, there is something paranormal about the paratelevisual in the very position it occupies in the field of television. Furthermore, based on this structural difference, I also argue that, in its relative freedom from the commercial pressures of regularly scheduled programming, the paratelevisual often assumes an uncanny, disturbing, or just simply weird air. Most importantly, as I examine further in the following chapter in relation to a series of Parks Canada public service announcements that are horrific companions to Michael Snow's *La Région Centrale* (1971), the paratelevisual has the capacity to haunt us. Once it has disappeared, it tends to stay with those who experienced it, with the slightest of mnemonic triggers being enough to reanimate and revivify it.[29]

Hinterland Remediations

Even before the spots themselves left the small screen, parodies and reworkings of them had started to appear. Most significantly, in an episode broadcast on NBC on 5 November 1982, SCTV presented a parody of *Hinterland Who's Who*. Chapter 3 looks at SCTV's history and paratelevisual innovations and archival richness in greater detail. For now, it suffices to say that the comedic force of SCTV's take on *Hinterland Who's Who* derives in part from the show's structuring conceit. At the heart of SCTV is the idea that all of television is subject to satire, from the programming to the stuff that appears in between. Furthermore, SCTV extends its satire from content to flow, generating laughs not simply by rendering note-perfect parodies of particular content but also by denaturalizing ideas of the program day. In SCTV's woodchuck spot, a janitor's strike shuts down production at the station. To fill airtime, station manager Guy Caballero (Joe Flaherty) brokers a deal that allows SCTV to pick up the CBC feed. After a quick station identification featuring the classic "exploding pizza" logo designed by Burton Kramer for the network in 1974, the *Hinterland Who's Who* spot begins, with John Candy beginning the narration: "The woodchuck is found in open woods and ravines across Canada and the northeast United States. [pause] A terrestrial day-active animal, the woodchuck hibernates in snowy climes. [extended pause] For more information, contact Parks and Recreation Canada, Ottawa." The humour of the spot derives in part from Candy's attempt to echo the dispassionate delivery that characterizes the original *Hinterland Who's Who* shorts. But perhaps the real source of comedy here is the silence that punctuates the piece. The extended pauses and the shots of woodchucks mostly just staring into the distance and sniffing combine to produce a short that parodies the original by ever so slightly emphasizing the quirks rather than indulging in overblown exaggeration.

The narration of the original *Hinterland Who's Who* spot from 1972 delivers a more coherent account of the woodchuck's story, yet it is still very much distinguished by the extended pauses and the randomness of the facts that it provides, which the SCTV parody identifies and exploits:

> The woodchuck, also called the groundhog, is one of the larger Canadian rodents. A mature adult may weigh up to 17 pounds. [pause] In winter it depends almost entirely on body fat, until April when new plant food reappears. [pause] Like the beaver, the woodchuck's front gnawing teeth grow continuously, except during hibernation. Constant grinding trims them down. [pause] The breeding period lasts three months, and from four to five young are usual. [pause] In May, at about seven weeks, the young are weaned and cautiously begin to forage on their own. However, they still rely almost entirely on their mother to warn them of impending danger. For more information on the woodchuck, contact the Canadian Wildlife Service in Ottawa.

Beyond the off pacing of the narration and the weird focus on the woodchuck's weight, what I find particularly striking about the official clip is the slightly menacing note with which the voiceover closes. Accompanied by a shot of a woodchuck standing watch over her four chucklings, the suggestion of "impending danger" points to a possible horrific moment that falls just beyond the spot itself but retroactively haunts it. It is striking how many of the *Hinterland Who's Who* shorts include the suggestion of proleptic peril, and this feature somehow evokes the dominant mood or structure of feeling of the period, which, as I explore in chapter 2, was awash with a sense of the end, whether it would come as a consequence of environmental degradation or nuclear catastrophe.

Of course, SCTV's *Hinterland Who's Who* parody was perceived differently by its initial American audience on NBC – not discounting the Canadians who would have watched this episode on cable or in communities proximate enough to the border to pick up the broadcast off-air – and by its later Canadian audience on the CBC. For the former, the humour derives from how the sheer boringness and banality of the woodchuck clip represents a kind of Canadian public service broadcasting decidedly out of sync with the brashness and energy of American commercial broadcasting. For Canadian viewers, the humour comes from the estrangement that the spot allows. It makes audible and visible the weirdness of the *Hinterland Who's Who* spots themselves in its identification and exploitation of their formal features and distinctive tone. The SCTV parody serves as a good lesson in how a remediation transforms the original. Once viewed, it is virtually impossible to see the originals in the same way again or to hear the narrator's voice without the satiric shadow of John Candy's more mellowed tones.

More recently, *This Hour Has 22 Minutes* (CBC, 1993–present) has produced a series of *Hinterland Who's Who* parodies that document a variety of Canadian types and figures, from the "Reluctant Shoveler" to the "Winter Cyclist." Whereas the SCTV spoof zeroed in specifically on the formal features of the *Hinterland* spots to generate its humour, *22 Minutes* takes hold of the general formula and seeks laughs in the shift from the natural to the social. Although I am predictably partial to SCTV's metatelevisual approach, I fully understand that the popularity and power of the *22 Minutes* spots derives not just from their soft satire of social types but also from their adaption and reproduction of many of *Hinterland*'s conventional features. For instance, the spot on the "Club Hopper," voiced by Cathy Jones, adopts the phrasing and pacing of the *Hinterland* originals but also pinpoints the precision with which they used a scientific vocabulary as part of their pedagogical aims:

"The high-heeled, black-dressed club hopper is a Canadian subspecies who refuses to don layers of warm covering during the winter months, choosing instead to retain her summer plumage. She can be spotted on weekends in small groups, emerging from a taxi, waiting hours in line in the bitter cold, risking frostbite just to avoid paying two dollars for the coat check. Despite these peculiarities, she remains highly desirable to her male counterpart, the open-shirted, gold-necklaced, cologne-soaked jabroni. For more information on the club hopper, watch a Drake video." So even though 22 *Minutes* strips the spots of their unsettling silences and elegiac air, its satire captures something of *Hinterland*'s feel and function. Perhaps more importantly, it remediates and recirculates the form of the clips, further consolidating their cultural weight and significance. This process, to borrow from Will Straw's analysis of how the recirculation of older cultural products in a way resuscitates them, has the effect of "carrying them forward in time and [...] extending the cultural space that they occupy."[30] The 22 *Minutes* satirical take on the *Hinterland* clips reveals the connection between remediation and memory in the ways that satire sustains. But it also delivers the more general lesson that the relationship between past and present is reciprocal. Remediations draw some of their energy from cultural familiarity with the original, but the original is reinvigorated each and every time it is recovered and recirculated.

Contemporary reworkings of *Hinterland Who's Who* are by no means restricted to popular culture and television satire. Contemporary artists have also used the *Hinterland* format and made allusions to the series to interrogate the elisions, exclusions, and inequities that have marked Canadian culture from the 1960s and 1970s to the present. Perhaps most notably, Shawna Dempsey and Lorri Millan have drawn extensively on *Hinterland* in their *Lesbian National Parks and Services*, an ongoing performance project launched as part of a Banff Centre residency in 1997. As Jennifer Fisher explains, this work "is comprised of a complex discursive masquerade involving uniforms, social interactions, brochures, field reports, and a book-length *Field Guide to North America*."[31] The power, force, and humour of the *Lesbian National Parks and Services* project derive in large part from Dempsey and Millan's committed performance as lesbian park rangers who are eager in their study of lesbian populations and keen to recruit new rangers to the ranks. This straight-faced immersion in the ranger roles is in fact a queering of the mid-century archetype of the helpful park warden and his civic – or to be more blunt, colonial – commitment to pedagogy and the stewardship of nature.

Following on the Banff Centre residency, Dempsey and Millan made a film documenting the activities and initiatives of the lesbian rangers. *Lesbian National Parks and Services: A Force of Nature* (2002) mobilizes all the conventional features of the mid-century government-sponsored documentary to question and unsettle received ideas about gender, nation, and the natural environment. Opening with images of Rangers Dempsey and Millan canoeing down a river as the melancholic call of the loon echoes in the air, *A Force of Nature* quickly turns to an account of the formation of Lesbian National Parks and Services (LNPS). An English-accented and calmly authoritative male voice delivers this story, its timbre reminiscent of NFB productions from the 1950s and 1960s. The narration, both arch and amusing, is magnificently rich with double entendres:

> Avid outdoorswomen Shawna Dempsey and Lorri Millan have long experienced frustration in the bush. Scientists and conservationists have allowed lesbian flora and fauna to wither and decline, to survive in isolated communities often invisible to a casual observer. Such official indifference perturbed these conscientious naturalists. However, during a sortie through the lesbian wetlands, they struck upon an idea that would change the face of conservation history. What if, they wondered, an organization existed to service and protect the lesbian wild. This question inflamed their minds as they paddled resolutely on. Each punishing stroke carried them closer to their destiny. Future lesbian rangers Dempsey and Millan knew that they were no longer simply traversing lake, stream, and bog. They had begun a nobler journey that would lead to the fulfilment of a lifelong dream: to wear a uniform.

The gloriously overwrought prose of this origin story mimics the tone and feel of celebratory informational films about the national park system from the postwar period as well as other promotional works about governmental agencies and initiatives. Further sequences in the film detail the rigorous training that lesbian ranger recruits must undergo in order to join the force and the extensive fieldwork that is involved in LNPS's efforts, as the narrator puts it, "to increase awareness and sensitivity to the complex, varied, and sometimes fragile lesbian ecosystem." The film documents the ways that the Banff Centre project intervened to reframe and unsettle heteronormative and white, settler colonial experiences of nature. But it also extends this work, revealing the role that documentary practices and conventions from the postwar period, especially those deployed in sponsored films and wildlife films, played in producing ideas of nation and nature that gloss over the violence of homophobia and colonialism.[32]

Dempsey and Millan extended the lesbian ranger universe in 2009 with *Lesbian National Parks and Services Presents: Endangered Species*, a set of public service announcements commissioned by Pride Toronto that detail three disappearing or at risk "lesbian species": the "Marxist-Feminist," the "Lesbian Separatist," and the "Bull-Dykus Americanus." Whereas *A Force of Nature* is in broad critical dialogue with forms of sponsored film and wildlife documentary, the 2009 public service announcements draw tangibly on the legacy of *Hinterland Who's Who*, from the familiar soothing voiceover to the montage of habits and habitats to the concluding invitation to contact Lesbian National Parks and Services for further information. Dempsey and Millan substitute softly plucked acoustic guitar for Cacavas's flute melody but reproduce with uncanny accuracy the pauses and phrasings that characterize the *Hinterland* series. In their focus on endangered lesbian species, these public service announcements echo *Hinterland*'s 1970s anxieties about extinction and environmental degradation, but they do so in order to think historically about transformations within the lesbian community itself and about the disappearance of social types and specific queer identities (see figure 1.2). The clip for the Bull-Dykus Americanus is the most lovingly done, with images of Millan herself walking through a city park, metal thermos and hardhat in hand, before settling down on a bench to eat lunch alone. The voiceover accentuates the melancholy of these images, exploiting a scientific vocabulary to softly satirize:

> Almost forgotten among the world's most threatened species is the Bull-Dykus Americanus. [pause] Virtually eradicated by habitat

loss and poaching, naturalists and conservationalists have long believed these stout, biped megafauna to be extinct. [pause] The recent discovery of a few small clusters of bull-dykes isolated by deforestation and habitat erosion has led to calls for careful species management, including the controversial proposal for the reintroduction of the bull-dyke into former habitats. [pause] You can help the beleaguered bull-dyke. Report sightings. Positive identification can be made based on boastful bravado, masculine camouflage, and a fierceness that belies a soft underbelly.

What is particularly striking about this public service announcement is how it replicates the formal features of the original *Hinterland* shorts but also their call to conserve and foster. Consequently, far from merely mobilizing the form for satiric purposes or isolating for critique the state-led settler colonial environmental stewardship of an earlier period, the LNPS clips function in a more complex manner. They draw on the political energies and aspirations of the long '70s, extending arguments for the protection and conservation of the environment into the realm of identity politics. This move firmly identifies the occlusions that marked and defined the earlier period. The reproduction of both the voice and the formal features, but with a difference, throws *Hinterland* and the historical moment that it metonymically represents into stark relief, making visible the occlusions and inequities that structure and define it.[33]

There is also a potential connection to be made between the *Hinterland* series and the work of KC Adams, an Oji-Cree multimedia artist based in Winnipeg. Adams's *Perception* (2014) is a portrait series that features images of Indigenous people in diptych. On the left side of the diptych, the image of the unsmiling subject is accompanied by a racial slur or common anti-Indigenous stereotype framed as a question, with the text below the image inviting the viewer to "Look Again." As Adams explains, for this image, she asked her subjects "to think of a time when they experienced racism or discrimination, and to think about how they felt at that time."[34] This invitation leads to the right side of the diptych, which shows the same subject smiling beneath text detailing who he or she really is, a smile that Adams prompted by "ask[ing] them to think of something positive – maybe the first time

1.2. Shawna Dempsey and Lorri Millan's *Lesbian National Parks and Services Presents: Endangered Species* (2009). The conventional features of the *Hinterland* clips make them susceptible to such remixing and remediation.

they kissed their partner, or a really special time in their lives."[35] Adams herself participated in the project, with her unsmiling image captioned with the anti-Indigenous slur "Squaw?" The portrait of a smiling Adams immediately alongside the first one overturns this racist stereotype, providing both her name and nation, along with the information that she is a "wife, mother, twin, artist, educator, homeowner, tax payer, curler, who paid for university herself." As with televised public service announcements like *Hinterland Who's Who*, the power of the series derives in large part from its repetition and seriality. There were a total of 130 images for the initial Winnipeg version of the project, which saw large-format posters displayed throughout the downtown area on billboards, on transit shelters, in traditional advertising spaces, and via postering. My interest here is in the way that Adams's intervention can be understood as a mobilization of the format of the public service announcement. Adams liberates the public service announcement from its usual use as an expression of, and promotion for, the liberal state, overturning it in order to speak against the anti-Indigenous racism with which the state ultimately is complicit. Particularly striking is Adams's use of the phrase "Look Again." This phrase motivates the overturning of racist stereotype that comes when the viewer looks to the second of the two images that constitute the poster, which is the "actual representation of the person," as Adams herself puts it.[36] The phrase, perhaps unexpectedly, echoes the invitation used in a public service announcement on biodiversity that dates to the *Hinterland* period and asks viewers to see the natural environment differently. Sponsored by Environment Canada, the clip states, "If you think a marsh isn't good for anything, think again." It then proceeds to list the ecological benefits of marshlands, as well as naming the animals that depend on such areas for survival. It warns that filling in a marsh may not seem like the end of the world but explains that, for the animals who rely on a marsh, it would be the "end of their world, [pause] and our world would be poorer." Then, after an extended pause, it concludes with the stern injunction, both said and presented in video graphics on-screen, to "take another look." This Environment Canada ad fits with the anxious and elegiac tone of the *Hinterland* series but also addresses a widespread and unthinking civic ignorance about the environment, its value, and the consequences of our negligence toward it. The specific injunction to "take another look" anticipates Adams's *Perception* series, especially in the way that it asks its viewer to see differently in order to perceive what is usually obscured or obliterated by the distorting lens of racism that plagues Canadian culture. And although Adams has not specifically cited this clip as an influence, it nevertheless resonates with her project, not least in the way that *Perception* mobilizes the form of the public service announcement to think through the politics of vision and the history of anti-Indigenous racism in the settler colonial state.

The work by Dempsey and Millan as well as Adams reveals the ways that contemporary visual artists have taken up the form and function of the public service announcement and mobilized it for powerful political ends. Yet, alongside these pointedly political remediations, recent years have also witnessed the embrace of the *Hinterland* form online as part of the popular and participatory culture that YouTube in particular has facilitated. Homemade *Hinterland* parodies have populated the site almost since its launch in 2005, with users bending the conventions to cover everything from the "Hoser" to the "Sasquatch." By using the *Hinterland* form, these spoofs double down on ideas of nation and dominant fantasies of national identity. *Hinterland Who's Who* itself now stands as representative of Canadianness, so to use the form to satirize stereotypical Canadian types and figures is at once self-reflexively ironic and deeply sentimental. Such sentimentality is, of course, problematic, not least in the way that it functions through a series of exclusions and occlusions in what it considers typically Canadian and thus suitable for parody. But it can also inch toward something more compelling when it draws in elements that reveal the artificiality of those borders. Amateur parodies scarcely have the political bite of Dempsey and Millan's *Endangered Species* series, but sometimes, in their sheer absurdity, they can expose the strangeness of ideas of nature and nation. An example of this is a spoof *Hinterland* on the "Lion Pug." For this parody, pug owner Jay Roach has attached a fake lion's mane to his pet pug and documented its everyday activities. The humour comes through the video's attention to formal detail, from the clipped precision of the narrator's voice to the static shots of the lion pug simply staring into the distance. The parody is sweet, even sentimental, the kind of cute animal video that is YouTube's stock in trade. Yet, in exploiting the flexibility of the *Hinterland* form, this clip reveals the ways that ideas of nation and nature are produced rather than naturally occurring – that the subject matter of the *Hinterland* clips is fungible rather than fixed.

So Lonely

I conclude this chapter by looking at a more oblique set of connections, a method that anticipates the chapter that follows, which adopts this approach to understand Michael Snow's classic experimental film *La Région Centrale* through a series of unusual, and perhaps unexpected, associations with other cultural texts and forms, from the disaster film to the paintings of Peter Doig. Here, I want to think a little about sound, not just in terms of the narrator's voice but also with regard to *Hinterland*'s use of animal calls and communication. The clip for the loon is emblematic here. The loon's familiar calls are heard throughout, punctuating the voiceover and lending the clip a somewhat eerie quality. The narration, of course, addresses the symbolic significance of the sound of the loon but accentuates its unsettling strangeness in its very phrasing, delivery, and syntax: "The calls of the loon, and it has several calls in its repertoire, have come to symbolize Canada's wilderness because of their lonely, [weird pause and emphasis] *haunting* quality." The narration pauses in order to make this loneliness audible, setting a kind of *Hinterland* standard – this is one of the earliest clips that was made – in terms of allowing, even in the limited duration of a 60-second short, the space for ambient wilderness to be heard. *Hinterland Who's Who* conveys ideas of nature, and notions of the nation as a largely uninhabited wilderness, in its selection of animals (mostly wild and ex-urban, except for the raccoon and the robin) and in its tendency to photograph them as far from developed areas as possible. This characteristic is accentuated by the sound design, which produces the idea of the isolated wild in the stretches of space that it allows for the sounds of an ambient natural soundscape captured by a sensitive field recording.

Perhaps an even more striking use of sound comes at the very beginning of the clip when the call of the loon is mixed with the *Hinterland* theme. The familiar, trilling tremolo of the loon fits perfectly with Cacavas's flute melody, the mournful seamlessness integrating with the melancholic. Given that this mix was there even in the original black-and-white version of the Loon short made in 1964, it would be anachronistic to think of this sound effect in terms of a remix or mash-up, yet it does anticipate a classic Canadian disco track that dates to 1979, just after the final *Hinterland* cycle wrapped production and while the loon public service announcement still aired on Canadian television. "So Lonely" is, in some ways, a minor track on Gino Soccio's debut album, *Outline*. The single that preceded the album, "Dancer," which spent six weeks at the top of the Billboard disco charts, is given pride of place as the album's opening track. The deep-funk groove of "Dancer" threatens to overwhelm all that follows, yet the downtempo, impressionistic "So Lonely," with its bell chimes and piano stabs, manages to stand out for different reasons. Most notably, Soccio punctuates the track with the full repertoire of loon calls: tremolo, wail, yodel, and hoot. Soccio's decision to include the sounds of the loon in the song is perhaps due to its title and theme. The lyrics of the song amount to nothing more than the title repeated thirty-two times in sets of four, with alternate sets punctuated by a "yeah" that somehow evokes both blissed-out ecstasy and exhaustion or enervation. Because of the loon's symbolic significance in the Canadian cultural imaginary, the calls certainly contribute to the song's thematic meditation on loneliness and isolation. Yet it feels as though this simple connection does not fully exhaust their meaning and significance.

Soccio's loons evoke something of a mood or feeling tied to both place and period, and their mournful calls invite a deeper consideration of how they evoke the melancholy that characterized the twilight of the 1970s. Disco registers this structure of feeling very precisely. On the one hand, in the popular imagination, disco captures the euphoria of the moment, the disappearance into the beat that also constitutes a liberation from the world's burdens. On the other hand, at the same time, so many disco songs register something of the sadness of the world as well.[37] Released in late 1978, but ascendant in the charts throughout the spring of 1979 just as Soccio entered the scene, Gloria Gaynor's "I Will Survive" is emblematic here. The song's triumphant conclusion is in every way haunted by the trials and tribulations catalogued in its opening phases. And in the wider world of disco-inflected pop, the late period work of Abba is an extended study in sadness, from the road-weariness documented in "Super Trouper" (1980) to the grim fatalism of "All Is Said and Done" (1981). Canadian disco had long flirted with the sense that behind the genre's euphoria lurked loneliness and despair. Even in as exultant a song as Patsy Gallant's "From New York to L.A." (1976), a staple of 1970s Canadian AM radio and a favourite of New York discos, the celebration of fame is offset by moments of devastating self-doubt. The drained comedown vibe of "So Lonely" immediately places it in the sad disco category, but it is the loons that make it sound truly forlorn. Stripped of the narrative dimension that defines the Gaynor and Gallant songs, Soccio's track relies on the calls of the loon to intensify the song's sense of abject aloneness. "So Lonely" evokes the melancholy of the morning after, forming part of a deep catalogue of disco tracks dedicated to this feeling, but it also suggests the end of something more. And here we are back to the sense that *Hinterland*'s call for preservation is somehow already too late, that the environmental catastrophe it gestures toward in mood, tone, and feeling is already too far advanced. The loon's call at the end of the 1970s, in both *Hinterland* and Soccio, signals a recognition of the irreversibility of things, that the beginning of the end, both for disco and for the world, has already arrived. In Canada the end of the 1970s was marked by this sense of weariness and no clear sense of what the future could or should be. "So Lonely" and its loons arrived when Pierre Elliott Trudeau's Liberal government was on its last legs and when only Joe Clark's short-lived minority Conservative government was on the horizon. As a result, Soccio's loons, with their echo of the *Hinterland* series, condense and communicate a complex structure of feeling that resonates on both a decennial and national level.

I would like to be able to conclude with the detail that Soccio sampled his loons from the *Hinterland* short itself, but, alas, any close listen to the track confirms that this is not the case. Soccio's sample was more likely gleaned from a wildlife record of some sort, which were in plentiful supply in the 1970s thanks to organizations such as National Geographic, and not haphazardly recorded off the television. Nevertheless, I do not think it is reckless to speculate that Soccio would have seen the *Hinterland* short or perhaps, since he lived in Montreal, the *Merveilles de la faune* version. Even if it did not constitute a conscious influence on the track, it does form part of the larger, late-1970s repertoire of sounds that circulated within the Canadian sonic imaginary. Following Soccio, the loon call has become a surprisingly common feature in contemporary electronic music. As Philip Sherburne explains, the presence of the loon in a whole series of tracks from the mid-1980s onward comes down to a sample of a loon's call being included as part of the library of sounds available to use with the E-MU Emulator II, a sampling keyboard that has had an immense impact on contemporary electronic music as well as on pop and dance. But, as Sherburne also notes, the Emulator dates to the mid-1980s, so Soccio's work predates it: "long before the sampler was invented, Gino Soccio laced his single 'So Lonely' with the bird's eerie cackle, way back in 1979. (That feels significant, if only because Soccio made Italo-disco, yet hailed from Montreal, within the loon's own natural habitat.)"[38] As a result, Soccio's track, a link between the electronic and the environmental, serves as a kind of urtext for all the loon samples that follow. It haunts Manchester-based 808 State's "Pacific 202" (1989), the defining track of the Second Summer of Love, which erupted in the United Kingdom in the late 1980s and resounds throughout Sueño Latino's "Sueno Latino," a classic Italo-house track released in 1989 that was a staple in the clubs of Ibiza, Spain, throughout the 1990s. On these tracks, Sherburne suggests, "the loon sound serves as both a rhythmic accent and a spot of tone color."[39] But beyond these sonic attributes, the call inevitably comes with a whole set of cultural and historical connections as well. Used most often on ambient and chill-out tracks, the loon evokes a whole range of New Age artists and eco-sensitive classical composers from the 1970s, including Canada's own R. Murray Schafer, and is an echo of the mind-expanding environmental consciousness that characterizes the period across forms and genres.[40] This connection brings things full circle, from Soccio to the clubs of Europe and back to the Canadian 1970s. From Soccio's initial use, the sound of the loon has travelled far and wide, and no matter how far it flies from its natural habitat, whether into the packed and sweaty confines of Manchester's Haçienda or onto the sun-soaked beaches of Ibiza, contained within its call is a connection to the *Hinterland* short and the long '70s in Canada.

I pick up on various thematic threads from this chapter – horror, remediation, and even loons – further along in *Hinterland Remixed*, but

I end this chapter with the idea that *Hinterland Who's Who* continues to have a force and power in the present. The "cultural residue" from the 1960s, 1970s, and early 1980s may appear to contemporary eyes as abject and pathetic or as cute, funny, and harmless, yet it still holds a certain power in that it is a reminder that meaningful change was once thought possible and that political intervention, even by the state itself, was understood to be a positive thing, even worthwhile and necessary. It is not that this sense of revolutionary transformation or utopian aspiration has been completely liquidated from the present. Yet such is the precarity of hope that those bits of the past that carry it forward into the present are ever more precious and alluring. The *Hinterland Who's Who* shorts do this cultural and political work. They may seem like innocuous, outmoded vignettes, yet there is a weirdness and energy to them that is brought into the present as they are remembered and recirculated.

2. "A record of the last wilderness on earth": *La Région Centrale*, Landscape, and the Long '70s

Filmed in northern Quebec, Michael Snow's *La Région Centrale* (1971) is a classic of experimental landscape cinema. Shot with a 16-millimetre camera mounted on a gyroscopic device, it captures, through a programmed set of rotations, the rocky, barren surroundings and the sky above them in almost their entirety. At 180 minutes long, Snow's film is a real test of spectatorial stamina, but it is also an engaging and thoroughly mesmerizing cinematic experience. The film is divided into seventeen sections that vary in length from just a few minutes to nearly thirty. The transition between sections is marked by an illuminated X, or cross, that occupies the whole of the film frame and remains on-screen for just a few seconds. In some of the shots, Snow's camera crawls over the landscape and drifts across the sky, enabling a deep consideration of the spaces and surfaces that appear before it. In other shots, the camera spins and swirls at an incredible speed, transforming the landscape and the sky above into a blur of colour, movement, and form. Given its key place in the history of experimental film, it is no surprise that much has been written about *La Région Centrale*. Accounts of the initial screenings of the film, by critics such as Peter Gidal, John W. Locke, and Tony Rayns, are particularly fascinating, not least for their effort to convey its sensory intensity.[1] Later critical analyses by Annette Michelson,

P. Adams Sitney, Bruce Elder, Bart Testa, Bill Simon, and William C. Wees are equally compelling for the ways that they wrestle with the impact of Snow's work on the world of experimental film.[2] My effort here to look awry at the film is no slight to this previous work. In fact, I draw quite extensively on it, looking especially for those moments when the critical focus on the film's formal and structural innovations, and the perceptual and philosophical ideas related to them, gives way to some sense that the film is in complex dialogue with both place and period.

Filmed after his 45-minute slow zoom masterpiece *Wavelength* (1967) and his 50-minute series of pans in ↔, *or Back and Forth* (1969), *La Région Centrale* continues Snow's fascination with, and exploration of, filmic space and camera movement. In his proposal for funding submitted to the Canadian Film Development Corporation (CFDC), Snow wrote, "I would like to make a three-hour film 'orchestrating' all the possibilities of camera movement and the various relationships between it and what is being photographed [...] I want to make a gigantic landscape film equal in terms of film to the great landscape paintings of Cézanne, Poussin, Corot, Monet, Matisse and in Canada the Group of Seven."[3] In order to achieve this feat, Snow commissioned Pierre Abbeloos, a technician and engineer who worked at the National Film Board in Montreal, to construct, from Snow's own sketches and designs, a camera mount whose movements could be controlled remotely and electronically. While Abbeloos worked on the apparatus, Snow searched for an appropriate location. An initial hunt turned up a few promising spots north of Montreal that would be accessible by car, but Snow was set on a site that evoked an absolute sense of wilderness, a terrain without sign or mark of human intervention. After consulting topographical maps and aerial photographs as well as undertaking an initial site visit, he settled on a spot 130 kilometres north of Sept-Îles, Quebec, that could be reached only by helicopter. It was, as Snow described, "a mountaintop strewn with extraordinary boulders [...] some of the kinds of slopes I wanted and a long deep vista of mountains. It's not a travel-poster beauty, but it's a unique place, arctic-like, rocky, no trees."[4] Snow's chosen location differs greatly from the landscapes that populate the history of painting he invoked in his proposal, but it was perfectly suited for the "gigantic landscape film" he imagined as being the cinematic extension of their legacy.[5] *La Région Centrale* marked Snow's return to Canada after years working primarily in New York City. He was drawn back by the actual Canadian landscape since it offered him the barrenness that his formal experiment demanded as well as the opportunity to engage with a specifically Canadian history of landscape representation. But he was also drawn back by changes to the Canadian cinematic landscape and by opportunities to undertake a film project on a larger scale and of greater logistical complexity than the works he had completed up to that point.

The federal government had launched the CFDC in 1967, and Snow submitted his funding application for *La Région Centrale* in March 1969. The film received $15,000 of its eventual $27,000 budget from the CFDC. The other $12,000 in funding came from Famous Players, a Canadian cinema chain. In a 1971 interview with *Take One*, Snow made clear that the funds he received from Famous Players were an investment and that "they want to get their money back."[6] Nevertheless, he immediately conceded that the CFDC and Famous Players "were all pretty good about it. They made the money available at the lab and pretty well left me alone."[7] His funders viewed him first and foremost as an important Canadian artist, and a financial return on their investment was not necessarily their primary concern. As Snow joked, "I guess I have a rather peculiar status, sort of like McLaren at the Film Board – a kook who they sponsor. I don't think they expect to make any money from the film."[8] So, as much as *La Région Centrale* marks Snow's engagement with the history of Canadian landscape painting and the work of the Group of Seven in particular, the way he funded the film also links him to the changing commercial landscape of Canadian cinema in the 1970s. This connection makes him a perhaps unexpected precursor to David Cronenberg, Ivan Reitman, and Bob Clark, as well as making *La Région Centrale* a notable antecedent to these directors' respective films *Shivers* (1976), *Meatballs* (1979), and *Porky's* (1982), all of which likewise received CFDC funding.

La Région Centrale was shot over the course of five days in September 1970. Snow had wanted to film in spring or summer, but various delays had pushed back the shooting schedule to dangerously late in the season. Dropped off by a helicopter, the crew of four included Snow, Abbeloos, Bernard Goussard, and Snow's wife, Joyce Wieland, herself a renowned artist and filmmaker whose photos documenting the shoot are both striking and extraordinary.⁹ The first day of the shoot was dedicated to installing the camera apparatus and setting up the operating panel and generator behind a nearby rock (see figure 2.1). This work was followed by three days of shooting virtually around the clock. On the fifth and final day, snow disrupted the shoot, and filming had to be abandoned. Over the years, critics have identified a series of different production dates for *La Région Centrale*, but based on details in the Snow Fonds at the Art Gallery of Ontario, Kenneth White proposes that the shoot took place between 14 and 20 September 1970.[10] This would mean that the setup of the apparatus took place on Monday, 14 September, that the film was shot from 15 to 17 September, and that Snow and his crew were snowed out on Friday, 18 September. As Snow confirmed in a 1972 interview with George Csaba Koller for *Cinema Canada*, the crew "got stuck in a snowstorm" and "the helicopter didn't come when it was supposed to."[11] This circumstance, perhaps, accounts for the later than expected return on Sunday, 20 September, that White's investigations suggest. Such details may seem incidental, yet Snow's film is not simply a record of the landscape and the camera movements that capture it but also a partial record, at least, of the light and meteorological conditions at that precise location at that particular moment in time. As evocative as the landscape is, I am always struck when watching the film by both the equinoctial quality of the sunlight and the vibrancy of the moon. And there is good reason for these features, which derive from the specific dates that Snow and his crew were filming: autumn equinox took place on 23 September 1970, just a few days after shooting was complete, and the moon was full from 14 to 17 September, the three nights that the crew is most likely to have shot through the night. Even though I am not going to muster an argument that *La Région Centrale* is first and foremost a film about the weather, I do take seriously the idea that it is a film about the conditions and the light, and later in the chapter, I return to the sun, including its significance and how the film captures it.

Snow arrived back in Montreal with five hours of footage, and during a ten-week residency at the Nova Scotia College of Art and Design in Halifax in the fall of 1970, he assembled a three-hour cut of the film.[12] This initial version included a half-hour opening segment that shows the crew on-site, having assembled the camera, put it in place, and set

2.1 Michael Snow with camera apparatus specially designed for
La Région Centrale (1971) as photographed on location
by Joyce Wieland.

it in motion. This material was eventually jettisoned, however, as Snow decided it was unnecessary, that the sensory experience of the film was amplified if the viewer was simply thrown into it without this prologue. It is hard to disagree with Snow's decision, and I will have more to say below about the consequences of this evacuation of humans from the film, yet I wonder what is lost with the excision of this material. As Snow himself explains in an interview that he gave while editing the film in Halifax, this sequence frames the film that follows in a very particular way: "The first 30 minutes shows us the four people who have set the camera and machine in motion doing various things, talking, looking, but after that we are gone and the remaining two and a half hours is entirely made by the machinery (you?). There are no other people but you (the machinery?) and the extraordinary wilderness. Alone."[13] What is striking about this description is that it can easily be read as a pitch for a horror film or as a prospectus for an experimental one. The film as originally conceived and cut by Snow encourages the spectator to imagine, from one perspective at least, being airlifted to a remote spot, affixed to a gyroscopic machine, and abandoned in the wilderness. The remainder of the film records the landscape as seen by this person, condemned to a cold and lonely death, spun round by a preprogrammed, unthinking machine. The horror is generated in part by the mystery of the mechanical apparatus itself. In Snow's revised and released cut of the film, we never actually see the thing, only its shadow. And when its shadow does appear, however briefly and fleetingly, it somehow manages to convey only the cold indifference of the machine to the living eye that has been strapped to it in the horrific scenario sketched above and that is being sadistically subjugated to its programmed, mechanical rotations.

I am not suggesting here that Snow's film has secretly, all along, unbeknownst to all commentators and critics, been an oblique kind of horror film and absolutely must be read as such. My much more modest claim is that the film, even in its final version and shorn of what would have been a fairly creepy prologue, contains many elements that would populate genre cinema such as horror, science fiction, and the environmental disaster film in the 1970s and early 1980s, especially as they were made in Canada.[14] It is less a matter of direct influence, with genre directors wishing to enrich their trashy films with images, motifs, and tropes drawn from or directly inspired by Snow's film, and more a matter of a shared desire to reveal something of the strangeness of the Canadian landscape, or at least some parts of it, and to use this strangeness for specifically cinematic ends. For those familiar with Canadian literature and literary criticism, such ideas are old hat. After all, Northrop Frye, in his "Conclusion to the First Edition of *Literary History of Canada*" (1965), identifies this wilderness dread as a key component of the Canadian cultural imagination: "I have long been impressed in Canadian poetry by a tone of deep terror in regard to nature [...] It is not a terror of the dangers or discomforts or even the mysteries of nature, but a terror of the soul at something that these things manifest. The human mind has nothing but human and moral values to cling to if it is to preserve its integrity or even its sanity, yet the vast unconsciousness of nature in front of it seems an unanswerable denial of those values."[15] The ease with which one can replace "poetry" with "film" here – "I have long been impressed in Canadian *film* by a tone of deep terror in regard to nature" – speaks to the way that Frye's observation in this 1965 essay, like those of Margaret Atwood in *Survival* (1972), forms part of a larger, and precisely periodized, "structure of feeling"[16] that also includes *La Région Centrale*, various public service announcements, and a whole slew of low-budget, location-shot horror films.[17]

Although obvious shortcomings are evident in the sort of thematic reading of a national literature and culture that Frye and Atwood deliver, there are ways that the reductions and oversimplifications involved in thematic criticism retain an element of truth, even in their wrongness, and are all the more influential because of it. As Gina Freitag and André Loiselle argue in their edited volume on Canadian horror cinema, which draws extensively on Frye's work and takes "terror of the soul" as both its subtitle and the title of its introduction, "It is very possible that Frye's reading of the Canadian mentality is a woefully inaccurate interpretation of the way the people of Canada *actually are*. But it does not really matter. The fact of the matter is that – real or imaginary – tension between the 'terrifying outside' and the 'unbearable inside' has had such a deep influence on how intellectuals and artists have envisioned Canadian culture that it has come to express something of the Canadian ethos: a terror of the soul at what we *fantasize* ourselves to be."[18] Freitag and Loiselle, as well as the contributors to the volume, catalogue the various ways that this fantasy of nation and identity has given rise to a specifically Canadian type of horror cinema from the 1970s until the present day, tracing the legacy, impact, and influence of Frye's and Atwood's ideas on the Canadian cultural imagination.

When it comes to *La Région Centrale*, what is most fascinating is the film's contemporaneousness with these efforts to define Canada and demarcate its cultural preoccupations. Snow's film, for all its formal rigour and despite his understanding of it primarily as an experiment in motion, perception, and representation, participates in Canada's Centennial and post-Centennial conversations about culture and identity. Indeed, as funded by the CFDC, the film is directly linked to Centennial initiatives to define and develop a specifically Canadian culture. As a result, *La Région Centrale* is very much a product of the Canadian 1960s and 1970s. It records an actual landscape, but its meaning and significance are wrapped up in the way that it originally related to, and intervened in, a cinematic, cultural, and political landscape as well. Now, nearly fifty years after it was made, it forms part of the landscape of national cultural memory. The seeming barrenness of the landscape that it records belies the complexity with which it delivers the past into the present.

La Région Centrale as Experimental Science Fiction

My approach here is perhaps a little unorthodox in the way that it imagines *La Région Centrale* as a vehicle that carries a unique historical set of ambitions, fears, and concerns from the past into the present. Snow's film has largely been understood as being in dialogue primarily with other forms of experimental filmmaking, a history of landscape painting, and even late-modern experiments in land art, from Robert Smithson's *Spiral Jetty* (1970) to Robert Morris's *Observatory* (1971), both of which are near contemporaries of Snow's cinematic experiment. But to think through the specifically national cultural and political significance of *La Région Centrale* and to think about the ways that the historical moment of which it forms a part persists in national cultural memory, I want to place it alongside other types of Canadian filmmaking from the 1970s that are not commonly understood to have anything to do with Snow's film: the shorts and public service announcements produced by the National Film Board (NFB) for Parks Canada and a handful of genre films made under the Capital Cost Allowance scheme that the Canadian Film Development Corporation introduced in 1974 (five years after Snow had applied for funding for *La Région Centrale*), which sought to encourage commercial feature filmmaking in Canada by offering a 100 per cent write-off of investments against taxes.[19] What binds together these very different kinds of filmmaking – educational film, experimental film, and exploitation film – are their frequent efforts to fathom the importance and significance of wilderness not simply in a cultural moment of high nationalism but also in an era of seemingly imminent ecological or nuclear catastrophe. The "terror of the soul" (to borrow Frye's phrase once more) that the natural environment is capable of triggering is wrapped up in a series of historically specific anxieties, aspirations, and preoccupations that extend beyond the nation but are, for a variety of reasons, felt with particular acuity and intensity in Canada.

By the time that Snow screened a 25-minute excerpt of *La Région Centrale* at the Anthology Film Archives in New York in May 1971, he had decided that the prologue must go and that what would remain would be a full 180 minutes of the camera eye recording the stony terrain and sky above it. The landscape is perhaps most readily described as lunar, which somehow immediately situates the film as belonging to the moment of the moon landing and the collective cultural fascination with the extraplanetary. As Annette Michelson argues, this specific context shapes the spectator's experience of the film. Deprived of grounding in either gravity or character, the spectator is let loose from the traditional certainties of perception and identification. As Michelson observes, "Snow's film conveys most powerfully the euphoria of the weightless state."[20] But it also, in the way that it invites, even demands, identification with the camera, provides a "mimesis of and gloss upon spatial exploration" that "gives new meaning to the notion of science fiction."[21] Although Michelson focuses on the analogy to weightlessness and the sensory experience of floating in space, there is also a way that the film is about the landing as well. Indeed, the opening slow spin of *La Région Centrale* tracks along the ground as though it were the surface of another planet and the images were the transmissions of a just landed passengerless explorer very slowly becoming operational. In an interview with *Cinema Canada* shortly after the film first screened in Toronto in August 1971, George Csaba Koller pressed Snow on possible connections to science fiction. Like a number of early critics of the film, Koller told Snow that *La Région Centrale* reminded him of Stanley Kubrick's *2001: A Space Odyssey* (1968), but more interestingly, he asked Snow specifically about Erich von Däniken's *Chariots of the Gods?* (1968). Von Däniken's book was made into a documentary film in 1970, which was released in North America in 1971 around the same time that Snow first screened an excerpt of *La Région Centrale* in New York. The book is a classic of the era of the mass-market paperback, and the film, nominated for an Academy Award for best documentary, extended the impact and reach of von Däniken's argument. In *Chariots of the Gods?*, von Däniken proposed that extraterrestrial beings visited earth and influenced ancient cultures, passing on technologies that enabled the building of the Pyramids and of Stonehenge. Although von Däniken's assertions were quickly rejected and easily refuted by scholars, their mix of the cosmic and the conceptual gripped the popular imagination. Snow responded bluntly to Koller's suggestion that *La Région Centrale* may share something with the ambition of *Chariots of the Gods?* to think about the earth, the history of civilization, and the immensity of the cosmos, saying, "Well, see, I don't work with ideas like that."[22] Snow insisted that *La Région Centrale* "comes out of a line of things I've been doing," and he situated it as just another step in his experimentation with the camera.[23] When Koller reduced this focus to a "preoccupation with technique," Snow insisted, "That's not technique, that's making the film. Like talking about Chariots of the Gods doesn't have anything to do with anything. You can make a film about anything, but ... that's the kind of reading you can make from phenomena which I made and okay, you're right. But it is not something that is on the screen."[24] Snow conceded that there is a certain interpretive legitimacy to the claim that *La Région Centrale* is in incidental dialogue with *Chariots of the Gods?* yet insisted that any such dialogue occurs beyond, rather than on, the screen.[25] I respect Snow's commitment to a strict formalism – his insistence that *La Région Centrale* is quite simply what appears on the screen and nothing more. For Snow, *La Région Centrale* was the camera movements and the resulting images that occupy the screen space over the course of its 180-minute running time. Nevertheless, I am fascinated by the way that those images connect to the fears and anxieties as well as the passions and preoccupations of the era in which the film was made and transport them into the present. Furthermore, and in a neat irony, it is Snow's formal investigations into movement and duration that open up the very space that enables the spectator to make these cultural connections. This may all just sound like a confession that I have let my mind wander during screenings of Snow's film. And, to a certain extent, it is; yet I would like to think that when my mind has wandered, it has wandered into the space of the film rather than away from it, that the connections I make between *La Région Centrale* and other film and television from the Canadian 1970s are not simply *catalyzed* by the film but *contained* within it.

Not only do the images of *La Région Centrale* invite comparisons to science fiction film, but so too does the soundtrack. The electronic sounds serve as an audio analogue to the film's visual experiment, as both resist film's tendency to anthropomorphize audiovisual representations by making them seem the product of human eyes and ears. As William C. Wees explains, the soundtrack "is another element that helps to dehumanize the mise-en-scène. Instead of windy silence punctuated by the occasional distant birdcall, the soundtrack duplicates the sine waves and electronic pulses that controlled the camera's movements [...] ranging from high, quick beeps, to long, low sonorous drones and tinny hums and buzzes like a ringing in the ears."[26] Wees argues that this sound-image split draws attention away from the landscape itself as part of Snow's formal ambition to transform landscape into image. But, for me, the bleeps, buzzes, drones, and hums echo the sound of long-range communications or guidance technologies and, as a result, make the film seem part of a cultural moment in which such sounds were becoming naturalized through broadcasts of space exploration and science fiction films such as *2001: A Space Odyssey* and Andrei Tarkovsky's *Solaris* (1972) that were deeply interested in the technologies of space travel. Seeing the opening images especially, I imagine the camera apparatus on a far-away planet being remotely controlled and monitored by a NASA crew on earth; yet in truth, Snow,

Abbeloos, and the others were mere metres away, crouching comically behind a large rock while their camera spun and whirled.

As much as the opening moments of *La Région Centrale* suggest lunar or extraplanetary exploration, there is also the sense, as the film proceeds, of the images being of a desolate and damaged earth. The treeless terrain evokes a sense of ecological devastation, perhaps even a catastrophe so immense that humanity has been wiped out or the earth has had to be evacuated. The absence of civilization is, in this scenario, a matter of Snow finding not so much a landscape unsullied by human industry as one that looks to have been destroyed by it. There are moments in *La Région Centrale* when it feels as though the camera is simply continuing a preprogrammed set of rotations sometime long after those who did the programming have died or disappeared. Consequently, *La Région Centrale* participates in a long history of catastrophic and postapocalyptic fictions that fantasize about population collapse or human extinction. These sorts of narratives are inextricably linked to anxieties about modernization, urbanization, and technological development. Mary Shelley's *The Last Man* (1826) certainly counts as a foundational fiction in this regard, but it is Richard Jefferies's *After London, or Wild England* (1885) that inaugurates the modern fascination with infrastructural collapse and the way that nature might reclaim cities and towns emptied of their human inhabitants. The barren landscape of *La Région Centrale*'s rocky, treeless terrain is nearly the opposite of Jefferies's verdant renaturalization, yet it can be understood as part of the same subgenre that either invites spectators to delve deep into the past or projects them into what might be a frighteningly near future in order to imagine the "world without us." Jefferies and most of those who have followed in his wake do not generally explore a scenario of absolute depopulation or human extinction, instead retaining a small group of survivors to reflect on the causes of catastrophe and to repopulate the planet. The absence of the human and the presence of the machine make *La Région Centrale* a far more terrifying proposition. Each spin and rotation, as well as each minute that passes, drives home the realization that the world is not dependent on us, that it will continue even if its human population disappears. The trace of the human remains only in the machine that unsentimentally continues its preprogrammed tasks even after the death of its programmer.

Although the camera apparatus that Snow designed and Abbeloos built for *La Région Centrale* is vastly different from the fictional and animated eponymous garbage-collecting protagonist of Andrew Stanton's WALL-E (2008), both films confront collective cultural anxieties about human death and machine life. Even though one is seen only in its shadow and the other is the sentimentalized centre of the film itself, the two machines share what is an unsettling and unnerving technological autonomy. They are a stark reminder that in our absence not only will nature continue on without us, but so too will the things we have constructed, programmed, and set in motion.

Terrain, Territory, and Time: *La Région Centrale* as Indigenous Land

Of course, in Canada the supposed emptiness of the landscape and even dystopian fantasies about the extinction of human life on earth are in complex dialogue with a history of imperialism and the genocide of Indigenous peoples. This traumatic history haunts the hinterland horror genre that flourished in the 1970s, even when the films do not seem to be about it at all. Perhaps more significantly, it shapes and informs the environmental disaster film, which, from one perspective at least, is always about the death and destruction that are the inevitable consequence of capitalist and colonialist expansion. The structuring formal absence in Snow's film is the camera itself, but perhaps the far more important on-screen absence is the Indigenous population of northeastern Quebec and central Labrador, the Innu, to whom the land represented in *La Région Centrale* ultimately belongs. Their traditional nomadic way of life would have taken them across this landscape that Snow's camera, over the four days of filming at least, found empty. There is certainly a way in which Snow's film might be understood to participate in, even contribute to and continue, the erasure of Indigenous peoples in representations of the Canadian landscape that have long served as a kind of ideological justification for imperial expansion and resource exploitation.[27] Yet the dystopian tone of the film and the image of a destroyed earth that it presents can also be understood, in exactly the opposite way, as an expression of sympathy and solidarity with those who are experiencing something like this future catastrophe in the present as part of a longer history of colonial domination and destruction. In an early interview about the film, Snow emphasized his desire for the crew's visit to this remote place to have as little impact on the terrain as possible. He said, "In this film I recorded the visit of our minds and bodies and machinery to a wild place but I didn't colonize it, enslave it. I hardly even borrowed it."[28] Even though Snow's use of "colonize" here refers to a relationship with the land rather than the people to whom it rightly belongs, I do think there is something in this statement that signals a recognition of the devastating consequences of settler colonialism for both the environment and those subject to its genocidal logic. Although the film to some degree perpetuates fantasies about untouched and untamed wilderness, it also recognizes the catastrophic consequences of colonial exploration and domination and resists any unthinking participation in that process. I am fully aware that this kind of "it's complicated" assessment of the film's ideological commitments and consequences is both irritating and unsatisfying, but it does seem to me that the precise political significance of Snow's film is both complex and contradictory.

Whatever the complications in assessing the precise relationship of *La Région Centrale* to a history of landscape representations that are caught up in a history of colonial expansion, I am struck by the convergence of Indigeneity, ecology, and the planetary in North American culture between 1970 and 1972 and definitely argue that Snow's film is an oblique part of this knot of images and ideas, if only by way of its absences and elisions. The most notable example of this convergence, perhaps, is the legendary "Keep America Beautiful" public service announcement, which made its television debut on 22 April 1971 to mark the inaugural Earth Day. This date was just a month before excerpts from Snow's film were first screened in New York City. This clip, popularly known as the "Crying Indian" ad, featured a non–Native American actor, Iron Eyes Cody, as its central figure, but it had an immediate impact and remains an important cultural touchstone, especially for its central image of the noble chief canoeing amid industrial pollution and household garbage. If this ad pictures a dying earth, Buffy Sainte-Marie's "Moonshot," released less than a year later in April 1972, wishes a wry bon voyage to lunar explorers leaving the earth behind on a voyage of discovery that will get them, she sings, no farther than Indigenous people have already been. Sainte-Marie's song, as Matthew D. Tribbe argues, crystallizes connections between a resurgent sense of Indigenous identity – related, perhaps, to the emergence of the American Indian Movement as a potent political force – the utopian countercultural aspirations of the long '60s, and the omnipresence of NASA in the Western cultural imagination:

> The most revealing connection between Indian spirituality, neo-romanticism, and Apollo, however, came from the singer Buffy Sainte-Marie, a Cree Indian who was inspired to write about Apollo in her 1972 song, "Moonshot," after "a conversation with Christian scholars who didn't realize that indigenous people had already been in contact with the Creator before Europeans conquered them." Sainte-Marie chided NASA and the culture it represented for assuming its rationalist approach was the only way to touch the stars. While NASA and its backers touted the advanced communications technologies it employed to converse with astronauts a quarter-million miles away, Sainte-Marie pointed out, "I know a boy from a tribe so primitive, he can call me up with no telephone."[29]

The story that "Moonshot" tells, of a journey into the future where the travellers will be welcomed upon arrival by the very people they think they have left behind, weirdly resonates with *La Région Centrale*'s visit to a place that appears to be both distant past and imagined future simultaneously. This is a loose set of connections, to be sure, but thinking about *La Région Centrale* as part of a historical moment that sees the convergence of the Indigenous and the astronomical, of ecological fears and extraplanetary aspirations, makes it resonate in unexpected and extraordinary ways.

The terrain, territory, and time of *La Région Centrale*, which bind it to an Indigenous imaginary exemplified by Sainte-Marie, are not alone in collapsing the distinction between past and future with the aim of transforming the politics of its present, the early 1970s. The title itself has this effect as well, albeit in an oblique and allegorical way. Given its focus on landscape, the title of Snow's film might initially be understood in a geographical or topographical way as naming the location that is depicted, an interior landmass with no coasts or shorelines visible. But the title can also be taken to have national, psychological, and symbolic significance: it records a part of Canada that, although isolated, barren, and depopulated, can be understood as central to the Canadian cultural imagination for precisely these reasons – an idea to which I return in the final chapter when I look at Geronimo Inutiq's remediations of Glenn Gould's radio documentary *The Idea of North* (1967) in his installation ARCTICNOISE (2015). Yet, as Snow would explain, the title actually came from Wieland, who had spotted the phrase in a physics book in a Quebec City bookstore and had suggested to Snow that he use it.[30] Although I do not think this technical origin of the title entirely precludes or negates the toponymic and symbolic associations that I suggest above, it does point to the way that Snow's machine, as cold, unblinking, and seemingly objective as it seems to be, might still be considered a mechanism for revelation. After all, it shows both what is there and what is not there, inviting the spectator to see both the landscape and its absences.

Winnipeg filmmaker Guy Maddin has picked up on the political significance of Snow and Abbeloos's apparatus and the political potential of its redeployment. Maddin's *The Brian Sinclair Story*, which forms part of *Hauntings* (2010), Maddin's installation project that saw him remake lost films, focuses on an Indigenous man who died in a Winnipeg hospital waiting room after being ignored for nearly a day and half by doctors and staff. The force of the film comes not simply in depicting the shameful incident, which could have been done more directly in conventional documentary style, but also in Maddin's replication of *La Région Centrale*'s spins and rotations. As Maddin explains, Snow and Abbeloos's apparatus proved perfect for an inquiry into what is and is not seen in any landscape, whether topographical, political, or cultural:

> It was very simple. It was very glibly made, the decision to take Michael Snow's camera. I know Michael Snow a bit and asked him if he'd ever lost a movie. He said he lost 20 minutes from *La Région Centrale*. So I asked if we could use his camera to shoot something. We planned to shoot *Never the Twain*, a Brad Grinter sexploitation film about a man convinced he's the reincarnation of Mark

Twain while visiting the 1974 Miss Nude World pageant. So we wanted to test out the camera first. I put it to the real-life tragedy of Brian Sinclair, who was ignored by hospital staff till he died and then basically ignored by our country. What better way to film him than the unblinking eye of the *La Région Centrale* camera? It really should've been 33 hours long, which is the length of time Sinclair sat in the waiting room. That's my only regret about it.[31]

Even in its brief 4-minute span, Maddin's film reveals how this specific Indigenous man, a wheelchair-using double amputee whose death could have been prevented with a simple catheter change and some antibiotics, died as a result of his invisibility to the hospital staff.[32] Sinclair's invisibility serves as a metonym for the way that Canada more generally refuses to see Indigenous people, whether in terms of acknowledging their basic rights or honouring treaties and agreements. The power of Maddin's film is that it reveals, via the mechanism of Snow and Abbeloos's unblinking camera eye, how what is there can nevertheless still not be seen.[33] This revelation loops back and reshapes how we might think about the politics of seeing in *La Région Centrale* itself. In Snow's film, what is not there can nevertheless still be seen through its very absence. Even though it might seem that Snow's film participates in a problematic erasure of Indigenous people that long haunts the genre of landscape painting, there is a way in which *La Région Centrale*'s precise and prolonged focus on this absence mitigates this problem and opens up the space to recognize the presence of the structuring absence at the very heart of the Canadian cultural imaginary and Canadian cultural memory.

To bring this analysis full circle, I want to point to a visual work that shares at least some of Snow's desire to see the landscape anew and represents an efflorescence of contemporary Indigenous politics that very much draws on the legacy of Sainte-Marie. Consisting largely of drone shots of the familiar lake-rich, forested, and rocky terrain of the Canadian Shield, the video for A Tribe Called Red's "We Are the Halluci Nation" (2016), the opening track on their album of the same name, is perhaps more reminiscent of 1970s work by IMAX pioneer Graeme Ferguson such as *North of Superior* (1971) than *La Région Centrale*.[34] Yet how we retrospectively understand or interpret Snow's film should surely be affected by the video's crawl over the landscape, which culminates in an overhead shot punctuated by kaleidoscopic effects as it slowly zooms in on the band's crest and seal draped over an immense boulder. The track's opening line, "We are the tribe they cannot see," very much speaks to the (in)visibility of Indigenous peoples in the history of landscape representations, including Snow's. But it also points to the contradictory place that Indigenous people occupy in the contemporary Canadian cultural imagination as well, where they are politically ignored yet resurgent, turning their invisibility into a weapon that will allow them to strike back against settler colonial structures with real effect. This sense of a "Halluci Nation" on the rise is very much tied up in the album's use of science fiction conventions and tropes, with colonization being represented as an alien invasion that has temporarily driven Indigenous people underground, only to see them re-emerge in the present ready to strike back at the invading force in order to reclaim what is rightly theirs. The seal on the rock, shot from above, materializes, visualizes, and confirms what is not seen in *La Région Centrale*, namely that this is Indigenous land.[35]

Eco-Disaster and Environmental Loss

As I have already suggested, the 1970s were a rich period for disaster cinema, with fiction film becoming a space in which the worst-case scenarios of environmental catastrophe could be imagined and represented. In some cases, these scenarios were catalyzed by fears of nuclear annihilation, whereas in others they were a response to the energy crisis and to the growing public consciousness of the effects of industrial pollution. A key Canadian contribution to this genre is Timothy Bond's *Deadly Harvest* (1977), an eco-thriller that is, to be honest, not a great film: it is poorly acted, clunkily directed, clumsily shot, and unimaginatively scripted. Despite these problems, it is completely fascinating, not least for the way that it uses the Canadian countryside in winter to evoke a sense of ecological destruction and desperation. The leaden grey bleakness that, in the world of the film, now counts as summer is equal in tone and temperature to certain parts of *La Région Centrale*'s autumnal record of northern Quebec, especially those sections where the weather has taken a turn for the worse and Snow's camera captures just how cold and blustery the rock on which it is mounted must be. The soundtrack to *Deadly Harvest* was composed by John Mills-Cockell and consists largely of synthesized drones not dissimilar to Snow's experiments with electronic pulses and bleeps. The artificial – some would even say unnatural – sound of the synthesizer is used in the 1970s eco-disaster film to give tonal form to the catastrophic consequences of humanity's alienation from the natural environment. Snow's film anticipates this effect, and on this sonic basis alone, there are moments throughout when, from the vantage point of the present, it feels like an early, bold example of the environmental catastrophe film.[36]

In the 1971 interview with Koller for *Cinema Canada*, it is quite clear that the environment was on Snow's mind, especially as it related to a sense of Canadian national identity. When Koller floated the idea that the terrain of *La Région Centrale* seems like that of another planet, Snow turned things back to earth: "Yeah, that really is fantastic. But if anything, I was really trying to show a place that hadn't been touched by us and to record it in a way, because when everything's covered by concrete, maybe that'll be interesting to see. I hope it never happens, but I mean that was an aspect of it because I'm really interested in the idea of preserving as much wilderness as possible in Canada. I mean that's one of the things we have that is really a fantastic thing and it's disappearing."[37] Two comments in this statement are striking. The first is Snow's vision of his film, at least in part, as an archive of a landscape in addition to being an experiment in camera movement. Given that there is a long history of the time capsule, a sense of the importance of archival preservation is not by any means specific to the 1970s, but I do think that the fears of environmental loss and even the possibility of human extinction make the decade one in which such projects were taken on with a sense of both urgency and anxiety, as well as finding figuration in fiction. Douglas Trumbull's *Silent Running* (1972) crafts a scenario in which the earth can no longer sustain plant life, so specimens are preserved in geodesic domes – an echo of the Biosphere that Buckminster Fuller designed for Expo 67 in Montreal – that form part of a space fleet just beyond Saturn's orbit. The film literalizes the notion of a landscape capsule, taking the plants themselves into space rather than simply images of either them or the landscape. But beyond fiction, the most notable capsules of the era are the golden records affixed to the *Voyager 1* and *Voyager 2* spacecrafts, which were launched by NASA in 1977 and contained, in addition to messages from American president Jimmy Carter and United Nations secretary general Kurt Waldheim, a series of sounds and images of the earth, including landscapes. In 1969 Snow quite uncannily anticipated the *Voyager* capsules in his proposal to the Canadian Film Development Corporation. He saw some hope for the future in the idea that the machine that he and Abbeloos had designed and built would serve to image the moon's surface, but he also recognized that its present purpose was to record a wilderness that he felt was surely going to disappear: "The film will become a kind of absolute record of a piece of wilderness. Eventually the effect of the mechanized movement will be what I imagine [for] the first rigorous filming of the moon surface. *But* this will feel like a record of the last wilderness on earth, a film to be taken into outer space as a souvenir of what nature once was. I want to convey a feeling of absolute aloneness, a kind of Goodbye to Earth which I believe we are living through."[38] The second thing that strikes me is the proximity between Snow's impassioned plea for wilderness preservation, especially in Canada, and popular articulations of environmental consciousness from that era. There was, of course, the Earth Day public service announcement of 1971, but there was also Joni Mitchell's "Big Yellow Taxi" (1970), which formed part of the national soundtrack of the year in which Snow prepared and filmed *La Région Centrale*. Snow echoed Mitchell's dystopic vision of a world in which paradise is paved and replaced with a parking lot in his sense that soon everything would be "covered with concrete."[39] In these statements, Snow conveyed his conceptual and aesthetic ambitions for the film, but he also voiced a clear political intent and communicated an affinity with the era's environment movement. With his speculation that the ultimate audience of *La Région Centrale* might be an extraterrestrial one, Snow constructed an entire narrative frame for his film that saw it launched into space, one that very much anticipated both the science fiction and ecological disaster cinema of the 1970s (see figure 2.2).[40]

The barren treelessness of *La Région Centrale* is weirdly unsettling in the way that it suggests wholesale crop collapse or ecological catastrophe. In another strange synchronicity, Cornel Wilde's cinematic

2.2 Landscape in Michael Snow's *La Région Centrale* (1971).

adaptation of John Christopher's novel *The Death of Grass* (1956), retitled *No Blade of Grass* (1970) for the screen version, was released just weeks after Snow's crew completed filming. As much as I find the rocky desolation of Snow's landscape unnerving, it is the lack of animal life that truly unsettles me, especially the absence of birds. This may seem like a personal idiosyncrasy of some sort, yet birds played a role in both experimental cinema and cult cinema of the time that was significant enough for their absence in Snow's film to fit more broadly within a structure of feeling in which they occupy a symbolic place. Another important Canadian experimental film from the era, David Rimmer's *Migration* (1969), uses the repeated image of a bird in flight silhouetted against the sky and intercuts it with shots of other animals (including a dead deer), trees, rocks, the sun, and the shoreline. As Colin Browne notes in a review of a 1980s retrospective of Rimmer's films at the Vancouver Art Gallery, "[*Migration*] tends to be very heavy on symbolism à la the sixties, juxtaposing images of dead animals and dead vegetation with, among other things, diving sea lions, revolving thorns, soaring birds and flickering, fiery water which becomes stars. This is the most consciously 'poetic' of the films shown, even down to the fact that Rimmer uses the camera to 'write' across the encountered world of death and rebirth."[41] Rimmer himself refers to *Migration* as "mainly an editing film,"[42] and there is no doubt that it is virtuosic in the speed and fineness of its cuts and in its array of "[s]wish-pans, sudden tilts and snap zooms,"[43] some of which, in the way that they skirt and invert the horizon, weirdly anticipate *La Région Centrale*. Yet the imagery itself makes it more than a mere cinematic exercise. The soaring seagull especially links the film to the *Hinterland Who's Who* short on the herring gull, which was one of the first in the series to be made in colour in 1966.[44] Even though this *Hinterland* public service announcement by no means functions as a meditation on lifecycles, nature, death, and mortality in the way Rimmer's film does, its images of gulls against the sky do function similarly to his as representative of nature and, in the grace of flight and the contrast between shape and sky, are strikingly cinematic. Rimmer's film does not take up *Hinterland*'s litany of facts about the gull, but he does represent it as part of a complex natural web and as a species that bridges the natural and developed landscape. Even though it is not a public service announcement or nature film of a conventional sort, it does communicate something of a love for nature and an anxiety about its fragility. As a result, it fits within a broader public consciousness common to this precise historical moment, especially in Canada but elsewhere as well, that the environment is both under threat and worth saving. *Hinterland Who's Who* is part of this consciousness, but so too are programs such as *The Nature of Things* (CBC, 1960–present) and *Wild Kingdom* (NBC, 1963–1971, syndicated 1971–1988, and aired by the CBC in Canada intermittently during this period).[45] As well, linked by the distorted image of a soaring gull that served as the cover for its soundtrack album, Frédéric Rossif's *L'Apocalypse des Animaux* (1970), a six-part French television series, aired internationally in the years that followed.[46] Vangelis's proto-ambient score for Rossif's series is very different from either Snow's electronic bleeps and pulses for *La Région Centrale* or Phil Werren's noisier electronic experiments in *Migrations*, but they all stand as early 1970s efforts to rethink the relationship between sound and nature, with electronic instrumentation and its specific tones and textures serving as a means to convey the sense of a world out of balance. This soundscape is something that experimental film shares with both the low-budget horror films and the disaster cinema of the period, where electronic sounds frequently represent not simply alienation but also annihilation, whether by apocalypse or axe.

Finally, and to bring this discussion back round to Snow once more, in his interview with Koller shortly after *La Région Centrale* first screened, Snow commented, "I have a real thing about eagles. In my next film there's a thing about birds. When you start thinking about eagles, its really fantastic. Just think about those big wings and the size that they are and how far away they are from us."[47] Although birds play no part in what was Snow's next film, *Breakfast (Table-Top Dolly)* (1972–76), they do feature prominently in *Presents* (1982), in some cases silhouetted against the sky in a way that brings to mind not only *Migrations* but these other examples as well.[48] And, needless to say, birds are also central to what is perhaps Snow's most significant piece of public art and the work that rounded out the decade in which he made *La Région Centrale*. *Flight Stop* (1979) is a sculptural installation of sixty Canada geese hung in the galleria of Toronto's Eaton Centre. Flying as a flock with wings outstretched, Snow's geese, seen from the various levels of the mall below, actualize Snow's enthusiasm for the eagle and its avian form: "I mean, they're really big things."[49] Thus, even though *La Région Centrale* is distinguished by its birdlessness, the film is haunted by the sense that this absence is caused not just by isolation but also by some greater devastation, aligning it with the environmental anxieties of the period and with the eco-disaster thrillers that form part of the same structure of feeling.

National Park Nightmares

Beyond the treelessness and birdlessness, I think that *La Région Centrale* evokes a sense of horror due to the landscape itself, which, in its sheer immensity, emptiness, and indifference, becomes a source of terror. This effect is exemplified in the way that its barrenness is echoed by *Deadly Harvest*, but below I will point to a Canuxploitation classic in order to consider how Snow's film resonates unexpectedly with horror cinema that followed in its wake. First, however, I want to connect *La Région Centrale*'s portrayal of the hinterlands to a series of Canadian public service announcements that promoted the protection of a set of similarly isolated and remote landscapes. These 60-second television spots were commissioned by Parks Canada and produced by the National Film Board in the early 1980s. They feature four national parks from across Canada: Prince Albert National Park in Saskatchewan, Point Pelee National Park in Ontario, Auyuittuq National Park Reserve in the Northwest Territories (now Nunavut), and Kluane National Park and Reserve in the Yukon. These shorts are distinguished by the way they combine an eerie electronic score, composed by Alain Clavier, with ambient environmental noises. As Michael Brendan Baker argues, the sonic audacity and adventurousness of Clavier's work at the NFB distinguishes him from both his peers and his predecessors.[50] Clavier was a participant in Maurice Blackburn's Concept Sound Studio and collaborated with his mentor on the soundtrack of Peter Foldès's *Metadata* (1971), an early experimental computer-animated work.[51] Despite these collaborations and connections, there is very much a distinctive Clavier sound, which is now almost inextricably associated with the Canadian 1970s and 1980s for anyone who saw NFB works

2.3 "The poor image." Parks Canada vignette for Kluane National Park and Reserve.

(or related commissions such as the Parks Canada interstitials) at that time. As Baker suggests, the Clavier sound does not simply score the work but also shapes it in a powerful way: "Clavier's sonic palette was often suffocating and dark, atonal and discordant, discontinuous and disruptive – the viewer, overwhelmed by the soundtrack, has no choice but to submit to the image-track."[52] That seems especially true of the Parks Canada interstitials, which seem to have had a particular mnemonic hold on those who saw and heard them in the early to mid-1980s, precisely because of the way that Clavier's unsettling score frames the images and generates unease and anxiety (see figure 2.3).

Located in the Yukon, Kluane National Park and Reserve is far from where Snow shot his film, yet it shares a similar subarctic terrain. The Kluane short features none of the formal experimentation of *La Région Centrale*, yet there are a few slow pans across the horizon that correspond to, even echo, one of Snow's programmed rotations. For a clip that was meant to promote ecologically sensitive tourism at a nationally protected site, it is surprisingly unsettling. In an interview given while editing *La Région Centrale*, Snow remarked on the way that his film frames images of nature and landscape that point, both spatially and temporally, to everything that lies beyond them, "the cosmic continuity which is beautiful, but tragic; it just goes on without us."[53] There is a similar sense of nature's indifference to its representation, and of the limits of the seeing subject, in the Kluane public service announcement. Even though 179 minutes and over 4,000 kilometres separate them, both films evoke a sense of the sublime.

As much as these films reveal something about the workings of the sublime, they also offer a good lesson in the functioning of cultural memory, especially how it changes in the transition from an analogue to a digital culture. As I argued in the opening chapter in relation to the *Hinterland Who's Who* public service announcements, people do not simply remember the big events from any specific historical period but often, it seems, also experience the much more tenacious hold exerted by those everyday and incidental things, which, in their banality and repetition, burrow their way into subconscious cultural memory. Once their cultural moment has passed, whether it is a television theme tune or the set of gestures in, say, doing a Rubik's Cube, they are half-forgotten, only to be brought back to mind intermittently in a flush of nostalgia or a randomly triggered memory. In some cases, the subject may begin to harbour doubts about whether the thing was exactly as remembered or whether it existed at all. Although they appeared frequently on Canadian television in the early to mid-1980s, Parks Canada interstitials were, like the *Hinterland Who's Who* spots, withdrawn from circulation at some point in the late 1980s. After that, as time passed, they entered the zone of unsure remembrance, a collective uncertainty about whether they actually existed. I think this occurrence was in large part due to the eerie strangeness of Clavier's music, whose pitch-shifted weirdness makes the spots seem unreal or oneiric. Although the advent of YouTube in 2005 would see the re-emergence of these clips as people scoured old VHS tapes and uploaded them, their persistence in cultural memory in the years prior to that was helped along by the music of Boards of Canada, whose work, especially their album *Music Has the Right to Children* (1998), replicates and reproduces Clavier's distinctive sound. As Baker observes, the "blissed-out analog glow of Michael Sandison and Marcus Eoin's work is a dead ringer for Clavier's warmer, more melodic compositions."[54] Key to the Boards of Canada sound is an equation between the distortions of both remembering and remediation. The nearness of the Boards of Canada sound to Clavier's work aligns the uncertainty of memory with the instability of media. As a result, Boards of Canada tracks such as "Wildlife Analysis" (1996) and "Kaini Industries" (1998), which are both roughly the length of a 60-second public service announcement, sound like Clavier but not quite, as if they were done from imperfect memory and done in a way meant to emphasize the imperfections of analogue storage and preservation. The warp and static of the sounds ensure that the tracks do not sound entirely like Clavier or half-remembered Clavier but instead like Clavier as heard on a malfunctioning 16-millimetre projector, as transmitted through the small speakers of a tube television, or as brought into the present on a low-grade VHS cassette. And, indeed, when these spots reappeared online, they did so in poor quality, gleaned from tapes that had only incidentally preserved them in the ad breaks of the shows actually being recorded. Finally, in a nice irony, these interstitials share something with *La Région Centrale*. As much as Snow's film screens worldwide and is a staple of experimental film programming, its unavailability on DVD has, almost inevitably, ensured its appearance online and on YouTube. The version there, split into two parts, has a digital on-screen graphic that suggests it was taped from Rai Tre, one of the channels of Italy's government broadcasting agency. I do not know the date or the circumstances in which *La Région Centrale* would have been shown on television, but how extraordinary that it was. This poor copy of *La Région Centrale* functions in a similar way to the rediscovered interstitials. If the cinematic experience of Snow's film is overwhelming and its immensity almost incomprehensible, its presence online in a poor copy is nevertheless reassurance that it actually exists and is as you remember it.[55]

What makes the Kluane public service announcement especially unnerving is the way the human figures trekking across the tundra are isolated in long shots against the snowy landscape. The slow reverse zoom suggests being watched menacingly from afar. The stalking, unseen threat in the wilderness is a staple of 1970s horror cinema and is particularly common, perhaps not surprisingly, in Canadian examples of the genre. Peter Carter's *Rituals* (1977), also known as *The Creeper*, is a tax shelter horror film made in the forests of northern Ontario. For their annual summer getaway, five doctors are dropped off by floatplane deep in the wilds of the Canadian Shield. They plan to fish, drink, and over the course of five days, hike back through the woods to the nearest town. Things, predictably, begin to go horribly wrong almost immediately, and it eventually becomes clear that they are being targeted by a madman in the woods seeking revenge, they later learn, for the past professional indiscretions of one of the doctors. More interesting than this inferior rendering of the plotline of John Boorman's *Deliverance* (1972), however, is the way that the film uses and presents the landscape. As Caelum Vatnsdal puts it, "The horror in *Rituals* is based on reality, almost obsessively so. Nothing could be more Canadian – it's like a documentary about suffering in the woods."[56] In the film's early scenes, the density of the brush generates a sense of claustrophobia, suggesting a constant yet obscured threat, but further on in the film the men trek across an open, barren landscape eerily reminiscent of Snow's vista in *La Région Centrale*. There is something about this landscape's contours and wide-openness that utterly terrifies. Since the film was shot outside Sault Ste Marie, Ontario, this terrain is most likely the result of strip mining or soil erosion, yet it assumes, within the logic of the film, an air of absolute menace. As a manifestation of the immediate threat and peril the men face, the landscape is the visible terrain of the unseen madman, whom, almost conspiratorially, it hides. Later, when the remaining men reach the abandoned hydroelectric dam that they hope will offer them safety, they spot the madman on the horizon.[57] For me, this is not only one of the most terrifying moments in all of Canadian cinema but also one that, each time I watch Snow's film, I weirdly expect to be replicated, even though I know this is an irrational expectation. The possibility of a madman popping up on the horizon in full view of Snow's camera only to be gone when the rotation comes round again was unlikely when I first saw the film, and I would think that the likelihood diminishes each subsequent time I watch it. Nevertheless, the tone and atmosphere of Snow's film ensure that I always keep an eye out for him, and as a result, his nonappearance in *La Région Centrale* does not, in a strange way, preclude his presence there in the horizon of my expectations.

The abandoned dam in *Rituals* invites another way of thinking about the landscape in *La Région Centrale*. Even though no facility is visible in Snow's film, the area in which it was shot occupies a significant place in the history of Canadian hydroelectric development. Built between 1967 and 1974, the Churchill Falls Generating Station in Labrador is distant from the spot where Snow shot his film, yet the lines that transport the electricity from Churchill Falls to the broader North American grid run through the very terrain Snow captures in *La Région Centrale*. Even though these electrical lines are not visible in Snow's frame, they are very much part of the larger context of the film. They are precisely the sort of "manmade" installation that he sought to avoid in shooting *La Région Centrale*. Snow's sense of urgency in filming absolute wilderness before it disappeared coincided with the accelerated development of hydroelectric facilities and transmission towers and lines across Canada in the 1960s and 1970s, which, as Daniel Macfarlane argues, is very much connected to a sense of national identity. In considering Canada's attachment to hydro developments in the postwar period, Macfarlane writes, "Nor should we discount the nation-building aspects of these developments, including cultural affinities and various forms of hydro/hydraulic nationalism. The ubiquity of hydroelectric generation in Canada is revealed by the fact that Canadians, especially in Ontario, tend to call all electricity 'hydro' regardless of its source ('how much's your hydro bill, eh?'). And hydroelectricity is clearly tied to identity in other provinces, especially Quebec."[58] As a result, hydro installations, like the "hydro/hydraulic nationalism" that they represent, haunt the space of *La Région Centrale*, even though they are situated out of view or perhaps only in the future of the particular patch of land it captures.

Of course, the story of hydroelectric development in Quebec and in Canada, including its place in the accelerated modernization that characterized the postwar period, is closely tied to the Indigenous politics of that moment and to the widescale dispossession of land that generating stations and hydro corridors require. As the Churchill Falls development moved forward, the Province of Quebec announced plans, in April 1971, for another generating station, at James Bay, in the western part of the province. It did so without consulting, or even really considering, the impact of such a development on the Cree communities in the area. In the wake of the announcement, these communities mobilized to block the construction of the dam. An injunction against the province was granted in 1973, leading to the signing of the James Bay and Northern Quebec Agreement in 1975. The James Bay protests are a major landmark in the history of Indigenous opposition in Canada, and accounts of the struggle occupy an important place in the history of Canadian cinema.[59] The NFB, perhaps not surprisingly, was quick to capture the struggle as it unfolded. Boyce Richardson and Tony Ianzelo's *Our Land Is Our Life* (1974) and *Cree Hunters of Mistassini* (1974) both convey the importance of the land to the Cree, and Alanis Obomsawin's *Amisk* (1977) alternates between performances at a festival held to raise funds for the Cree communities fighting the development and meetings in which Cree discuss the connections between their traditions and their future. Later documentaries, such as Boyce Richardson's *Flooding Job's Garden* (1991) and Magnus Isaacson's *Power* (1996), look back at the historical importance of Indigenous opposition to both the James Bay I and James Bay II developments and situate these struggles as central to the Canadian 1970s and 1980s. Although *La Région Centrale*'s sights are set on the opposite side of the province, its proximity to the Churchill Falls lines and its documentation of a landscape that, however isolated it may appear, is at the very heart of Canada's "hydro/hydraulic nationalism" of the high-nationalism era make it part of a broader set of works about national identity, natural resources, Indigenous resistance, and the wilderness scattered throughout the history of Canadian cinema.[60]

A Strikingly Gorgeous Yet Eerie Calm

To draw this chapter to a close, I want to turn briefly to a more contemporary artist, Peter Doig, whose paintings mediate between Snow and 1970s horror cinema in a way that renders the original connection between them two or three decades earlier readily visible. Doig is a Scottish Canadian artist born in Edinburgh, raised in Montreal, and now living in Trinidad whose work bears the imprint of a youth watching horror cinema.[61] A number of his paintings draw on Sean S. Cunningham's slasher classic *Friday the 13th* (1980), which, although clearly influenced by 1970s Canadian wilderness horror, is an American film. Nevertheless, Doig's depictions of key scenes from the film capture that moment when the threat has seemingly been neutralized and a sense of calm descends: *Canoe Lake* (1997–98) shows protagonist Alice drifting listlessly on the lake at the end of the film, and *Echo Lake* (1998) shows a policeman on the shoreline from Alice's perspective in the canoe. The latter especially captures the lingering threat that resides within eerie calmness, as the human figure is immersed in the ink-black murkiness of both the forest and its reflection in the placid lake.[62]

The same unnerving calmness defines the Parks Canada public service announcement for Prince Albert National Park in Saskatchewan, which, like the one for Kluane, dates from the early 1980s. The multiple canoes that appear in the spot are a tangible link to the Doig paintings, wilderness horror, and even the "Crying Indian" ad of 1971 mentioned earlier. There is also a shot as the camera makes its way through the leafy forest undergrowth that, despite the soothing and hypnotic music, is almost unbearably creepy and unsettling. A similar calmness descends on Snow's landscape as the film enters its third hour. Snow structures *La Région Centrale* on a 24-hour cycle, beginning at noon one day and ending just short of a full rotation at 11:00 a.m. the next.

The sun is out at dusk, and as the camera spirals and spins, there are lens flares that produce strikingly gorgeous images. I am not sure if anyone has worked through the semiotics of lens flare, but for me the effect is inextricably associated with both the 1970s and film itself, and it tends to represent a tranquility that should be cherished but is under threat. Although it may just be an optical phenomenon generated by the interaction of lens and light, when it appears in *La Région Centrale*, in the Parks Canada public service announcement for Point Pelee National Park, and in *Rituals*, the lens flare becomes a visual trope of an uneasy and fragile relation to the natural environment. It evokes the whole structure of feeling of a precise historical moment when ecological anxiety manifested itself across a variety of cinematic forms.

In her analysis of *La Région Centrale*, Johanne Sloan argues that Snow manages at once to push the technical and conceptual limits of landscape representation and stay true to the genre's conventions: "What is most striking about *La Région Centrale*, I want to emphasize, is precisely that this dehumanized, machinic, inexpressive process *fails* to result in a landscape image that is entirely drained of narrative, affect, and memory. And Snow knew it would fail in this respect, that it had to fail in some sense as a structural film and as a bachelor machine, if it was going to measure up to the great landscape art of the past."[63] One of my interests in this chapter has been to think through the ways that Snow's landscape film is rich with precisely the "narrative, affect, and memory" that Sloan identifies. Not only are there a whole set of cultural connections that ground and embed Snow's film within the wider Canadian cinematic, cultural, and political context of the 1970s, but it is also a film that is deeply engaged with the central and defining social, political, and environmental questions of the decade. *La Région Centrale* is a very moving film, not simply because it spins its audience around for three hours but also because it opens up a cinematic space, in terms of both duration and subject, for memory and emotion as well as engagement and contemplation. Its continued force resides in the way that it brings the past into the present. *La Région Centrale* is both a landmark of experimental landscape cinema and a remarkable document of both period and place.

3 "SCTV now begins its programming day": Television, Satire, and the Archive

Produced between 1976 and 1984 and airing on a variety of channels in both Canada and the United States, SCTV is a landmark of television comedy and essential to any account of the history of satire on the small screen. It stands alongside the early seasons of *Saturday Night Live* (NBC, 1975–present) as one of the key sketch comedy shows of its era, and it launched the careers of numerous actors and comedians – John Candy, Andrea Martin, Dave Thomas, Joe Flaherty, Catherine O'Hara, Harold Ramis, Rick Moranis, Eugene Levy, and Martin Short – who would go on to shape film and television humour in the years and decades that followed. My concern in this chapter is less with SCTV's role in the history of television comedy than with the way that it now functions as an archive of televisual form and a catalyst for cultural memory. Its usefulness as an archive derives from the show's structuring conceit: SCTV spoofed not simply the distinctive programming of its era but also the mechanics of television itself, punctuating its satire of familiar television genres and forms with everything from ad breaks and station identifications to public service announcements and teasers for upcoming programs. As a result, and in the face of the relative indifference that official archives show to this type of incidental or ephemeral televisual material, SCTV serves as a rich resource for those wanting to understand the feeling and experience of being a viewer in the 1970s and early 1980s, a largely pre-cable era of broadcasting defined by idiosyncratic programming, regional oddities, jarring juxtapositions, and the structured ebb and flow of the broadcast day from sign-on to sign-off.

Set in fictional Melonville, SCTV presents a satirical behind-the-scenes look at the daily operations of a small-market television station that, quite inexplicably, imagines itself to be a rival, competitor, and equal of the big networks. A good deal of SCTV's comedy derives from this basic sitcom format. It is, from one angle at least, a simple workplace comedy shot through with elements of farce and a commitment to the absurd. The interactions between characters, such as network president Guy Caballero (Flaherty), programming maven Edith Prickley (Martin), union leader Sid Dithers (Levy), and gregarious on-air personality Johnny LaRue (Candy), provide a sitcom frame through which SCTV satirizes the business of television, making it the contemporary of other broadcast media sitcoms of the era, such as *The Mary Tyler Moore Show* (CBS, 1970–77) and *WKRP in Cincinnati* (CBS, 1978–82).

For all the comedic possibilities inherent in a sitcom set at a struggling television station, the real power of SCTV resides in the way that it combines this backstage satire with the sketches and spoofs that make up the station's on-air content. Given the show's origins as an offshoot of The Second City, a Chicago theatrical institution that opened a Toronto location in 1973 and specialized in topical, satirical, semi-improvised comedy revues, it is perhaps not surprising that the show's creators devised a format that would allow for both extended sketches and short comedic bits. But the striking thing about SCTV, and what makes it invaluable to those interested in the 1970s and 1980s, is its fidelity to the televisual universe it creates. Beyond the backstage conflicts, blunders, and mishaps, SCTV consists of programming from the fictional network. As a result, it is able to satirize the business of television as well as the medium's form and content. SCTV certainly takes aim at the exhausted genres and overworked formulas that populated late-1970s and early 1980s television, from game shows to police dramas, and perhaps just as importantly it spoofs the ads, newsbreaks, public service announcements, and promos that punctuated these programs. Adapting Gérard Genette, who uses the term "paratext" to name all those elements of a book that are not the primary text, I use "paratelevisual" here, as I did in Chapter 1, to identify all the structuring elements of broadcast television that are not usually recognized or thought of as its proper content.[1] SCTV satirizes both the content and the construction of television, resulting in the need for a term that distinguishes it from more straightforward parody shows that merely spoof generic forms and program formats. This attention to television's form and flow make SCTV, whatever distortions come as a consequence of its satiric impulses and comedic exaggerations, a kind of time capsule that preserves a surprisingly complete televisual experience of the period. It does so in a way that, for the most part, runs counter to the parcelization of the televisual past that occurs when it is preserved in official archives or packaged for commercial sale. SCTV's decision to compress the broadcast day into individual episodes may have been a simple matter of playing to comedic strengths and opening up satiric possibilities, but it resulted in a show that preserves that most ephemeral aspect of television: the experience of watching it.[2]

In this chapter, I am going to explore three specific ways that I think SCTV preserves the televisual past. First, it functions as a kind of historical snapshot of televisual flow, capturing something of the form and feel of television of its era, even as it compresses and lampoons it. Second, SCTV serves as an archive of lost or disappearing generic forms. In its presentation of program parodies, spoof ads, and fake promos for shows that will never actually appear, SCTV provides a fairly comprehensive overview of the types of content that appeared on television in the late 1970s and early 1980s, including many forms that, even by then, seemed old hat and part of television's past. Third, SCTV operates as a record of place. This is most true of the episodes that were shot in Edmonton as a result of a deal with the owner of ITV, a regional television network, to move production there from Toronto. As a consequence of this relocation at the beginning of its third series, SCTV records the precise look of a provincial Canadian city of the period and captures more generally the growth and expansion of suburban Canada. In addition to this representation of a real landscape, it also presents a vision of the North American televisual landscape from the vantage point of a local station, a peripheral player located far away from the major centres and desperately generating any kind of programming whatsoever to fill its schedule. These three modes of preservation – a history of flow, an archive of forms, and a record of place – all interact and intertwine, of course, but I treat them separately and in sequence in an effort to identify precisely how media and memory converge in SCTV.

A History of Televisual Flow

One of the most memorable sequences from SCTV comes in one version of its opening credits.[3] Against a backdrop of dozens of television sets being thrown from the windows of a large apartment block and crashing on the sidewalk below, a voiceover announcer declares, "The SCTV Television Network now begins its programming day. SCTV is now on the air!" This announcement transports the spectator to the fictional world that SCTV inhabits, while alerting them that this small, strange broadcaster has taken over the network they are currently watching, whether it was Global in the early years, NBC or the CBC in its prime, or by its final series, HBO/Cinemax. There is clearly a Brechtian aspect to the announcement and to the other metatelevisual elements interspersed throughout the show. By reproducing and satirizing the continuity segments of network television, SCTV makes them strange, rendering them noticeable to a contemporary audience for whom they have become completely naturalized as part of the everyday experience of watching television. By foregrounding these component parts of the broadcast infrastructure, SCTV estranges its viewers from the act of watching television itself.

There were, of course, antecedents to SCTV's metatelevisual tomfoolery. In the 1960s, programs such as *That Was the Week That Was* (BBC, 1962–63) and *This Hour Has Seven Days* (CBC, 1964–66) pushed the limits of news and current affairs programming in their tastes for controversial topics and their sharp satirical sense. But they also played with the conventions of television itself, mobilizing common forms, such as the man-in-the-street interview, only to undermine or exploit them for comedic and political ends. Perhaps a more direct influence on SCTV's metatelevisual experimentation is *Monty Python's Flying Circus* (BBC 1, 1969–73; BBC 2, 1974), which, beyond its parody of familiar genres, frequently took apart and reorganized the grammar of the television program: closing credits would sometimes appear part way through an episode or at its beginning, segments would be broken up by fake continuity announcements, station identifications, and news flashes, and sketches would be cut off to join something else already in progress. Finally, there is SCTV's near contemporary *Saturday Night Live*, which, from its very beginning in 1975, featured "Weekend Update," a parody of nightly network news broadcasts, as well as frequent commercial spoofs. I am sure there are plenty of other examples in the history of television comedy that also indulge in some level of metatelevisual play, but what makes SCTV particularly interesting is that its core premise rests on a media-specific self-reflexivity. It is television about television, but more precisely, it is television that interrogates both the stuff and structure of television.[4]

SCTV's self-reflexivity is certainly a sign or feature of the televisual postmodernism that was emergent in the 1970s, but I find it more productive to think about the show's innovations using the language of Raymond Williams, whose landmark *Television: Technology and Cultural Form* (1974) was published just two years before SCTV hit the air. Williams argues that the analysis of television, both popular and academic, too often focuses on individual programs abstracted from the larger context of the broadcast schedule of which they are a part. He encourages a shift in analytical focus in television reviewing and in the emerging discipline of television studies from the interpretation of shows in isolation to a consideration of the programmed flow that structures the experience of watching television. As Williams argues, "In all developed broadcasting systems the characteristic organisation, and therefore the characteristic experience, is one of sequence or flow. This phenomenon, of planned flow, is then perhaps the defining characteristic of broadcasting, simultaneously as a technology and as a cultural form."[5] SCTV goes beyond parodying television programming to satirize the "planned flow" that Williams identifies and names. As Williams explains in his preface, the structure of television became fully visible to him only when he was a visiting professor at Stanford in 1973 and found himself, as he puts it, "in a very different television situation" from that to which he was accustomed in the United Kingdom.[6] Through its compressions and satiric distortions,

SCTV likewise defamiliarizes the experience of television and might be imagined as a kind of unexpected and unintentional ally of Williams. In estranging television, SCTV encourages its audience to recognize that the naturalized sequence of the programming day is very much an artificial construct, a planned flow designed to capture them as an audience. There is a seeming irony here, in the sense that SCTV is itself the product of commercial television and subject to its commodity logic, but this fact is mitigated somewhat by the way that the show encourages a kind of boundary confusion between its fake programming, advertising, and promotional bumpers and the real stuff that appears before, after, and during them. SCTV's satire of screen culture is characterized as much by admiration as by acidity (I discuss the show's telephilia and cinephilia below), yet this ambivalence does not detract from the structural insights that its satire enables.

From the vantage point of the present, even if seen through the lens of SCTV's satire, the structure and conventions of 1970s and early 1980s televisual flow seem especially strange and wonderful. What struck me immediately when I returned to SCTV on DVD is the extent to which the kind of formal sign-on that begins each episode now needs to be historicized. Such a performative declaration was part of the formal architecture of television transmission in an era before the advent of 24-hour programming. It, along with the corresponding sign-off announcement at the end of the broadcast day, with its listing of transmitters, retransmitters, and the playing of the national anthem, now metonymically represents a whole era of broadcasting that has been eclipsed and belongs to the past. The CBC, for instance, switched to a 24-hour format on 9 October 2006, which meant the loss of a set of sign-off protocols that had long been in place. This type of paratelevisual material, for a long time, was simply inaccessible once it left the air. Unlike the popular programs of the past, some of which have at least found their way back into circulation through VHS or DVD reissues and more recently on streaming websites, this material was largely condemned to the archives, the cost of its preservation, if it was saved at all, being its inaccessibility.

This kind of paratelevisual material is now a source of fascination for many, and I do not think that its allure should be written off as mere nostalgia. Rather, it needs to be understood in terms of a form of cultural memory that organizes itself around the minor rather than monumental, the incidental rather than important. In terms of how this operates, there is perhaps no better example than the national anthem, which conventionally signalled the end of the program day. SCTV parodied this broadcast staple in series 3, episode 12 (show 64), which aired on 5 December 1980.[7] This episode concludes with renditions of both the American and Canadian national anthems. The first is sung by Mel Tormé (Rick Moranis). He starts off with the familiar "Oh say can you," but, being Tormé, can scarcely resist drawing "see" out into "seebadeebadeebadeebadee." From then on, Moranis delivers a scat jazz version of the anthem, interspersing the standard lyrics with improvisations drawn from American popular song, including "Chattanooga Choo Choo" (1941) and "Brother, Can You Spare a Dime?" (1930). He concludes with a classic Tormé flourish, landing with jazzy emphasis on the final word: "And the home of the BRAVE!" In one way, the joke simply draws on the familiar formula that is one of the staples of impression comedy: imagine if *this* person was singing *that* song. In this regard, it is a well-crafted bit. Moranis captures the absurdity of Tormé singing "The Star-Spangled Banner" in full Tormé mode. But he also exploits Tormé's superannuatedness: by 1980 Tormé was still well enough known to be trotted out on talk shows and to work the revival circuit, but he properly belonged to an earlier period. I will have more to say below about the complex temporality of SCTV – the way that it was not only in sync with its cultural moment but also, through its soft and loving satire of figures like Tormé, able to serve as an archive of slightly earlier ones as well. For now, I simply emphasize the way that the sign-off anthem sketch both exploits and extends Tormé's celebrity and is very compassionate in its identification of his corniness. The sketch also estranges the sign-off anthem itself by making it into something to be noticed rather than a mere part of the sign-off protocol.

Following Moranis's take on Tormé singing "The Star-Spangled Banner," the SCTV continuity announcer says, "And now the Canadian anthem, as selected by Bob and Doug Mackenzie" (Moranis and Thomas). Like the Tormé bit, it begins with the anthem's standard opening but very soon goes astray. Doug throws things off track with a refrain from the song "Take Off," recorded on the album *The Great*

White North (1981), singing "Cooo, loo, coo, coo, coo, coo, coo, coooo! / Cooo, loo, coo, coo, coo, coo, coo, coooo!" The remainder of the anthem consists of a mash-up, avant la lettre, of a series of Canadian songs, from Joni Mitchell's "Raised on Robbery" (1974) and Stompin' Tom Connors's "Snowmobile Song" (1971) to Gordon Lightfoot's "Sundown" (1974) and Gilles Vigneault's "Mon pays" (1964). The joke resides in the development of a parallel between Moranis's uncontrollable appeals to the great American songbook in his transformation of "The Star-Spangled Banner" into a show-stopping medley à la Tormé and the construction of a Canadian equivalent that consists largely of the folk-inflected Canadian pop hits of the 1960s and 1970s. The sketch was aired not so long after the 1971 implementation of the Canadian Radio and Television Commission's MAPL rules, which stipulated that at least 25 per cent of radio airplay had to be dedicated to Canadian content, a fact that sharpens the bit's satirical edge.[8] *SCTV* was, at once, the beneficiary of similar content rules for television – it is unlikely Global would have funded the initial run of the show if not for these rules – and rather acerbic about it. When the CBC picked up *SCTV* at the start of the third series, it requested an additional two minutes of "distinctly Canadian" material for each episode.[9] This resulted in "The Great White North" segments, making Bob and Doug Mackenzie, as Erin Hanna notes, both a product and satire of these regulations: "What was meant to be a sarcastic snipe at the CBC became a North American phenomenon."[10] The fact that Bob and Doug by and large do nothing during these segments – frequently indulging in aimless conversation or providing inane tips, in the spirit of public service announcements, about how to use a microwave oven or properly cook back bacon – is both an expression of their resentment about having to create these characters in the first place and a satire of the regulatory demand for specifically Canadian content. Something of this acidity is there in the Canadian anthem sketch as well, given that many of the songs that have been specifically "selected" by Bob and Doug largely consist of the most benign and banal examples of Canadian content, from the saccharine sweetness of Anne Murray's "Snowbird" (1969), which starts the whole thing off, to the empty sing-along bombast of Bachman Turner Overdrive's "Takin' Care of Business" (1973), which brings it to a close.

Although the sketch invites a conversation about the cultivation of Canadian culture in the 1970s through the implementation of regulatory mechanisms, it also demands a consideration of the role, impact, and lasting mnemonic legacy of the sign-off anthem. Long a staple of televisual infrastructure, the sign-off anthem occupies a strange place in cultural memory. Transmitted at the end of the broadcast day, and quite often very late at night, the anthem perhaps hit viewers at their most sleepy, susceptible, and sentimental. This timing, combined with the standard vocabulary of images and the melodramatic strains of the anthem itself, made it an oddly powerful television experience that sticks in cultural memory more persistently than might be expected. SCTV's parody of the sign-off anthem appeared around the same time that a new one appeared on regular Canadian television. Made for the National Film Board (NFB), Ted Remerowski's *O Canada #1: National Anthem: "With Glowing Hearts"* (1979) delivers a standard set of predictably patriotic images drawn from NFB stock and other NFB productions. Nevertheless, it is a powerful film that at once embodies and transcends the expectations for the sign-off anthem. It begins with aerial landscape shots of tundra, prairie, and mountains, before moving on to seascapes, shorelines, and urban scenes. When people appear, they are the benign representatives of order (a traffic cop) and industry (a rather hunky young miner), and what follows are images of a wedding on Parliament Hill, pedestrians trudging through a snowstorm, schoolchildren in tuques and scarves at a playground, and a canoeist braving river rapids. Hockey turns up around the halfway mark, the Snowbirds make an appearance, and nature is represented by a shot of a golden eagle soaring in front of a jagged cliff-face. The Canada that the short presents is a white one, with only the images of a solitary Inuk woman drawing and a single black Canadian kid in the schoolyard to break the hegemonic whiteness.[11] But it is in its final phase, as the anthem reaches it crescendo, that Remerowski's film delivers its most powerful sequence. This effect is, at least in part, due to the music itself. The film uses Vic Vogel's arrangement of "O Canada," which was commissioned for the 1976 Olympics in Montreal. This specific version of the anthem, from its rumbling, brass-rich introduction to the soaring strings of its finale, is inextricably linked to the 1970s and 1980s for those who watched television during this era or experienced the Olympic enthusiasm that overtook the nation in 1976.[12] This attachment is something that is probably unregistered and unrecognized by the vast majority of those familiar with this specific version, yet this kind of indexation of arrangement and era plays its role, I think, in the unconscious operations of cultural memory.[13] The affective force of this attachment is intensified as a consequence of the images with which Remerowski concludes his film. After a stunning slow-motion overhead shot of a diver twisting off the 10-metre tower, the film shows the leap that won Greg Joy the silver medal in the high jump at the Montreal Olympics. The surge of national pride that this triggers is in no way diminished by the fact that Joy won the silver medal rather than gold. In fact, those feelings might actually be intensified by this second standing, necessarily so, since, in 1976, Canada became the sole host nation of the Summer Olympics that failed to win a gold medal. As Joy himself remarked in 2012, "The nation embraced the moment [...] It became almost surreal. But the memory of it is like any distant memory. It's more of an image than a memory now."[14] Although the passage of time perhaps explains Joy's alienation from his own experience and the transformation of memory into image, the repetition of the same sequence in the sign-off anthem has likewise transformed the event for viewers as well. As the Montreal Olympics receded into the past, the connection between the games and Joy's long, loping stride and subsequent leap eroded. As a result, this sequence in Remerowski's film brings together image and arrangement in a powerful affective knot that retains its power even after its precise referent is lost. The film's concluding image, captured in the moment that Joy secured the silver medal, is of an androgynous child, presumably in the crowd at Montreal's Olympic Stadium, hugging his or her younger sibling. It is an obvious final shot in the sense that it imagines the futurity of nationhood in the image of the child, but it is also a complex one. The child's haircut is strangely similar to Joy's own, a standard 1970s pudding-bowl style seemingly appropriate for all ages and genders. There is also something uncanny in the kid's fair features. They are weirdly suggestive of the children in Wolf Rilla's film *Village of the Damned* (1960), his adaptation of John Wyndham's novel *The Midwich Cuckoos* (1956), or more contemporaneously, the youth in Stephen King's short story "Children of the Corn" (1977), which Fritz Kiersch would not make into a film until 1983. These horror connections return me to an observation from my opening chapter: there is often something deeply unsettling about the aggressive ordinariness of the 1970s. But they also point to the complex interrelatedness of memory and repetition: the image of that child over and over again every night at sign-off intensifies its affective force as well as opening up the possibility of its mutation and distortion. What initially seems to be an indisputably joyful image can, through repetition, become something that is unexpectedly unsettling.

I have somewhat drifted away from SCTV at the moment, yet it is important to recognize that the show, especially in its parody of interstitials and the infrastructure of television, is part of a dense cultural web that binds it deeply to its cultural moment. Furthermore, SCTV and the incidental televisual bits that it plays with and parodies form an important part of national cultural memory that persists into the present and is subject to a variety of reworkings and remediations by contemporary artists and filmmakers. So, before returning to SCTV proper, I want to discuss briefly Brett Bell's *Sign-Off* (2010), a short film that inherits SCTV's irreverence toward "O Canada" and similarly plays with the forced solemnity of the anthem's appearance at the end of the broadcast day. *Sign-Off* begins with the monotone announcement that "we now conclude our programming day" before launching into a series of images of landscapes, animals, and Canadian symbols, from the Bluenose to the giant nickel in Sudbury, Ontario. The viewer's eye is guided toward this cavalcade of Canadiana by a clip, drawn from Gilles Carle's *Percé on the Rocks* (1964), of a young woman peering through a telescope. The instrumental arrangement of "O Canada" that Bell uses is a particularly lugubrious one, and once it reaches the very phrase "with glowing hearts," from which Remerowski's film takes its title, it begins to distend and distort, lending the film an almost nightmarish quality. Images of the natural world give way, at first, to what looks like an industrial film about libraries, archives, or information management, but the images soon become more frenetic, violent, unrelated, and odd: a rider is thrown from a bull, a battleship lists and sinks, teenagers have a road accident, a young boy wanders down an urban alley wearing only his underpants, a fish dies and sinks to the bottom of an aquarium (see figure 3.1). The short is a found-footage experiment in juxtaposition that derives from a tradition that includes Bruce Conner's *A Movie*

(1958) but draws as well on a strain of television comedy that similarly revels in the absurdity of decontextualized stock footage. However, it is the inclusion of the footage of card catalogues and early computers that is especially striking, as it points to the ways that cultural memory differs from archival storage. If the rows and rows of shelves, alongside the data-processing machines and interfaces from the industrial film, are an idealized vision of archival preservation and accessibility, the flurry of often discontinuous images that make up the rest of *Sign-Off* points to the randomness and haphazardness of memory itself. Bell's film reproduces something like the half-remembered experience of a half-awake viewing of the sign-off anthem, in which the majestic landscapes and expected symbols of the nation metamorphosize into something darker and more menacing. The film's conclusion, an abrupt cut from a sunset and the final notes of "O Canada" to the brightness of the test pattern and the abrasiveness of the test tone, is perfect in the way that it replicates the now vanished experience of being jarred awake, groggy and confused, in front of the television as the broadcast day ends.

Even though Remerowski's film is safely archived and accessible online via the National Film Board, this is not the case with other sign-off versions of "O Canada." For those, viewers must rely on YouTube and the work of amateurs and enthusiasts who scour old VHS tapes in the hope of finding these missing elements of Canada's audiovisual heritage. As a result, YouTube has become a provisional repository, constantly in flux, for these minor works that often fall beyond the scope, means, and mandate of official archives but nevertheless occupy an important place in national cultural memory. The need for alternative archives of various sorts is particularly acute in Canada, where there has been little official effort to collect, catalogue, and make publicly available the nation's television history. As Michele Byers and Jennifer VanderBurgh argue, "the backbone of television research" in Canada for a long time was "[t]he circulation of personal television collections" on VHS, a practice they term "trafficking" because of its contravention of Canada's copyright laws.[15] Throughout the 1980s, 1990s, and into the 2000s, this samizdat exchange of tapes was one of the few ways that one could access SCTV in Canada. Scholars and fans of the show were fortunate in that a half-hour syndicated version appeared regularly on

3.1 Brett Bell's *Sign-Off* (2010).

the Comedy Network in Canada throughout the 1990s and 2000s, a syndicated afterlife that, as Byers and VanderBurgh detail, is denied to the vast majority of Canadian productions. SCTV became readily accessible for study only in 2005 when Shout Factory, an American DVD distributor, released a boxset of twenty-one DVDs. This release, however, contains only series 4 and 5, the NBC years, in their entirety. A selection of episodes from series 2 and 3 are available on a *Best of the Early Years* compilation, also released by Shout Factory, but the twenty-six episodes of series 1 and eighteen episodes of series 6 remain unavailable in any format. It is in the context of this larger archival absence that the available episodes of SCTV seem especially valuable in reconstructing something of the experience of watching television in the 1970s and early 1980s. They cannot displace those tapes out there where someone, with either uncanny historical foresight or simply by mistake, taped some of the flow of broadcast television at that time, but they can supplement and second them.

YouTube has gone some way to ameliorate this lamentable archival situation, as amateur enthusiasts have scoured taped-from-broadcast VHS cassettes to salvage those bits of flow that were most likely recorded unintentionally.[16] These efforts are unsystematic and inevitably produce only a fractional record of the past. Nevertheless, it is fascinating to think not only about how an inadvertent archive comes into existence on the basis of, in the first instance, widespread technological ineptitude (not being able to set one's VCR timer properly), but also about the problem of time in an era before the personal video recorder's digital network synchronization (having to give wide berth to timer settings so as not to cut off either the beginning or the end of a program). In many cases, I suspect, the bits of flow recorded and preserved on the basis of these difficulties and frustrations are now more interesting than the programs that were ostensibly being taped. As Charles Acland suggests, a partial and incomplete, yet valuable and horribly at risk, history of VCR-era television is scattered in basements, attics, junk shops, and thrift stores throughout the world. He writes that "buried in the shallow grave of those vernacular archives of video recordings are an extraordinarily rich, if haphazard and idiosyncratic, assembly of broadcasting oddities. One-time broadcasting events and anomalies, rare local commercials, station identifications, and sign-off notices. Bumpers, news inserts, and weather alerts announce that one is not just watching, for instance, *Force of Evil* (1948), but a specific late-night broadcast by a particular station of that classic noir."[17] Acland's description of the treasures that might be found at the end of a T-120 VHS containing mostly programs that seemed tape-worthy at the time, but are of little or no historical interest, very much sounds like any individual episode of *SCTV*.

To take an example more or less at random, the episode of *SCTV* titled "Walter Cronkite's Brain," which aired on NBC on 6 November 1981, contains just about all of the elements Acland names. The show begins with *SCTV*'s opening credits and sign-on but also includes a K-Tel parody ad for a "best of" album by the 5 Neat Guys; Count Floyd (Flaherty) introducing the trailer for that week's *Monster Chiller Horror Theatre* selection, *Slinky: Toy from Hell*; a promo for *Small Town Dick*, a detective show; an episode of *Pre-Teen World* that features Rough Trade performing "High School Confidential" and a band interview by the enthusiastic but extremely nervous pubescent hosts; various bumpers that remind the viewer that he or she is watching SCTV; a parody of the "Pepsi Challenge" commercials of the era that features Andrea Martin as incomprehensible immigrant Perini Scleroso; and Dr Tongue (Candy) and Woody Tobias Jr (Levy) giving a lesson on screen acting on the early morning educational program *Sunrise Semester*. Even this partial inventory of the episode's content points to the way that *SCTV* functions as a kind of archive of flow. Taken in isolation, these are all funny bits, but their real force comes in their sequencing and juxtaposition, which replicates the idiosyncrasy of the era's programming, especially on local, independent channels or network affiliates. For those who want to imagine the experience of watching television in the 1970s and early 1980s or simply be reminded of what it was like, *SCTV* provides and preserves a rough approximation of it.

An Archive of Disappearing Forms

In addition to preserving something of the characteristic flow of an earlier era of television broadcasting, *SCTV* also acts as an archive of generic forms. The show's satire relies heavily upon the formulaic familiarity of television programming, both in terms of the shows themselves and in terms of interstitial material such as ads, idents, promos, and public service announcements. The experience of watching SCTV today is one of recognizing the mutability, even mortality, of form. And, as with flow, the show's satirical intent facilitates rather than compromises its archival capacity. Through exaggeration, SCTV renders the generic conventions of specific program formats and individual paratelevisual elements readily visible. As a result, it is a valuable resource for the television historian interested in the particularities of period style and the mutation of generic forms.

A survey of SCTV's broadcast schedule quickly turns up a whole host of program types that have since disappeared or changed beyond recognition: nothing so chaotic as the drunken chat and variety format parodied in *The Sammy Maudlin Show* exists anymore; the topical melodramas of the SCTV *Movie of the Week* have largely migrated to the digital enclave of the Hallmark Channel; the weekend teenage thrills of Count Floyd's *Monster Chiller Horror Theatre* are inextricably associated with the 1950s, 1960s, and 1970s; SCTV *Boogie*, SCTV *Disco*, and *Mel's Rock Pile* all spoof the kind of television dance show that was a staple of local affiliate stations. Perhaps the most interesting of the outmoded formats that SCTV lampoons is the high school quiz show. *Reach for the Top* (CBC, 1965–85) was a fixture on CBC affiliates across Canada. Once the regional and provincial competitions were complete, the winners faced off in a series of nationally broadcast shows to determine the overall champion. Alex Trebek hosted the CBC Toronto affiliate's version of *Reach for the Top* for several years, beginning in 1966, and his normally affable demeanour as quizmaster is the starting point for *High Q*, SCTV's parody of the high school quiz show format.[18] *High Q* features Eugene Levy as Alex Trebel, and the sketch sees him grow more and more frustrated with the young contestants as they prevent him from properly executing his role as quizmaster through their disruptive behaviour (see figure 3.2). The comic force of the sketch derives from Levy's note-perfect turn as the beleaguered Trebel as well as from Catherine O'Hara's performance as the nervous, buzzer-happy, and somewhat dim Parkdale High student Margaret Meehan. *High Q* hearkens back to an era when in-house productions of regional and affiliate stations occupied a greater portion of the program schedule.

3.2 SCTV's high school quiz show, *High Q* (1978).

These shows, understandably, did not always have the production sheen of full network broadcasts, yet they were an integral, and often beloved, part of the local television schedules, not least because they often featured ordinary people from the community and offered them their moment of televisual fame. There is a larger story to be told about the erosion of regional production in Canada, especially at the CBC, as the network experienced cuts from the mid-1980s onward. I will say more about this change in the television industry below, but for my purposes here, what is key is the way that SCTV captures the feel and conserves the format of this type of programming as a consequence of its structuring conceit.

Another striking element of *High Q* is how out of place it would seem on television today, even with the contemporary fascination for competition shows of all sorts. Although something like *University Challenge* (ITV, 1962–87; BBC2 1997–present) persists in the United Kingdom, the sight of anxious and often untelegenic high school students taking up screen time in Canada seems highly unlikely. Despite the fact that *Reach for the Top* was revived in the late 1980s and broadcast in part on various cable and educational channels right up until 2009, the program and its format, I think it is fair to say, belong resolutely to the past. A search of the CBC's online archives turns up a clip or two of classic-era *Reach for the Top*, and there surely must exist videocassettes that preserve the youthful screen appearances of many who were on the program, even if those tapes are languishing in basements or attics at this point as the technology needed to watch them quickly disappears from the homes themselves. Given this situation, the SCTV parody plays some part in preserving the cultural memory of the program. The fact that the show was considered familiar enough to be the stuff of parody suggests its relative centrality in the cultural landscape of the period, and its preservation on SCTV in parodic form further consolidates, even amplifies, that claim. The example of *Reach for the Top* and *High Q* demonstrates not only the way that cultural memories of a specific historical moment are shaped by what was satirized during that moment but also how, in the absence of an accessible and reasonably comprehensive television archive, the satire becomes unexpectedly important in preserving these forms and giving shape to those cultural memories.

In "Embedded Memories," Will Straw argues that film can act as a "container of cultural knowledges [...] a storage device, through which a set of historical references are held, delivered to various places, and allowed to occupy cultural space."[19] He establishes this idea of a "desubjectif[ied]" process of cultural intelligibility through a reading of Jay Roach's *Austin Powers in Goldmember* (2002) that understands the film's frenzy of historical references to the 1960s and 1970s as part of a process through which a certain understanding of the recent cultural past is both preserved and perpetuated.[20] I am making a similar claim for SCTV here, which likewise serves as a container of the type Straw identifies. Through its satire, it stores and salvages a history of television formats and flow from the period of its production, the 1970s and early 1980s. Since television of that era was defined, far more strongly than I think it is today, by a mixing of temporalities – classic Hollywood movies scheduled alongside both syndicated reruns and contemporary productions – SCTV serves as a synoptic, satiric history of television more generally. It shapes the cultural memory of the televisual past that it shares with the present at the same time that it preserves for the present the 1970s and early 1980s televisual landscape that it observed and occupied.

The telephilia and cinephilia of the cast of SCTV are readily apparent in the sheer range of satirical references. They have a particular fondness for classic Hollywood cinema, which is somehow appropriate given that the show shared its late-night broadcast terrain with films from the 1930s, 1940s, and 1950s, licensed in bulk by the CBC as well as by network affiliates in the United States as a form of cheap programming. Beyond the classic and contemporary film parodies, the cast of SCTV also seems wholly versed in the history of television. SCTV's broadcast schedule is distinguished by the same mixing of temporalities that characterized television more generally in the era. A single SCTV episode might mix together a hokey 1950s sitcom, a syndicated wildlife program from the 1960s, and a contemporary but completely out of date 1970s-style variety show by an aging Bob Hope. This atopicality plays a part in SCTV's ability to preserve a sense of the televisual landscape of the period. The temporality of TV is always uneven and mixed, with a number of different times existing side by side as part of televisual flow. That is, however, especially true of the precise period when SCTV was on the air. After the advent of specialty channels, especially ones organized around the broadcast of archive or retro material such as Turner Classic Movies or TV Land, older material played less and less a role in broadcast schedules of both network and independent television. SCTV archives the era immediately prior to this relegation of the past to the niche markets of the cable dial. It makes visible the way that the television of the period, especially the semi-desperate programming of independent stations and small-town affiliates, is distinguished by a rather chaotic historical heterogeneity markedly different from the increased temporal homogeneity that seems far more dominant today.

This process of recollection and conservation of the mixed temporality and program heterogeneity of television holds true for the paratelevisual material and commercial content on SCTV as well. The bumpers, promos, and public service announcements replicate the period form and feel of these genres, but perhaps more importantly, the era's televisual grammar, pace, and flow are invoked by the precise placement of this paratelevisual content between program parodies and before and after the breaks where the real advertisements would have been. The station identification is a particularly powerful marker of period. In her consideration of how the BBC used a number of retro idents in its promotion of the 1970s-set series *Life on Mars* (2006–07), Amy Holdsworth pinpoints the connection between affect and association: "The channel ident has the potential to become an evocative marker of television memory through its repetitious use by a channel across a specific period of time. The distinctive use of graphics, music and sound which work to distinguish the channel identity for the viewer on its reappearance arguably crystallises memory and summons a series of associations with the period."[21] The SCTV logo and synthesized audio identification from the second cycle of series 4 onward, in particular, reproduces the video-influenced graphic design of the period and captures the era's corporate enthusiasm for electronic music signatures. Seen again on DVD, it reminds viewers of the general grammar of 1970s station identifications, perhaps conjuring up some nostalgic feelings about them in the process. At the same time, the SCTV logo and soundmark are in themselves now a marker of period, serving as both satire and exemplar simultaneously. SCTV's ad parodies similarly play with the forms that are familiar to viewers of the period but that, in many cases, have disappeared in the intervening years. Scattered throughout the entire run of SCTV, for instance, are commercials for fake K-Tel song collections. These allow the cast to make the most of their talent for musical parody and impression but also offer a penetrating insight into the state of the music industry at that time, especially the role of television in promoting novelty acts, exploiting trends such as disco through hastily pieced together compilation albums, and squeezing further revenue out of a label's back catalogue.

Perhaps the best of the K-Tel parodies is *Gordon Lightfoot Sings Every Song Ever Written*, in which Rick Moranis delivers an eerily perfect Lightfoot impression and Dave Thomas mimics the rapid patter of a K-Tel announcer. The parody plays on Lightfoot's transformation from folk luminary in the 1960s to a middle-of-the-road performer by the early 1980s, and it indexes all the conventional features of the K-Tel collections' television advertisements: the scrolling list of song titles speedily voiced by the announcer, the clips from the included tracks as performed by the artist, the "wait, there's more" moment when it is revealed that the collection is an even better bargain than it initially seemed, and finally, at the very end and usually repeated several times, the notification of the differential pricing for the album as opposed to the tape and cassette: "tape and cassette $4.99, LP $6.99." Such an ad parody is, on the one hand, merely mnemonic, as it reminds contemporary viewers that such commercials were a television staple throughout the 1970s and 1980s and archives their conventions, but it is also metonymic, being representative of an entire "structure of feeling," to borrow Raymond Williams's term once again,[22] as it manifested itself in the form and flow of television.

In terms of remembering the form and flow of Canadian television specifically, SCTV's series 5, cycle 4, episode 1 (show 106), broadcast on 5 November 1982, is particularly invaluable. When the janitors go on strike, station manager Guy Caballero (Flaherty) decides to pick up the CBC satellite feed to fill SCTV airtime. The station's usual run of programming is replaced with Canadian staples, such as *The Journal*, a parody of the CBC's news magazine program of the same name, which was hosted by Barbara Frum (1982–92), and the topical, panel-oriented game show *Headline Challenge*, modelled on the CBC's long-running *Front Page Challenge* (1957–96). More interesting than these direct satires of Canadian programming are the interstitial elements, which are done with precision and bite. I have already examined SCTV's parody of the *Hinterland Who's Who* public service announcement in chapter 1, but there are several other interstitial elements from this episode that, taken together, reproduce the form and feeling of late-1970s and early 1980s Canadian flow. First up, there is an extended promo for *Monday Night Curling*, a satire of the famed Saturday night fixture *Hockey Night in Canada*. Hosted by Gord McLellan (Levy) and Gord McKee (Candy), with tips from Howie McMeeker (Short) and commentary by Dandy Dick Bellows (Flaherty), *Monday Night Curling* references a couple of real Canadian sports television personalities from the era, Howie Meeker and Dick Beddoes, and acidly stereotypes hockey play-by-play men as an endless series of Gords. It also perfectly replicates the pace and style of the sports promo that punctuated Saturday programming at the time. SCTV's CBC feed also features an NFB vignette. Vignettes were a series of short interstitials that the NFB made specifically for television from 1978 to 1982. Over 100 were made on a wide variety of cultural, historical, and social topics. Perhaps the most famous of the series is John Weldon's *The Log Driver's Waltz* (1979), an animation that brings to life the folksong performed by Kate McGarrigle and Anna McGarrigle while they were members of the Mountain City Four. Even though the SCTV parody reimagines Norman McLaren's short film *A Chairy Tale* (1956) as a vignette – it never was – its presence as part of the fictional CBC feed sediments its important place as part of Canadian televisual flow of the period and provides a reminder of the contexts and conditions under which these films were screened and experienced.[23] Lastly, and perhaps most importantly, twice in the CBC segment, the CBC network identification appears with its familiar audio identification, voiceover announcement, and animation. Designed by Burton Kramer in 1974 as part of a modernization of the CBC's graphic identity, the "exploding pizza" logo, as it is colloquially known, is inextricably tied to the Canadian 1970s and 1980s and, like Vic Vogel's arrangement of "O Canada," forms a key part of the era's structure of feeling, being an ambient presence that both suffuses and defines the cultural moment. Although station identifications remain an integral part of television broadcasting, the fondness that many Canadians have for this specific version of the CBC logo demonstrates the crucial place that interstitial material occupies in the national cultural memory, as well as the way that SCTV archives its presence and placement in the televisual flow of a period.[24]

A Record of Place

One of the reasons that SCTV was so adept at reproducing the look and feel of a small-market independent television station and its in-house productions was that, for a significant portion of its run, the show was produced using the facilities of small-market independent television stations. The first two series were produced in Toronto from 1976 to 1979 using the studios of Global. These early years made do with basic sets and little location shooting, the program driven by the inventiveness of the writing and the strength of the performers, who had honed their skills onstage at The Second City. The third series and first two cycles of series 4 (a total of twenty-six 30-minute episodes and eighteen 90-minute episodes) were filmed in 1980–81 at the studios of ITV in Edmonton after producer Andrew Alexander cut a deal with Charles Allard, the owner of the station. Although cast members were reluctant to move to Edmonton, the episodes filmed there suggest that they embraced both the makeshift studios made available to them and the surrounding locale. This taste for location shooting continued when the show returned to Toronto in early 1982 to shoot the final cycle of series 4 and remained there until the show wrapped up production at the end of series 6 in 1984.

Given this production history, it is not surprising that SCTV provides an ongoing commentary on the idiosyncrasies of local television stations and the endearing oddness of locally produced programming.[25] As much as the show is about a plucky little station that imagines itself to be a network in competition with the major players, it is also about the connection between programming and place. Local ads and programs structure the imagined community of Melonville in a way that has largely disappeared in Canada with cuts to regional broadcasting, the shutdown of local production centres, and the delocalization of the independents. SCTV is a reminder of an earlier era of television when there was a greater sense of locality. It is also a record of the peripheral places where the show was produced. In fact, it is perhaps not too much to hazard a correlation between the fictional station's cash-strapped inventiveness and desperation for content to fill the slots of the programming day and the real show's actual conditions of production, which were similarly characterized by rushed production schedules and making do with the facilities at hand.

The SCTV schedule features a number of programs and advertisements that ground the show in the fictional community of Melonville. Most obviously, perhaps, is the *SCTV News*, hosted by Floyd Robertson (Flaherty) and Earl Camembert (Levy). The tone of this newscast, briefly rebranded *Nightline Melonville* for a few episodes in series 4, was established in the very first episode of *SCTV* in 1976. Whereas Robertson reports on a number of stories of great significance and global importance, Camembert is stuck with banal local news items. Frustrated by the air of gravitas that these stories give his co-anchor, Camembert simply makes up a big story of his own about "a large rabies-ridden herd of caribou [pause] reportedly seen just 5 miles outside the city limits" of Melonville. As Robertson flips through his notes to find the story, Camembert grows more desperate, knowing that his lie is going to be exposed, and further claims the herd is "right down the 401 [highway], 6,000 of them, and one bite, you could die." The humour in this segment comes in part from Camembert's inferiority complex and the resulting passive aggressive hostility he directs toward his co-anchor. But it is also a satire of local news generally, which must conform to the seriousness of address required by convention but frequently does not have stories that merit it. Much of *SCTV*'s satire resides in the way that the station is caught between manager Guy Caballero's aspirations to head a proper national network, even if he demands that it all be done on the cheap, and the way that the station continually falls short of this goal and is mired in the banalities of the local.

Admittedly, the often inane ridiculousness of local newscasts is perhaps something that binds *SCTV* to the present rather than being something that makes it wholly part of the past. There are other Melonville-focused SCTV shows, however, that are exactly the sort of local programming that has largely disappeared from broadcast schedules or been relegated to city-specific community-service cable channels: the bare-bones local announcements program *Melonville*

Calendar, hosted by the soft-spoken Yolanda Devillbis (Martin); the digressive fireside chats delivered by soft-spoken and contemplative Melonville mayor Tommy Shanks (Candy); the local restaurant review program *Dining with LaRue* (Candy); and *Dialing for Dollars*, the intro show for the SCTV late-night movie, initially hosted by Moe Green (Ramis) but later by Walter Cronkite (Thomas), which offers a cash prize to the caller who can name that night's film and answer a skill-testing question. Each of these shows is distinguished by its simplicity and cheapness but also by its odd charm. They combine to create a sense of Melonville as a place but also serve as a reminder of an era when television was less poised and polished. *Melonville Calendar*, in particular, is the sort of community service broadcasting that seems, at this point, unbelievably dull and static but whose disappearance is often forgotten and certainly lamentable. SCTV's satire of such shows is far more caring than caustic and derives from an affection for these programs and places rather than simply taking aim at them.[26]

To get a true sense of how SCTV archives the idiosyncrasies of the local, one need look no further than the ad parodies. Local advertising was once a staple of regional affiliates and independent stations, but it has, to a large degree, vanished from television screens. Defined by their jaunty jingles, eccentric characters, and willingness to play with the available technology, they are a record of place but also of an enthusiasm for the medium of television itself. SCTV featured a number of ad parodies over the years, from those for Crazy Hy's, Melonville's own television and electronics warehouse, to those for Tex and Edna Boil's Warehouse and Curio Emporium, conveniently located, as the conventional phrasing always put it, 5 miles outside Melonville on Interstate 90. Both of these examples archive the endearing wackiness that characterized a particular sort of ad pitch once common on local television. Faced with the competition of chain electronics superstores, characters such as Crazy Hy have, by and large, disappeared, or at least migrated to local radio. And although warehouse and curio emporiums might still linger on the rural fringes just outside city limits, ads for them are no longer a television staple. What SCTV's ad parodies show is not simply that local ads provided these characters with a venue for their product and an opportunity to indulge their desire to perform but also that the form itself encouraged and cultivated this type of eccentric performance. In its ad parodies, SCTV documents a key moment in the history of local celebrity, one when the patter of a pitchman or, as in Edna Boil's case, a pitchwoman in a locally produced commercial became part of what bound a community together.

Something of SCTV's sentimentality and fondness for local affiliate or independent stations and their programming are captured in Seth's *George Sprott, 1894–1975*. This graphic novel or, as Seth himself puts it, "picture novella" was published serially in the *New York Times* throughout 2006 and gathered together in a single volume by Drawn & Quarterly in 2009. It recounts the life of its title character, an elderly curmudgeon. Nearing the end of his life, Sprott spends part of his time reminiscing about his heyday as a presenter on the small-town Ontario television station CKCK-TV. The book itself is meticulously designed: the front endpaper presents a 1950s-era CKCK test pattern, complete with smiling "Eskimo" at its centre, and the back endpaper features the contemporary test pattern comprised of the SMPTE colour bars, with the CKCK-TV logo emblazoned in the lower-right corner.[27] In the book itself, there are several pages and spreads that detail Sprott's life in broadcasting and the operations of CKCK-TV. On a page titled "Channel 10 on Your Dial," Seth presents a capsule history of the station, from its launch on 16 March 1952 – which would make it, were it real, Canada's oldest since Montreal's CBFT did not debut until 6 September of that year – to its decline in the 1980s. Illustrated with a row of imagined awards garnered by Sprott and the station, Seth correlates CKCK's fortunes to its celebrated on-air personality: "In the 1980s CKCK suffered a terrible decline from which it never recovered. Production simply became too expensive for such a little independent station. Only local news survived. The remaining airtime was filled with shitty American shows. Not that anyone cared! All those old shows are long forgotten anyway. Evaporated in the ether along with the folks who made them. In fact, just the other day an old timer at CKCK mentioned George's name ... Nobody in the room had heard of him."[28] Whereas SCTV imagines an independent local station that, despite its budgetary limitations, is the equal of the networks, *George Sprott*, with Seth's usual melancholy, traces the decline and disappearance of a similar station in roughly the same era. And even though *George Sprott* laments that its title character and his colleagues at CKCK have been forgotten, the book is, like SCTV, a vehicle for remembering, a "container," to appeal to Straw's terminology once again, that transports the past into the present.[29] As Candida Rifkind notes, in telling its title character's story, *George Sprott* preserves a moment in the history of broadcasting in Canada. Seth's book, she writes, "is as much an elegy for the ephemeral medium that brought George to the public as it is a biography of the man himself."[30] Sprott, his shows, and the extraordinary output of CKCK may be forgotten in the world that Seth creates, yet "[t]hey do survive," Rifkind argues, "in the pages of *George Sprott (1894–1975)*, a sizable print artifact that tells the story of the ephemerality of local television and its disappearance as a viable form."[31]

That CKCK is, like SCTV, a fictional creation does not neutralize or negate its suitability and value as a vehicle for cultural memory. For example, like SCTV's Count Floyd (Flaherty), Seth's Sir Grisly Gruesome preserves a broadcasting archetype and archives a history of the relationship between the horror film and late-night weekend programming on independent and affiliate stations. Seth's single-page "CKCK Viewer's Guide" for Thursday, 9 October 1975, provides a fascinating, if fictional, overview of a 1970s broadcast schedule. After the sign-on, CKCK's programming day begins with *Voice of the Farm* at 6:00 a.m. Following that, there are such highlights as the morning game show *Killjoys* and the noon-hour soap opera *Green River*. The after-school slot is filled by *Cartoon Parade (With Gus Goose)*, the supper-hour local news is anchored by Austin Wade, and the early evening hours are occupied by Sprott's own show, an arctic travelogue titled *Northern Hi-Lights*. The CKCK broadcast day concludes with the musical variety hour *Countrytime Jubilee*, the midnight-movie *Night-Owl Theater*, and the religious program *Altar of the Air-Waves* before shutdown at 2:30 a.m. It is, of course, possible to map this fictional CKCK schedule onto both other fictional analogues and real historical examples. Soap opera parodies are the staple of television satire, and CKCK's *Green River* is matched by SCTV's *The Days of the Week*. But beyond satire, there are obvious echoes of the real as well. *Countrytime Jubilee* is surely an homage to the very real *Don Messer's Jubilee* (CBC, 1957–69; syndicated 1969–73) and *The Tommy Hunter Show* (CBC, 1965–92), whereas *Busy Bob's Shoebox Showcase*, with its puppets and presenters, seems the station's equivalent to *The Friendly*

Giant (WHA-TV, 1953–58; CBC, 1958–85) or *Mr. Dressup* (CBC, 1967–96). Perhaps even more than these one-to-one connections and allusions, the power of Seth's "CKCK Viewer's Guide" resides in the way that it captures the flow, variety, and experience of the programming day, from the game shows and kids programs that populate the daytime to the entertainment and current affairs offerings that occupy the evening. Like SCTV's contraction of the programming day into a single episode, *George Sprott* presents not simply a series of show parodies but also a sense of their sequence and interrelation. Seth's staff photo of the CKCK on-air personalities likewise captures the heterogeneity of programming that was characterized by the experience of watching television in a pre-cable era: the prim and proper host of the afternoon women's program *Hen Party*, Flora Aiken, sits between Kingbo the Clown and Eddie Allan, "The Prairie Rambler." Even though *George Sprott* does not concern itself with the ads, public service announcements, bumpers, and station identifications that might have appeared on CKCK, Seth does conclude the book with a sign-off sequence that includes details about the location of its broadcast studio in Lakeside, Ontario, information about its transmitters and their wattage, and the availability of the station on the Superior Cable System. As Rifkind explains, this sign-off brings to a close the story of both Sprott and the station, and, after the announcer wishes the remaining viewers a good night, the close-down concludes with the national anthem.[32]

In addition to archiving the local as it manifests itself in programs and commercials, SCTV also documents a very particular landscape. During the show's stint in Edmonton, the cast frequently ventured out into the streets and surrounding countryside to film segments. As a result, SCTV is a compelling record of place. In the second cycle of series 4, Eugene Levy created his Al Peck character, a pitchman behind a series of cut-rate ventures, from his patented Sanitone dry-cleaning business to, more bizarrely, a used fruit market. Levy soft-shoed and sang his way through the commercials in an amusing fashion, but perhaps more interesting is the fact that these bits were shot on location and document the streetscapes of both Edmonton and Toronto. The dry-cleaning ad was shot along 17th Avenue in Edmonton, and this real locale gave material form to the fictional Melonville. It is somewhat weird to think that the rather ordinary streets of early 1980s Edmonton occupied network time when SCTV aired Friday nights on NBC, but, framed by the conceit of the show itself, these Edmonton streets became Melonville in the minds of viewers.

From a contemporary vantage point, it is tempting to look at this footage in the way that Thom Andersen scrutinizes scenes shot in Los Angeles in his archive-essay film *Los Angeles Plays Itself* (2003). In this film, Andersen encourages viewers to look beyond the primary action of a shot in order to see what lies in the background. Bracketing the narrative in this fashion opens up the filmed streetscape as a historical record of place. Whereas Andersen voices his frustration about the violence that film and television have done over the years to the real geography of Los Angeles as well as to the actual lived experience of its citizens, SCTV relies on scattered bits of Edmonton, Toronto, their suburbs, and their surrounding countrysides to piece together its fictional Melonville. And, although I understand Andersen's frustrations with cinematized Los Angeles, I find SCTV's archive of 1970s and 1980s Canadian spaces endlessly fascinating, not least for registering the ways that ordinary built space has changed in the intervening years. To take just one example, SCTV's spoof of George McCowan's Canadian film classic *Face-Off* (1971), renamed *Power Play* in the sketch itself, features a scene where new Toronto Bay Leaves signing Billy Stemhovichomski (Candy) is taken to the mall by the flashily dressed team captain known simply as The Chief (Moranis) to get a suit that befits his new status as a young hockey phenom. The scene is shot at a mall in Edmonton. It is more or less the standard issue 1970s-era brown and orange indoor retail space, yet the renovation or demolition of most of these spaces since then lends these images a historical value. They record a lost retail landscape, as the now defunct Canadian department store Eaton's lurks in the background, and also register a provincial, urban way of life that was only infrequently captured on tape or film.

As interesting as this location spotting may be, the cumulative effect of these real spaces is the production of the fictional Melonville. The precise location of Melonville is not clear. The nearby interstate suggests that it is in America, yet there are many references to Toronto streets scattered throughout the six series. This lack of geographical specificity is somehow appropriate, not least because SCTV, in some ways like English Canadian television itself in the 1970s and early 1980s, is caught between Britain and America. One example of this is a sketch from the first cycle of series 4, *Benny Hill Street Blues*. The sketch, as its title suggests, generates a satire of the quintessential hard-hitting yet sentimental American police drama of the era by introducing elements of lowbrow British sex comedy into it. Although *The Benny Hill Show* aired on numerous PBS affiliates throughout the United States in the 1970s, making the sketch accessible to SCTV's American viewers, I still argue that the very structure of the joke, the juxtaposition of English and American humour, can be understood as a consequence of the English Canadian cultural and televisual landscape of the 1960s and 1970s. The combination of colonial anglophilia and American influence not only shaped SCTV but also shaped English Canadian television more generally in the era just prior to and during the show's production. As a result, SCTV is a record of place in a couple of ways: it fleetingly documents the real landscape as captured on location by the unconscious eye of the camera, and it conveys the contours of the English Canadian cultural landscape through the juxtapositions and hybridizations that make up its satire of televisual flow.

In the next chapter, I move from the fictional Melonville to the very real city of Winnipeg, where, drawing on some of the satirical energy of SCTV, L'Atelier national du Manitoba crafted an operatic account of the tragedy of the Winnipeg Jets out of scraps of tape found in the local television station's dumpster. Whereas SCTV preserves the look, feel, and experience of Canada's long '70s in its paratelevisual playfulness, L'Atelier's *Death by Popcorn: The Tragedy of the Winnipeg Jets* (2005) revisits and remediates footage from the late 1970s and after as part of its efforts to understand a city caught in the grip of the past and unable to shake the sense that it is responsible for its own miseries and failures. So, even though the next chapter marks a shift in focus from the products of the long '70s to contemporary works that grapple with it legacies, the method remains the same: the impact and import of the long '70s in Canada reside in its traces and its unexpected connections and conjunctions.

4 Memory, Magnetic Tape, and *Death by Popcorn*

The work of the filmmaking collective L'Atelier national du Manitoba (2005–08) springs in part from the fortuitous discovery of a cache of deaccessioned tapes in a dumpster outside the offices of CTV Winnipeg. These tapes, jettisoned as the station was in the process of moving to its new downtown location, contained hours of footage of local news events, commercials, and current affairs programming stretching back to the mid-1970s. The collective, spearheaded by core members Matthew Rankin, Mike Maryniuk, and Walter Forsberg, used this discarded archive material, along with other scraps gleaned from yard sale VHS discoveries and newly shot material, to make *Death by Popcorn: The Tragedy of the Winnipeg Jets* (2005). *Death by Popcorn* sifts through the video remains of an earlier era and constructs a turbulent and trenchant video portrait of the city.

The hour-long video collage resists categorization. I am frequently going to refer to it as a film, despite its medium and format, in part to distinguish the overall work from its source video material but also because the concept of "film," somewhat counterintuitively, includes video of many sorts, particularly long-format works like *Death by Popcorn* that offer a story or argument or that document something. If format introduces a whole set of terminological problems, so too does genre. It is a historical documentary about the city's hockey franchise, but it is also an essay film about Winnipeg itself, from the city's golden period in the 1960s and early 1970s, fuelled by Centennial money and perhaps best represented by its successful hosting of the 1967 Pan Am Games and by the arrival of the Jets as a World Hockey Association franchise in 1972, to the city's economic decline and the onset of civic malaise in the 1980s and 1990s. The film's extensive use of archival material connects it to found-footage filmmaking, but its reliance on degraded and decaying analogue sources also makes it a kind of meditation on video specifically and on the medium's connection to history and to memory.[1] The film has a sharp satirical edge in the way that it pokes fun at the commonplace perception that the fate of the city is inextricably linked to the fortunes of its hockey team. Yet, at the same time, the operatic and overblown presentation of paranoid conspiracies about the Jets' departure from Winnipeg in 1996 is approached with the greatest seriousness. Far from simply mocking those who formulate vast conspiracies in an effort to understand the city, its historical predicament, and the suffering, resentment, and melancholy that structure its civic life, the film recognizes the weight and significance of this collective desire to account, in some way, for what have been experienced as insults and injustices. To do justice to the generic and aesthetic complexities of the work, this chapter both delves into the city's civic imaginary and draws on recent critical work on the history and significance of the videocassette. Far from inviting a separate line of inquiry, the work of L'Atelier national du Manitoba, I argue, is specifically about *video-era* Winnipeg, a period that stretches from the late 1970s to the late 1990s. This notion, I realize, makes what I have been calling the "long '70s" in Canada even longer. My aim is not to imagine some perpetual 1970s from which we have not yet escaped but to investigate the ways that we have not fully left it behind. The residues of the 1970s remain everywhere, whether stored, hidden, or naturalized as part of the present. *Death by Popcorn* invites a slight reperiodization, shifting the boundaries to examine how the first tenure of the Jets in Winnipeg, 1972–96, haunted the years that followed. Key to this approach is understanding the connection between format and feeling. The cultural memory of this era is mediated by magnetic tape, and *Death by Popcorn* reworks and reconfigures these video memories, drawing on abject and forlorn jettisoned cassettes to suggest that, as an intertitle near the beginning of the film puts it, "L'Histoire est écrite par ceux qui perdent."²

Since the making of *Death by Popcorn*, the Jets have, of course, returned to Winnipeg. After months of rumours and eager speculation, it was announced on 31 May 2011 that professional hockey would return to the city, with confirmation that the team once again would be called the Jets coming just weeks later. The new Jets played their first game against the Montreal Canadiens at home on 9 October 2011, losing 5–1. The redesign of the Jets' logo and jerseys, combined with the existence of a new, modern downtown arena, renders the images of the old Jets in *Death by Popcorn* all the more uncanny, remnants of a past that is now firmly past but somehow cannot be forgotten and still shapes the civic character. They are no longer traumatic reminders of unimaginable loss but catalysts for a kind of civic righteousness grounded in the idea that recent historical wrongs have now been righted. Nevertheless, the pain of remembering the years in the wilderness still remains and is often conveyed in the most melodramatic of terms. For instance, in conversation with the *New York Times* about the return of the city's hockey franchise, Winnipeg mayor Sam Katz describes the Jets' departure in strikingly gruesome terms: "When we lost the Jets, it was like someone smashed their fist through your rib cage, and while you were still conscious, pulled your heart out."³ The sheer effort by Katz here to convey the psychic pain of the city in the most grotesque, yet at the same time tremendously camp, physical terms is a testament to the central place that the loss of the Jets retains in the city's cultural imagination. This context makes *Death by Popcorn* an even more valuable document in the sense that it captures a city in the throes of a deep and profound melancholia and in the darkest night of its civic soul, fixated on the lost object and waiting for a new dawn that, at that point, did not seem to be on the horizon. It reveals the civic psychic scars that even the return of the Jets, the happy ending no one for a long time even thought imaginable, has not healed.⁴

Death by Popcorn begins with an extraordinary montage sequence that draws its soundtrack in part from the opening lines of Michael Radford's *Nineteen Eighty-Four* (1984), a cinematic adaptation of George Orwell's 1949 novel. As Big Brother speaks of a "land of peace and plenty, harmony and hope" under perpetual threat from the "dark armies" of elsewhere, the film presents a series of images of the Jets and their fans, and of local commercials for furniture stores, fast-food chicken outlets, and perogy makers, that satirically represents Manitoban cultural specificity, the cherished symbols of the local. The dark armies are represented by two figures, National Hockey League (NHL) president Gary Bettman and now retired hockey superstar Wayne Gretzky. The force of these images derives from the civic animosity that Winnipeg harbours toward these men, both of whom play a key role in the various conspiratorial fantasies that seek to explain the Jets' departure from Winnipeg in 1996.

The conventional understanding of the Jets' exit is that the city was betrayed by Bettman, who orchestrated the team's move to Phoenix as part of a larger effort to secure a greater share of the lucrative American sports market. But this corporate conspiracy is grounded in the fact that the Jets' unsustainability as a big league franchise had everything to do with the city's status as a small market with a sentimentalized but antiquated arena, incapable of generating sufficient revenue through ticket sales, the leasing of corporate boxes, or the licensing of television rights.[5] The team's failure throughout its history to capture the league's top honor, the Stanley Cup, is often explained as a direct consequence of this lack of a strong and significant revenue stream. Unlike its bitter rivals, the Edmonton Oilers, who won a series of league titles throughout the 1980s and early 1990s, Winnipeg seemed destined to always fall short of success, to be plucky but ineffectual, and to inevitably exit the league playoffs in the opening round. This failure on the ice seemed to manifest itself in a kind of provincial malaise, even resentment, as well. The Oilers' domination of the Jets throughout the team's history, during which Edmonton subjected Winnipeg to year after year of heartbreak and humiliation, came to represent, in the provincial cultural imagination, the position of Manitoba vis-à-vis the oil-rich and politically powerful province of Alberta. The use of Big Brother's speech in the film points to the proximity between provincial *ressentiment* and a more full-blown fear of and hostility toward outsiders. I should say from the beginning that the film does not assert that there is some fundamental xenophobia that defines Manitoba or Manitobans. Nevertheless, the film's satiric force does have a diagnostic edge in that it identifies what others think of it in the collective anxiety about the province's status in the world and documents the transformation of these anxieties into both resentment toward successful neighbours and a perverse and lacerating self-hatred.

L'Atelier was not alone in the mid-2000s in its efforts to understand the civic scars that the Jets' departure left. In *My Winnipeg* (2008), Guy Maddin also investigates the historical circumstances of their exodus and the demolition of the legendary Winnipeg Arena. By Maddin's own admission, *My Winnipeg* is a docu-fantasia, a film that leavens fact with fiction and indulges in fabrication to produce a truer history of the city than any orthodox documentary account of it would allow. That said, the section that deals with the departure of the Jets, the demolition of the Winnipeg Arena and the Eaton's department store, and the building of the new MTS Centre, named after the provincial telecom company, is Maddin at his most direct, passionate, and political. Maddin laments the city's failure to salvage the Eaton's building after the company went bankrupt in 1999 and castigates City Council for its cynical approval of a new, cut-rate arena on the very spot where Eaton's stood:

> Demolition is one of our city's few growth industries. Overnight, construction of a new arena on the old Eaton's site was announced. Curiously, after years of public fighting, with council resisting, refusing to build a new rink for the NHL Jets, allowing them to abandon us for Phoenix, our civic government rushed out this new architectural lie to Winnipeggers. The result – a sterile new thrift rink for minor-league hockey with too few seats to reach the NHL minimum, should a miracle ever give us another shot at playing in the big leagues. A ridiculous, politically motivated tragedy with the corporate name MT Centre.[6] I'm sure memories will accumulate in this MT Centre, which has nothing by low-priced newness to recommend it. Until then, this thoughtless new building just sits in the windswept downtown corner like a zombie in a cheap new suit.[7]

The sequence is both lyrical and lacerating. Maddin is clearly furious with the city for the way that it has betrayed both its hockey and retail history, but he also identifies a wider collapse of civic self-confidence.

Maddin implies that, in the wake of the Jets' departure, Winnipeg came to accept the shabby and the second-rate, mistaking the veneer of newness for legitimate revitalization or a sincere belief in the future. The final straw, for Maddin, comes with the demolition of the Winnipeg Arena on 26 March 2006. Drawing on the same footage as L'Atelier uses in *Death by Popcorn*, Maddin laments the destruction of "the most fabled, myth-and-memory-packed landmark in our city's history."[8] But, at the moment of the arena's destruction, something happens that allows Maddin to give voice to the regret and resentment that are at the heart of *Death by Popcorn*'s investigations as well:

> Kind of a strange victory. Only the part of the arena added in 1979 to accommodate the arrival of the NHL in town falls off the structure when the dynamite goes off. This I interpret as a sign, a sign that we should never have joined that league. I had really hoped that this would be some kind of stay of execution. But no, why did this happen? Why was this allowed to happen? The arena, my father, the paternal amphitheatre of our game, murdered, all because he lacked luxury boxes. Here we pride ourselves on the traditions of labour, and we allow our shrine to be outraged for its lack of luxury boxes. I'm ashamed of us. Ashamed to be a Winnipegger. Farewell. Farewell, beloved father.[9]

Like *Death by Popcorn*, Maddin here diagnoses a civic malady, the internalization of shame that is a consequence of the city's cynical indifference to its own history combined with the tawdry desire for the new, however cheap and crass. Bettman himself is not named, but the decision to join the NHL in 1979 is figured as the catalyst of civic downfall. The regret that Maddin names and identifies here is at the heart of L'Atelier's investigations as well. Throughout *Death by Popcorn*, L'Atelier shows how this regret is something that can quickly turn to resentment and rage when the internalization of shame becomes too much to bear.

These are topics to which I will return, but for now I will move on to the second bête noire in the story of *Death by Popcorn*. The film's demonization of Wayne Gretzky and its obsession with the role that he played in the downfall of the franchise are at the core of what the film has to say about the contemporary corporatization of professional hockey, the place the game occupies in the national cultural imagination, the importance of television and video in the Canadian 1970s, 1980s, and 1990s, and the contemporary function of the videocassette as the vehicle for the cultural memory of that time. Part of the humour of the film derives from its elevation of Gretzky to a position of absolute evil as the icon and embodiment of "the dark armies" that aim to destroy Winnipeg. Gretzky is shown throughout the film working his magic on the ice, he and his fellow Oilers scoring goal after goal against a series of demoralized Jets teams throughout the 1980s and 1990s, but the key images in the opening sequence are not from a highlight reel but from a commercial for ProStars, a breakfast cereal created in 1984 to capitalize on Gretzky's overwhelming popularity.

A probable source for the commercial is an aging videocassette most likely taped by some young hockey fan at the time that lay dormant in a damp basement or dry attic for many years only to be thrown out, given to Goodwill, or sold at a yard sale after the kid had gone off to college or university and those residual remnants of adolescence had become so much clutter weighing down a parental home. The static on the tape suggests this story or one like it, but it also fits with the paranoid and apocalyptic tone that the film establishes. The snow might be the result of poor reception at the time of taping, partial demagnetization while in storage, or simply the degradation of the tape itself over time, but the film transforms this visual noise into a signifier for otherness, as though these images of a feather-haired superstar are the intercepted transmissions of an enemy nation, recorded and retransmitted as part of a propaganda campaign. Gretzky, in both the media reality of modern Canada and the dystopian fantasy that the film constructs, is "The Great One." His deification everywhere else stands in stark contrast to his demonization in Winnipeg. When the film cuts between images of a young Gretzky on the ice, his talent already visible at the pee-wee level, and those of a frenzied crowd, the clip drawn from a Hollywood film of some sort but meant to represent impassioned Jets fans confronted with the image of their sworn enemy and baying for his blood, it shows the city, to its own detriment, to be isolated, out of sync and out of step with the course of history.[10]

Following this dystopian prologue, which establishes the basic parameters for the film's satiric analysis of recent history, *Death by Popcorn* settles into its investigation of Winnipeg's civic disposition, from its desperate search for saviours, both on the ice and in the boardroom, to its tendency toward melancholia and fatalism. This investigation is mediated by video, so I want to say more about the specificity of video as a medium, particularly the experience of watching an analogue format in a digital era. My sense is that video, with its formal attributes and the signs of its wear and tear situating it historically, now signifies in a very precise way. What I am calling the "video era" names that portion of history stretching from the late 1970s to the late 1990s when the lines of the video image, rather than the grain of the film image or the clarity of the digital image, signified the texture of the real. Of course, video itself has had a longer history than that, with early recordings dating back to the immediate postwar period and its residual use continuing today. Despite this longer history, I argue that the look of video is now inextricably associated with the late 1970s, 1980s, and 1990s in a way that desaturated 8-millimetre colour stock immediately invokes an imagined 1950s and 1960s or overcranked monochromatic silent images conjure a sped-up 1910s and 1920s.

The video era is a periodizing category that relies not simply on the visibility of technology and format that comes with the passing of time but also on their aestheticization. The look of video generates nostalgia, but there is something deeply uncanny about it as well, the scanlines estranging us from a past that is relatively recent yet is starting to feel shockingly distant. There have been a handful of studies in recent years that have sought to think through the dynamics of social change and cultural memory in terms of both materiality and mediality.[11] The videocassette has played a significant role in several of them. Will Straw's "Embedded Memories" stands out as a key contribution to what might be called "videocassette studies" in its assessment of how videocassettes serve as a vehicle for the circulation of "cultural knowledges"[12] at the same time that they, due to their tendency to pile up and accumulate, also function as the storage containers of, and triggers for, cultural memory. As Straw explains, "Like any container, the videocassette may serve to both transport and stockpile the cultural knowledges held within it. It will transport these across geographical and demographic boundaries, and, through such transportation, contribute to the mobility of contemporary cultural life. At the same time, in stockpiling those knowledges, the videocassette, like any medium of storage, allows them to pile up and to persist."[13] Although the videocassette may be, as Straw says, like any other container in its ability to circulate and its tendency to accumulate, it does stand, alongside its companion the audio cassette, as the privileged media container of the 1980s and 1990s.[14] As a consequence, the videocassette, perhaps the VHS tape in particular, stands as a key symbol of the era not because it remains the primary vehicle via which the sounds and images of the period circulate but because, even once transferred to digital and distributed online or via DVD, the material retains some textural trace of its source medium. Because of this, even in a digital age, the analogue consistency of video still filters our cultural memories of the late 1970s, 1980s, and 1990s. The texture of video can even trigger these memories, as format and feel become markers of pastness as much as content.[15]

VHS was not primarily a format designed for the creation of home videos. It was used for this purpose, but as Lucas Hilderbrand argues, it was a dependent technology whose principal use was taping broadcast television. As a consequence, there exists out there an incredible material archive of television from the late 1970s, 1980s, and 1990s on videocassette that is now in danger of disappearing and being destroyed. In terms of the endless number of primetime network television programs and marquee events that were taped, labelled, stored, and possibly never watched again, this loss would perhaps not be so catastrophic except that, as I argued about *SCTV* in chapter 3, the paratelevisual material that surrounded the programs themselves would become irretrievable. Charles Acland uses the term "vernacular moving image library" to describe these remnants of broadcast television that were captured on video: "[o]ne-time broadcasting events and anomalies, rare local commercials, station identifications, and sign-off notices."[16] This material sadly lies beyond the purview of most institutional archives, but it has become something of a YouTube phenomenon as enthusiasts sift through their video libraries for bits and pieces that are now in many ways far more interesting than the programs they were originally thought to have interrupted.[17]

L'Atelier was clearly a collector and archivist of this material. It collaborated initially with Winnipeg artist Daniel Barrow on a series of screenings that focused on local public access programming, advertising, and oddities from network affiliates, titled *Garbage Hill: A Showcase of Discarded Winnipeg Film and TV* (2005).[18] This three-day event was followed by a video compilation that unearthed a rich history of local television advertising, *Kubasa in a Glass: The Fetishised Winnipeg TV Commercial 1976–1992* (2006). *Death by Popcorn* manipulates and redeploys much of the material from these compilations and special screenings, interspersing it with the footage from the dumpster cassettes and supplementing it with home recordings of Jets games. Not only does the content historicize the images in the film, making it a eulogy both for a hockey team and for a bygone era, however recent, but so too does the texture of their technological reproduction. The dropouts, rainbow flares, skew errors, noise bars, and tracking interference, to adopt the technical vocabulary of video reproduction and quality control, likewise historicize the film, generating a sense of the pastness of the images and of the world being presented as much as the content does.

Death by Popcorn in particular and the work of L'Atelier more generally use format historicity and medium specificity to demarcate, investigate, and, to a certain degree, celebrate the video era. In this way, it should be considered complementary to the work of SCTV. Just as SCTV's satire betrays a fascination with local affiliates and regional broadcasting, L'Atelier's fascination with local access cable programming marks an archival effort to understand the importance of this type of material in the history of Canadian television and in the civic imagination of the city itself. The ads and local programming feature all kinds of oddballs and eccentrics of a sort rarely seen on television today, and their presence in itself is perhaps something to celebrate. *Math with Marty* is perhaps the iconic example here. The show largely consisted of its host, Martin Green, in front of an in-studio chalkboard enthusiastically working through math problems for the edification and enjoyment of his home audience. The show would become a cult favourite, perhaps down in part to Green's tendency to pick up his guitar and play a song or two in between equations. As much as the poor production values and lack of ease in front of the camera are the defining features of much of this material, there is also a good deal of inventiveness, playfulness, and wit. Above and beyond this characteristic, however, I want to follow Hilderbrand, who argues that

4.1 The distress of the analogue image in L'Atelier national du Manitoba's *Death by Popcorn: The Tragedy of the Winnipeg Jets* (2005).

there is an aesthetic dimension to video that is frequently overlooked and disregarded. Far from merely being a sign of technological failure or the format's limitations, these flaws also represent "an aesthetics of access" in that they are "historical records of audiences' interactions with the media objects."[19] What was taped is of interest, as are the signs that what was taped was watched. Part of the force of *Death by Popcorn* is that the poor quality of some of the material is precisely the index of its importance: skew lines at the top and bottom of the image, for instance, point to something rewound frequently and played repeatedly (see figure 4.1). This tape stress suggests both passion and pathology. In *Death by Popcorn*, moments of triumph bear these signs of repeated viewings, but so do sequences of failure, suggesting a compulsion not simply to figure out what went wrong but also to dwell on it in an almost pathological way.

The bizarre richness of 1980s and 1990s Winnipeg television returns me to the tragedy of the Jets. One way to explain the efflorescence of local programming during that time is the city's size. Winnipeg was large and isolated enough to need and demand its own in-house productions but small and peripheral enough to allow for a modicum of creative freedom and experimentation for those working in the field, including such local filmmaking luminaries as John Paizs and Guy Maddin, who were affiliated with the vibrant Winnipeg Film Group.[20] This mixture of necessity and opportunity generated a televisual culture that would largely disappear with changes to the Canadian Radio and Television Commission's regulations governing locally produced programming in the mid-1990s and with the end of local television advertising more generally as costs increased and viewership dwindled.[21] The Jets' tenure in the National Hockey League coincided with this moment of odd and extraordinary local televisual production. The history of the team, as well as the history of the city itself in that era, is not simply *on* video but is also primarily accessible *as* video. Video mediates but also becomes the texture and format of cultural memory itself, even for those who were there. This connection between medium and memory is, to my mind, as much the substance of *Death by Popcorn* as is the desire to tell the tragic tale of the Jets and the city that the team left behind.

Death by Popcorn is by no means the sole example in Canadian cinema of a film that explores the connection between memory, medium, and the long '70s. Brett Kashmere's video essay *Valery's Ankle* (2006) zeroes in on an act of hockey violence that perhaps, more than anything else, marks the beginnings of the modern game. The dominant image of the 1972 Summit Series between Canada and the Soviet Union is undoubtedly that of Paul Henderson celebrating his series-winning goal in the eighth and final game. Yet, as Kashmere shows, this triumphant image, which has come to occupy a key place in the Canadian cultural imagination as one that embodies and exemplifies the nation's heart and tenacity, obscures the spectacular levels of on-ice violence that set it up and made it possible. In game 6, with Canada down 3–1 in the series, Bobby Clarke brutally slashed Valery Kharlamov, taking aim at his already injured left ankle. Kharlamov's would miss game 7, and even though he returned in the final game of the series, his injured ankle prevented him from being the force he was in the earlier games. Kashmere's film asks, "What does this image say? At regular speed, it is nearly indiscernible. But stop the flow, split the second, and invisible evidence becomes visible. The two-handed slash, nearly unseen on video, but forceful enough to snap the blade of Clarke's stick, breaking Kharlamov's ankle." Video at once obscures the viciousness of this moment and makes Kashmere's investigation of it possible. By returning to the video footage, slowing it down, and zooming in on the point of impact until it breaks up, blurs, and pixelates, Kashmere opens up an inquiry into the connections between violence, masculinity, and nationalism. As Kashmere himself says in the film's voiceover, "I don't intend to speak about hockey. Rather, I want to ask questions. Questions about nationality and sport, about collective memory, cultural amnesia, and the formation of identity through a cinematic arrangement of researches, an archive of materials lost and found." Even though *Valery's Ankle* adopts a more sober and serious tone than *Death by Popcorn* and takes up questions of national mythologies rather than civic delusions, it shares an interest in video as a medium that transports the past into the present and an interest in how cultural memory is marked by the format that facilitates and mediates it. *Valery's Ankle* not only reveals how video serves as a medium for cultural memory but also carries in its textures and limitations the possibility of understanding history differently and disrupting deeply entrenched national mythologies:

The Summit Series occurred when video was becoming an international broadcast medium. The poor quality of the cameras and the television facilities used in Moscow caused several moments of picture loss. Besides representing obvious technological and economic disparities between the countries, I'd like to think these technical glitches signify the forgotten juvenile misbehaviour that occurred throughout the series. It's my assertion that Team Canada's performance, and Clarke's slash in particular, signify a discernible glitch in the production and presentation of Canadian nationalism, identity, and masculinity. This fissure disrupts Canadian self-identification as polite, peaceful, and sportsmanlike and enacts a shadow identity as frustrated, aggressive, and vengeful.

Although *Valery's Ankle* might seem far from L'Atelier's more playful and acerbic investigation of Winnipeg and the role hockey has played in the civic imaginary, the two films share a fascination with video, not simply as a medium but also as a metaphor. If, in *Valery's Ankle*, the glitches are a sign of the disjunction between national fantasies and brute reality, in *Death by Popcorn* they represent the gap between civic desire and the city as it actually exists.[22]

Alongside the experimental and essayistic remediations of *Valery's Ankle*, there are also more conventional narrative films that revisit 1970s hockey. Perhaps most obviously, Michael Dowse's *Goon* (2011) and its sequel, Jay Baruchel's *Goon: The Last of the Enforcers* (2017), pay homage to George Roy Hill's *Slap Shot* (1977). More interesting, however, is Atom Egoyan's *Gross Misconduct: The Life of Spinner Spencer* (1993). Made for the CBC, Egoyan's film uses video throughout to show how hockey, as a commodity, is mediated by broadcast and packaged as a product. In Egoyan's film, Spencer, a small-town kid from the British Columbia interior, is shown to be ill-equipped to deal with the machinations of professional hockey. As an enforcer, he has a key role on the various teams for which he plays, but he is also thoroughly expendable. His career overall is a downward spiral, from the achievement of his dream to play for the Toronto Maple Leafs to his early retirement to Florida, where he succumbs to drug and alcohol addiction. Egoyan's film shows how the violence that fuels Spencer's on-ice career also cuts it short, leaving him at its end without the resources to transition to life after hockey. But perhaps the key moment in the film comes at the very beginning of Spencer's career. Called up by the Maple Leafs, Spencer telephones his father to make sure he watches the game, which is scheduled for broadcast on *Hockey Night in Canada*. Egoyan cuts between a very nervous Spencer being interviewed between periods and scenes of his father back at home in British Columbia, furious that the local CBC affiliate is showing the Vancouver Canucks and the California Golden Seals matchup rather than the Leafs game. Taking things into his own hands, Spencer's father drives over 100 kilometres to Prince George and, at gunpoint, demands the station switch feeds so that he can see his son play. They do so but call the police as soon as Spencer's father leaves the station. He is shot and killed in a stand-off with officers shortly thereafter. Egoyan certainly shows how Spencer's father's rage and frustration might help to explain his son's character, career, and capacity for violence. Yet it is the video image of Spencer that is most memorable. Spencer is terrified in front of the camera and clearly out of his depth being interviewed in front of a national audience. Moreover, he is cruelly unaware of the tragic events unfolding back in British Columbia. In the video image of Spencer, Egoyan captures hockey as both national passion and pathology, with the specific quality of the televised image representing a transformation of sport into spectacle that has catastrophic consequences for Spencer and others like him.[23]

Like *Valery's Ankle* and *Gross Misconduct*, L'Atelier's *Death by Popcorn* is no simple exercise in soft or celebratory nostalgia for hockey of the 1970s, 1980s, and 1990s. Neither is it uncritically nostalgic for the Winnipeg of the era. Even as the film explores the aesthetic and cultural possibilities that opened up in the period due to the development of video technology and the particular fertility of Manitoba visual culture, it is also sharply diagnostic in its assessment of the province's collective anxieties and the city's civic failures. One of the most striking features of *Death by Popcorn* is its incisive analysis of Winnipeg's desire for a saviour, a player who might have counteracted the force of Gretzky or led the team to a Stanley Cup victory. Over the years, three figures emerged who nearly fit this bill: Dale Hawerchuk, Thomas Steen, and Teemu Selanne.

Hawerchuk is the earliest of these figures, selected by Winnipeg as the first overall pick in the 1981 NHL entry draft. The team at this point was desperate for a player who could turn their fortunes around. Having won the World Hockey Association's Avco Cup in 1979, Winnipeg struggled immensely after joining the NHL for the 1979–80 season. The film, anticipating Maddin's analysis in *My Winnipeg*, makes much of the Jets' 1979 victory in a league that was about to be dissolved. In a montage sequence set to Screamin' Jay Hawkins's "I Put a Spell on You" (1956), *Death by Popcorn* imagines the Avco Cup as a poisoned chalice, drinking from which doomed the team to failure during their existence in the NHL. The victory, ironically, was over the Oilers and their eighteen-year-old phenomenon, Wayne Gretzky, and the film suggests that he takes revenge throughout the 1980s for the disappointment of this early, traumatic loss. But the most resonant element of the clip is the observation from the play-by-play announcer that, if victorious, "Winnipeg will get permanent possession of the cup." The film loops and repeats this fragment, intensifying its force and transforming it into a terrifying prophecy that Winnipeg will suffer because of its success, that the city's golden age is over, and that it will not be able to succeed or survive in the harsher, more fiercely competitive NHL.

After this victory, a dreadful first two years in the NHL followed, and upon his arrival Hawerchuk did seem the saviour of the team and the city. He won the Calder Trophy for rookie of the year in his debut season and lifted the team from the bottom of the standings to a respectable finish and a place in the playoffs. The film does not dispute Hawerchuk's formidable talent on the ice but does take aim at the pressure the team and city placed on him as Winnipeg's answer to Gretzky. Whereas Gretzky exemplified the ease and charm of a sporting superstar and seemed wholly comfortable with his role as the league's pre-eminent player, Hawerchuk, a bit like Spencer but without the same tragic arc, seemed altogether less comfortable in the spotlight. The film reduces the speech Hawerchuk delivered when he was inducted into the Hockey Hall of Fame in 2001 to a string of conjunctions and hesitations, transforming it into a series of mumbled "um"s and "uh"s that stands in stark contrast to Gretzky's polished media fluency seen everywhere else in the film. Such an editing tactic is undoubtedly harsh on Hawerchuk, but it also humanizes him. Hawerchuk represents a humility and awkwardness of talent that is beloved in Winnipeg (and elsewhere), specifically because it is so different from the crafted, polished, and marketed superstardom of Gretzky.

This ironic celebration of Hawerchuk as the anti-Gretzky continues in a newly filmed sequence that sees Rankin speaking by telephone to Sylvain Séguin, the lead singer of the Québécois indie rock band Les Dales Hawerchuk. Séguin tells Rankin that the band got their name because when he was young his friends told him his style of play was reminiscent of the Jets' player. It is a tribute, then, and not in jest, as is their song "Dale Hawerchuk" (2005), the video for which *Death by Popcorn* absorbs and manipulates. The song is a tribute to Hawerchuk from the perspective of a weekend hockey player who fully embraces the comparison with the Jets' star and imagines that it gives him potency both on the ice and in the bedroom. The video has the band members – who are dressed in hockey gear, as though they just arrived home from the arena – parked in front of their television watching hockey highlights. *Death by Popcorn* augments the original video with footage of the Jets in action and other bits and pieces of Winnipeg-specific imagery.

The video concludes with a tape auto-ejecting from an old top-loading VHS player. This is significant since both sports and music videos were staples of VHS culture and the subject of much home taping.[24] The most significant connection between the VCR and the NHL is *Don Cherry's Rock'em Sock'em Hockey* franchise, a video series that compiles highlights from the league with a particular focus on spectacular goals and savage checks. A perennial bestseller in Canada, the first installment of the series was released on VHS in 1989.[25] In its montage sequences, *Death by Popcorn* participates in an ironic dialogue with the Cherry franchise.[26] But it specifically engages with one volume in particular. During the making of the film, the members of L'Atelier followed a list of seven rules. One of these rules identified the editor of *Rock'em Sock'em V* as an influence and inspiration:

> This unsung film genius is the veritable Walter Murch of direct-to-video bargain-basement hockey tapes. Mark Devitt is the subversive editor behind Don Cherry's only cinematic masterpiece, *Rock'em Sock'em V* (1993). While other works in the *Rock'em*

Sock'em canon might more accurately be termed as "procedural exercises," its fifth permutation is a highly-stylized work of early-1990s formalist wonder. In it, cloaked in red and obscured by dark glasses, Cherry is shown to preside over a sinister hockey underworld, rapping out his strict commandments from the eye of a swirly, analogue vortex of magnetic Brakhage-gasms. In one sequence, the dazed and devastated Winnipeg Jets spontaneously burst into frames in the middle of the ice as a cackling Cherry leaves them to writhe and scream in this punishing fibre-optic agony. With *Rock'em Sock'em V*, Devitt made the very idea of hockey look like a horrible, conspiratorial nightmare.[27]

Death by Popcorn's highlight sequences have much of the same energy that attracts hockey fans in general to the *Rock'em Sock'em* series, and they adhere to the Devittean model that L'Atelier themselves cite and explain. They interlace the action on the ice with an array of other images, from crying Jets fans to chopped and resequenced Kern Hill Furniture Co-op commercials, in order to parallel arena combat with the city's ongoing fight for survival in the face of an anticipated apocalypse. With both hockey highlights and music videos now essentially relocated to YouTube, the collective social practice of watching tapes of this sort has receded into memory. The video for "Dale Hawerchuk" captures the enthusiasm and electricity of watching something on tape, whether the experience of seeing something recorded on VCR and played over and over again or that of viewing a professionally assembled compilation as part of a ritual performed before or after a game.

The interview with Séguin also confirms a fascination with Québécois culture evident in the very name L'Atelier national du Manitoba. For the interview, Rankin wears a Quebec Nordiques jersey and sits in a room decorated with the Fleurdelisé and a Montreal Expos batting helmet alongside a Jets pennant. The mixing of this paraphernalia points to an imagined fraternity between the two provinces and a solidarity between Quebec City and Winnipeg as the two small-market Canadian cities that lost their NHL franchises during the 1990s. At the same time, however, it suggests a kind of provincial envy or admiration. Although Quebec City may have lost its franchise, the province still had its beloved Canadiens in Montreal. Furthermore, the strength and robustness of Québécois culture means that such a loss, however disappointing, was not as traumatic as it seemingly was for Winnipeg. This envy is not expressed by the ordinary Jets fans shown on-screen in *Death by Popcorn* but is articulated in the construction of the film itself and in the iconography that L'Atelier has adopted. Indeed, in "The Horizontalist Manifesto" (2005), the founding document of L'Atelier, the group claims, "Notre lutte est une lutte de liberté et de l'independence. Notre pays, la vraie patrie de notre Manitoba, c'est le Québec, pas le Canada."[28] I argue that the film offers a kind of reading of Manitoban political and cultural history by contrasting the province with Quebec but also by adopting Quebec as a model for cultural independence. *Death by Popcorn* suggests that Manitoba's contemporary malaise and anxiety are due in part to the fact that the province did not experience a cultural revolution of the Québécois sort and, as a result, retains a provincial, rather than national, identity.

In *Death by Popcorn*, this comparison between Manitoba and Quebec plays out, oddly enough, through the story of Teemu Selanne, another one of the promised franchise saviours, who arrived in 1992. Selanne's choice to stay in Winnipeg even though an offer from the Calgary Flames was on the table endeared him to Jets fans. The video clip of the news report on Selanne's decision to play for the Jets conveys both pride and incomprehension, once again pointing to the collective uncertainty about why anyone, if the opportunity was available to go anywhere else, would choose Winnipeg. Like Hawerchuk, Selanne had an immediate impact in his first season, setting the record for goals by a rookie. Jets fans nicknamed him "The Finnish Flash," but for the purposes of a montage sequence that imagines him as the European leader Charles de Gaulle, infamous in English Canada for his support of the slogan "Vive le Québec libre," *Death by Popcorn* creates the fiction that Selanne was known as "Général du Goal," who would inspire the team and the province to new heights.

After showing the highlights of a game in which Selanne almost single-handedly defeated the Oilers, the film switches to an extended clip of Québécois nationalist Pierre Bourgault speaking at a rally in the wake of General de Gaulle's visit to Montreal in 1967. Subtitles translate the speech but transform its meaning entirely by substituting "Winnipeg" for "Quebec." As a result, the film forces us to consider

Winnipeg as "fundamentally colonized" and a "ruined city." The force of the clip resides in Bourgault's assault on the sentimentalization of defeat. There is a spectacular moment when Bourgault tells the crowd that Quebec has no heroes, only martyrs. There are murmurs of disagreement from the audience, but he continues in the face of these jeers to argue that the lionization of martyrs can result only in an ongoing culture of defeat. General de Gaulle's visit, he argues, catalyzed a sense that Quebec could overturn its history of defeat, subordination, and colonization and become the winners of history. Bourgault names Louis-Joseph de Montcalm, Louis-Joseph Papineau, and Louis Riel among the martyrs of French Canada, the memory of whom must be overcome if Quebec is to move forward, but the subtitles substitute these names with the those of legendary Jets players Paul MacLean, Tie Domi, and Hawerchuk. And just as Bourgault paraphrases General de Gaulle's inspirational message to the people of Quebec as "never give up," so too does the film imagine that, in the early to mid-1990s at least, Selanne was the one who would inspire the city and help transform its perception of itself from losers to winners.

However absurd the comparison between General de Gaulle and Général du Goal seems, it does provide insight into the complexities of the film's political commitments and fantasies as well as into its understanding of recent history and the continuing force of the 1960s and 1970s in the national cultural imagination. Although it may on the face of it seem ridiculous to suggest that Manitoba could or should have a Quebec-like cultural revolution, the comparison itself reiterates the film's overall premise that there is a self-destructive aspect to Manitoban culture. After making *Death by Popcorn*, Rankin took up this theme in the experimental film essay *Hydro-Lévesque* (2007), which speculates on how the revolutionary energies of Quebec in the 1960s and 1970s might be transferred to and reanimated in contemporary Manitoba. As Rankin himself explains in an interview, the comparison between the two provinces comes out of the recognition that both "have something of a fetishized relationship with their own misfortune." But whereas Quebec was able to harness the energies of discontent in a period of accelerated modernization and the growth of a sovereigntist movement, modern Manitoba has thus far been unable to do the same. Rankin explains,

In the 1960s and 70s, Québec nationalism had a very heavy self-destructive streak to it. But, in large part because of René Lévesque, that electricity was re-channelled into a positive transmitter and today, in its best, most positive form, Québec nationalism is truly heroic and universal in its resilience. And I wanted that energy to be the force of good in my film. Winnipeg today is much like Québec was in the 1950s, except we are far more apathetic. Often we believe we are improving our city and affirming our collective worth as we commit the most profane acts of self-destruction. We demolish our icons, we vandalize our downtown with beautification projects, we curse the difficulty of our existence and long to be normal. To me, all of this is nihilism. So this was going to be the negative charge in my film. But in the end, I wanted Winnipeg to find its Lévesque. That's why, at the end, it is the electricity of Québec sovereignty that saves Winnipeg's life, like a transplanted heart.[29]

As a result, *Hydro-Lévesque* offers a kind of solution to the intractable dilemmas sketched out in *Death by Popcorn*. Whereas the later film offers a kind of sci-fi influenced political fantasy that imagines the re-animation of the province through the transplantation of energies from elsewhere, the former dwells satirically on the sense of imminent doom associated with the Jets' departure. The film follows the reinterpreted footage of Bourgault with a terrifying clip of *Survival* (1982–87), a local Winnipeg public access show that purported to be a preparation guide for the coming apocalypse. A hooded figure warns viewers, "People are living their lives now. They're preparing for a future. But they are preparing for a future of nothingness and death if they are not preparing to survive cataclysm." *Death by Popcorn* juxtaposes this survivalist satire with video images of rallies held in a desperate effort to keep the Jets in Winnipeg and call-in programs that feature local fans almost in tears over the announcement of the team's departure. On the one hand, the film sets up the loss of the Jets as the cataclysmic event for which Winnipeggers have been sternly instructed to prepare, but on the other hand, it suggests that the rallies of protest and ongoing efforts to save the Jets are precisely the fantasies of a future that will never be, the distraction from a cataclysm already in progress. That these rallies took place at the symbolic centre of Winnipeg, the much-mythologized intersection of Portage Avenue and Main Street, takes viewers to the heart of "the ruined city." Winnipeg's identity as a midwestern industrial city is marked by its history of suburbanization and the emptying out of its downtown. Successive efforts at city centre renewal throughout the 1980s and early 1990s – including the construction of MTS Centre, which Maddin laments – were distinguished by their complete misguidedness and almost total failure, and although the intersection of Portage and Main remains the city's symbolic centre due to its historical importance, it had been transformed by the mid-1990s into a symbol of urban decline, with the bank towers that mark the location quickly giving way on surrounding streets to parking lots, empty buildings, abject poverty, and other signs that the urban core had been politically and socially abandoned. The clip from *Survival* extends the apocalyptic imagery that runs through the film, but it also invites viewers to see life in contemporary Winnipeg as already post-apocalyptic, with videotapes of the Jets' past glory as the surviving remnants of life before the cataclysm.

Selanne was a success during his time as a Jet but was unable to lead the team to the victory it ultimately desired. He was traded to the Mighty Ducks of Anaheim in February 1996 as part of a fire sale that the Jets management launched once it realized that the franchise's move to Phoenix was inevitable. Numerous video clips from the time show a city already in mourning for a team still on the ice as fans suffer through the remainder of the 1995–96 season in a kind of living death. *Death by Popcorn* draws on a local sports call-in show and on street interviews to reveal the emotional and psychological impact that the announcement of the team's departure had on the city. Mass exodus is a particular fear of many callers and interviewees. Without the Jets, they ask, why would young people choose to stay in Winnipeg? Such worries are expressed in an overblown and melodramatic manner, yet they address the real fear of a provincial city that has long had to deal with outmigration. The title track of the Weakerthans' album *Left and Leaving* (2000) might be the exemplary expression of the melancholy of the abandoned, with its lyrical evocation of urban decline and psychic desolation and its images of a city that is "still breathing, but barely." The parking lots of downtown Winnipeg are absences that point to past glories, the demolished buildings that have, as the song says, "gone missing like teeth." *Death by Popcorn*, in its own satiric way, conveys a similar sense that, for all the hysteria and handwringing that the loss of the Jets caused, it did mark a watershed moment in the city's recent history in that it was a seeming sign of demotion or relegation to a lower level of urban desirability. As one tearful fan says, "I don't know what to do anymore. What can we watch in the winter now? What is Winnipeg now? It's just nothing."

This fear of undesirability and emptiness explains the city's affection for Thomas Steen, who completes the film's trio of player case studies. Although Steen's natural goal-scoring ability may not have matched either Hawerchuk's or Selanne's, he was a leader on the ice and a consummate playmaker. Yet the primary reason why Jets fans loved him so much seems to have been his attachment to the city itself. Steen spent his entire NHL career playing for the Jets, a commitment highly unusual in an era of free agency and the full marketization of sports labour. *Death by Popcorn* draws clips from the ceremony marking the retirement of Steen's jersey number in 1995. As Steen skates onto the ice for the award, the stadium announcer commends him for his commitment to the city itself: "This man and his wife and family embraced our city. Winnipeg became their home. They became involved in the community, spoke proudly about living here, and passionately defended the quality of life in Winnipeg from the many outside our area who love to knock this great place in which we live." *Death by Popcorn* intensifies the disturbing weirdness of the commendation's mix of incredulity and resentment by replaying it repeatedly. The phrasing echoes the speech from *Nineteen Eighty-Four* that opens the film but also establishes that Steen represents what a title card indicates is "Le rêve Winnipegois."[30] That dream is less one of victory than one of acceptance, a dream for someone to come from elsewhere and embrace the city. Steen, as such a figure, counters fears of outmigration and abandonment, but he does so as the representative of conservative domesticity. His professional afterlife as a Conservative candidate in the Winnipeg riding of Elmwood-Transcona in the 2008 federal election confirmed this symbolic status. He lost that election but was elected to Winnipeg City Council in 2010, before losing his seat in 2014. Steen's foray into politics was the subject of great enthusiasm in the local press, but it was also

4.2 Burton Cummings as the saviour of the Winnipeg Jets in L'Atelier national du Manitoba's *Death by Popcorn: The Tragedy of the Winnipeg Jets* (2005).

met with tempered criticism that had to dance around Steen's popularity as a former Jet in order to criticize him as a candidate.[31]

With tongue planted firmly in cheek, *Death by Popcorn* presents a fourth possible saviour of the Jets. This fourth figure was not a player but a performer. Since its inception, L'Atelier has had a fascination with Burton Cummings, the lead singer of Winnipeg's own The Guess Who. Perhaps most famous for the hit "American Woman" (1970), the first single by a Canadian band to reach number one on the Billboard Top 100, The Guess Who was in its heyday when the Jets were founded as a World Hockey Association franchise in 1972. Reviewing their album *Live at the Paramount* (1972) that year, Lester Bangs announced, "The Guess Who is God." He explained, "They have absolutely no taste at all, they don't even mind embarrassing everyone in the audience, they're real punks without even working too hard at it."[32] Bangs's ironic enthusiasm for "Canuck creep" Cummings surely must have been short-lived since, by the mid-1970s, The Guess Who had disbanded and Cummings had transformed himself into a power ballad crooner. Key to this transformation was Cummings's image. The combination of his curly hair, bushy mustache, and toothy smirk became iconic, at once signifying a soulful sensitivity, a mischievous eroticism, and a bizarre goofiness. L'Atelier seized upon this image in a postering and stickering campaign throughout 2005 and 2006, scattering a screen-printed image of Burton's face around Winnipeg with the title of his first solo hit, "Stand Tall" (1976), written underneath. In the midst of urban decline and dilapidation, this injunction seemed cruelly ironic, an impossible task both in a downtown that bore the scars of profound economic disenfranchisement and in a city largely defined by its economic marginalization (see figure 4.2).

Death by Popcorn draws on video footage of Burton suiting up for a Jets practice, a cheap publicity stunt that took place in the midst of the departure crisis. Cummings, like Steen, is loved for remaining in, or at least retaining ties to, Winnipeg despite his success, but ironically he is also mocked for it, as though choosing to retain a connection to Winnipeg is so inexplicable and embarrassing that the love must be counterbalanced with ridicule and scorn. Cummings's own relationship with the city is understandably fraught. His endorsement of the Jets and his playful media appearances in the 1990s documented in

Death by Popcorn show someone passionately committed to the city, as does his part ownership in Salisbury House, or Sal's, a local chain of burger restaurants. Yet Cummings is also known for his criticisms of the city, most notoriously his assessment in 1985, after a late-night incident in which he was hit on the head with a beer bottle at a North End 7-Eleven convenience store, that the Winnipeg he knew now belonged to the past and had been replaced by "Negativipeg." This ambivalence, this oscillation between passionate commitment to the city and frustrated and fed-up self-lacerating outbursts, is what makes Cummings the local icon he is, embodying as it does some key aspect of the city's psychic disposition.[33]

A montage sequence follows this desperate search for franchise saviours. Set to a fierce techno beat, it focuses in part on the "Winnipeg White Out," the tradition of Jets fans dressing entirely in white to create an intimidating atmosphere for teams visiting the Winnipeg Arena during playoff time. The practice is, at heart, an ironic embrace of Winnipeg's notoriously cold and snowy winters, but the film does point to its more sinister racist connotations, casting the Jets as "the Great White Brotherhood" and linking the rhetoric of civilizational survival and the fear of outsiders to the team's struggles on the ice. On a formal, technical level, the White Out posed certain challenges to video, which *Death by Popcorn* exposes and exploits. The footage from the late 1980s and early 1990s demonstrates just how unsuited video resolution was for capturing nuance in long shot. This limitation has been exacerbated with the passage of time, as the drop-outs from tape decay have whited out the White Out, rendering the historicity of the practice visible in the degradation of the image.

To conclude, I want to deal with the enigmatic title of the film itself. It refers to an incident during the 1990 Stanley Cup playoffs. The Jets led the Oilers three games to two in their opening-round series, were up three goals to one in game six, and seemed assured of victory over their now Gretzky-less but still formidable opponents. And then, late in the third period, a fan threw a box of popcorn on the ice. The moment is much mythologized and much lamented in Winnipeg hockey history, as it seemed to quash Winnipeg's momentum. The Oilers scored three quick goals to win the game, which turned the series around and saw the Jets once again eliminated from the playoffs by their archrivals. *Death by Popcorn* dedicates a newly shot sequence to this incident. It stages a nighttime, downtown, back alley meeting in the depths of winter between Rankin and a man who alleges to have been the one who threw the fateful box of popcorn. Dressed entirely in Oilers garb and snacking manically on a box of Nutty Club popcorn, an iconic local Winnipeg brand, the man seems slightly unhinged and over the course of the interview grows incandescent with rage. He explains that he communicates telepathically with Wayne Gretzky on a daily basis and that the Great One has passed a divine message on to him. This message, he explains, is that "Winnipeg is losers. Winnipeg is the worst. Winnipeg is a shit-cake of broken dreams!" He proceeds to launch an assault on a series of cherished Winnipeg icons, from former provincial Liberal Party leader Sharon Carstairs to legendary The Guess Who members Burton Cummings and Randy Bachman to furniture salesman Nick Kern, a staple of local television advertising (see figure 4.3). The unhinged and distraught man is played to perfection by Rob Vilar, a Winnipeg actor who has rightly assumed cult status as a result of his presence in a whole series of Winnipeg productions in the 2000s and 2010s. Vilar has been the subject of both a Cinematheque-hosted film festival (2007) and an experimental biographical documentary, Rhayne Vermette's *Rob What?* (2015). As Kier-La Janisse reveals in her analysis of Vilar's oeuvre, the actor is loved precisely for his capacity to steal scenes with unexpected but extraordinary improvisations. As Rankin tells Janisse, "The very best scenes in *Death by Popcorn* are the ones with Rob, and he is improvising all of his lines. I remember the explosive night in Winnipeg when we first showed that movie to a packed house at the Cinematheque and when Rob shouts out 'Winnipeg is a shit-cake of broken dreams!', the whole audience just went straight through the roof. That line really made the film. You just can't script what comes out of Rob's head! You can't even fully understand what it is that Rob seems to understand so perfectly. This is what makes him such a fascinating film persona."[34] As powerfully self-lacerating and astute as the "shit-cake" observation is, the true punchline of the sequence comes when Rankin asks him where he was born. The answer, of course, is "Winnipeg," satirizing and exemplifying the self-destructive self-loathing of Jets fans and Winnipeggers all in one fell swoop.

4.3 "Winnipeg is losers. Winnipeg is the worst. Winnipeg is a shit-cake of broken dreams." L'Atelier national du Manitoba's *Death by Popcorn: The Tragedy of the Winnipeg Jets* (2005).

The comic ferocity of the self-loathing is combined in the sequence with the pathos-drenched, fatalistic assessment of Jets president Barry Shenkarow, who claims that "everything was going our way; if that fan hadn't thrown the popcorn on the ice, we probably would have beaten Edmonton that year." This deeply held conviction, shared by many, illuminates the second part of the film's title. The tragedy of the Winnipeg Jets is that their fate is understood as tragedy, as the result of some fundamental flaw that condemned them to years of agonizing defeat and to their eventual disappearance. The box of popcorn thrown on the ice symbolizes the civic sense that Winnipeg is the cause of its own failures. And as much as the film examines how this becomes a kind of self-fulfilling prophecy, it also quite ruthlessly pushes it even further, showing how such thinking is debilitating and comforting in equal measure. *Death by Popcorn*'s most tender moment comes when the film returns to the conversation between Rankin and Séguin of Les Dales Hawerchuk near its end. Asked whether he has any message for Jets fans, Séguin says, "I'd tell them that they shouldn't give up their hopes of having an NHL hockey team again one day. You never know! And never think it's your fault for not having an NHL team. It's not Winnipeg's fault" (see figure 4.4). This statement is a clear echo of De Gaulle's message to Quebeckers not to give up, which Bourgault passionately relates, but more importantly it is a deeply compassionate message that recognizes the city's tendency for self-laceration and self-loathing and encourages healthy persistence rather than pathological fixation.

In the next chapter, I think more broadly about remediation and the return to the particular grain and texture of 1970s film as being a source of fascination in the digital age. But to bring this analysis of *Death by Popcorn* to a close, I want to emphasize the way that video is central to the film and, by extension, to what the city thinks itself to be. The tragedy of the Winnipeg Jets was not the stuff of the stage or even of film but the stuff of video, a format with which the team shares a lifespan and on which its highs and lows were captured. Piles of videocassettes archived the history of the team, and the signs of their wear and tear, including the decay and degradation of the video image, signify the civic passion felt for the franchise, the deep melancholy experienced upon its departure, and the passing of time itself. The Jets of the 1970s, 1980s, and 1990s will be distinguished from

4.4 Sylvain Séguin of the Québécois indie rock band Les Dales Hawerchuk consoles Winnipeg Jets fans who blame themselves for the city's loss of the team in L'Atelier national du Manitoba's *Death by Popcorn: The Tragedy of the Winnipeg Jets* (2005).

the team's new incarnation not simply by new uniforms, a new arena, and a different set of players and management but also by the textural difference between the new high-definition video technology that will capture the on-ice action and the desaturated, low-definition VHS and Betamax that now periodize its contents in a very specific way. *Death by Popcorn* salvages this forlorn material and, in revisiting the recent past, shows the inextricability of memory, magnetic tape, and the Manitoba of the 1970s, 1980s, and 1990s.

5 Remediating the Long '70s

The pervasiveness of remediation, as both a concept and a practice in the contemporary visual arts, has extended the cultural shadow of the long '70s both in Canada and worldwide. As artists rediscover, reuse, and rework audiovisual materials and everyday objects from Canada's postwar phase of accelerated modernization and explicit nation building, its "structure of feeling" is at once evoked and estranged.[1] The collective sense of the pastness of this period may grow more acute as it recedes into history; however, since Canada continues to live with the consequences of both the era's desires and its decisions, it still feels surprisingly present. This seems especially true of Canada's long '70s, whose remnants offer artists material with which to reconsider the nation today, as well as to track the contemporary state of national cultural formations back to their origins, or at least to an earlier moment of their formation, via their audiovisual traces and material residues.

In this chapter, I examine a trio of contemporary Canadian projects and installations that draw on the sonic and visual legacies of Canada's long '70s. At the centre of my analysis is Geronimo Inutiq's ARCTICNOISE (2015), an audiovisual installation that draws on Glenn Gould's experimental radio documentary *The Idea of North*, first broadcast on the CBC in 1967 and subsequently made into a 1970 CBC television documentary, directed by Judith Pearlman. *The Idea of North*, alongside

The Latecomers (1969) and *The Quiet in the Land* (1977), forms part of Gould's *Solitude Trilogy* (1967–77), a work that remains a high-water mark for experimental radio documentary and an important text for contemporary mythologies about Canadian nationhood and identity. Focusing on *The Idea of North*, Inutiq's work wrestles with Gould's formal inventiveness, the way that he pushed the boundaries of sound art in his radical radio experiment, but also turns a critical eye to the absence of Inuit voices in Gould's fantasies of nation-defining northernness. Yet, as in the preceding chapters, I seek out the continuities and connections between past and present via a series of associations, looking to other visual artists and filmmakers – Caroline Monnet, Paul Seesequasis, Kent Monkman, and Jeff Barnaby – whose work, like Inutiq's, extends and evaluates the impact and influence of the long '70s in the Canadian cultural imagination. The artists and filmmakers I examine in this chapter are all Indigenous. This fact signals the richness and importance of the work being done by Indigenous cultural producers today, but it is also a reminder that, when it comes to the practices of remediation and reconsiderations of the past, there is much more at stake culturally and politically for those who have been largely excised or excluded from dominant settler versions of history or violently subordinated within it.

The artistic remediation of archival materials characterizes much of the work I have examined throughout *Hinterland Remixed*, from the satiric reinventions of the *Hinterland Who's Who* shorts to L'Atelier national du Manitoba's videocassette salvage efforts, yet the artists and projects in this chapter point to the complexity of remediation and its metaphorical richness. Although the word "remediation," in the discourse of media studies, has come to signify the process whereby one medium is incorporated into, or represented within, another, it still bears the traces of its Latin origin and earlier English use.[2] To remediate is to remedy but also to redress, and both meanings have particular significance in Canada at this historical juncture, given that "reconciliation" is everywhere promised even as state commitment to actual compensation, whether in financial terms or in the form of increased autonomy or sovereignty, falls far short. But perhaps the most common contemporary use of the term "remediation" comes from the discourse of environmentalism, where it refers to the restoration of polluted sites and the removal of harmful contaminants from soil or water. Even though this scientific, technical use may seem distant from the term's contemporary political resonances and arguments for redress, reparations, or the restoration of land and autonomy, the combination of pipeline politics and environmental racism ensures that they are inextricably intertwined. Finally, to bring this consideration of remediation full circle, I argue that the artistic practices of remediation, especially when undertaken by Indigenous artists, DJs, and filmmakers, include and extend this cluster of meanings and resonances. To remediate is to remedy and to claim redress, but it is also potentially a process of decontamination, whereby the sounds and images of state archives (or of popular culture) are resignified and reclaimed. Whether in Inutiq's reworkings of Glenn Gould or in the work of the other Indigenous artists and filmmakers examined here, remediation includes decontamination since reusing materials from settler colonial archives reclaims them, potentially even decontaminates them, through a process of resignification that counters and challenges the roles they have played in the imperial and settler colonial imaginary.

The Idea of North and ARCTICNOISE

First exhibited at Vancouver's grunt gallery in August 2015, Geronimo Inutiq's ARCTICNOISE is a multimedia installation built out of elements of Glenn Gould's *The Idea of North*, the archive of Igloolik Isuma, a Nunavut-based production company perhaps best known for Zacharias Kunuk's award-winning *Atanarjuat: The Fast Runner* (2001), footage that Inutiq himself shot, and other archival and ephemeral images that Inutiq gathered and assembled. The precise setup and component parts of ARCTICNOISE have varied with each installation – the project travelled to both Trinity Square Video in Toronto and AKA Artist-Run Gallery in Saskatoon in the fall and winter of 2015 – but at its centre is a main room that immerses the spectator in a powerful audiovisual environment.[3] Running simultaneously, three separate video projections occupy the front, left, and right walls, with the audio track binding the visual elements together and immersing the auditor in a comprehensive sound world (see figure 5.1). The central feed features Inutiq's remix of material from the Igloolik Isuma archives and presents an Inuit-centred vision of the North that runs counter to Gould's romantic speculations. The left projection is an array of cultural images and materials referencing the North disrupted by both pixel and glitch. As Weiyi Chang explains, this wall is an altogether disorienting mix of material. The channel "cycles through a sequence of seemingly unrelated footage, including edited archives, pop-culture imagery, and cross-cultural references. Some clips are vaguely recognizable, such as the Warholian representation of a lone kayaker, while others are geometric abstractions and vividly rendered distortions that elude legibility and clarity."[4] On the opposite wall are images of travelling through a forested landscape. This is footage that Inutiq shot himself on a train journey north through La Vérendrye Wildlife Reserve in Quebec. This channel picks up on the narrative conceit of Gould's *The Idea of North*, that of a train journey northward from Winnipeg to Churchill aboard the Muskeg Express by a young man eager to learn about the North from southerners who have travelled there before him. The sound of the train echoes throughout Gould's radio documentary, and in the television version, scenes of the young man listening to the conductor tell tales of the North are punctuated by images of the landscape rolling past. By dedicating an entire channel to shots of the landscape gliding by, Inutiq ensures that in ARCTICNOISE the actual terrain of the North is continuously in dialogue with the people who live there and the history of its representations.[5]

The simple description of these component parts does not in any way capture the sensory experience of ARCTICNOISE, nor does it convey the ways that the piece activates the intellect through the senses. The surplus of audiovisual information pushes the capacity of the spectator to take it all in, yet the allure and energy of both sound and image, as well as the complexity of the mix, press the spectator into thinking about the historical and political questions about representation that are quite clearly in play. In this way, Inutiq's ARCTICNOISE shares something with John Akomfrah's recent multichannel audiovisual work in terms of both form and content. Like Akomfrah's *The Unfinished Conversation* (2012), a three-channel video installation about the political and intellectual impact of the great Stuart Hall, and like Akomfrah's *Vertigo Sea* (2016), a more recent three-channel investigation into the

5.1 Installation view of Geronimo Inutiq's *ARCTICNOISE* (2015).

connections between the global refugee crisis, climate change, and oceanic imaginary, Inutiq's work represents an effort to forge a new, multichannel cinematic language that reckons with the wreckage of the imperial past and its residues to speculate about possible futures. Such work, in its complexity, intensity, and extension, exceeds the capacity of a single channel and ultimately demands more than a single viewing. Both Akomfrah and Inutiq seek a new relationship between sound, image, and spectator that the three-channel setup makes possible. The three-channel form of ARCTICNOISE is fundamental to both its sensory and political impact and connects it to other decolonial interventions and projects elsewhere.

Of course, this provisional connection to work being done globally should not overshadow the ways that Inutiq's work is in dialogue with a history of Inuit art and the thriving field of Indigenous new media art more generally. The past two decades have witnessed an efflorescence of Indigenous new media art and a rich critical engagement with these works. Steven Loft and Kerry Swanson's edited collection *Coded Territories: Tracing Indigenous Pathways in New Media Art* (2014) is a ground-breaking book that thinks historically about the relationship between art and technology in Indigenous art practices while surveying the field of contemporary Indigenous artists who work with new or digital media. Particular mention must also be made of Heather Igloliorte, Julie Nagam, and Carla Taunton's edited collection *Indigenous Art: New Media and the Digital* (2016), published as a special issue of the journal *Public*, which not only features a number of articles that take up the connections between media art and Indigenous ways of thinking and being but also maps out several ways that new media artistic practices and interventions stand as a mode and means of Indigenous resistance. This issue of *Public* includes a series of images from Inutiq's LEFT_CHANNEL, which, as its title suggests, forms one part of the ARCTICNOISE installation. So, as much as Inutiq's work connects to decolonial artistic interventions happening globally right now, such as Akomfrah's, it is also important not to lose sight of the ways that it forms part of a broad and diverse set of contemporary Indigenous artistic practices that are grounded in a longer history of Indigenous life and resistance. As Igliolorte, Nagam, and Taunton note in their introduction, "Many of these texts [...] explore the ways in which 'technology' has always been a tool of Indigenous resilience, cultural continuity, and a conduit for storytelling."[6] That is equally true of Inutiq's work, and ARCTICNOISE stands as a particularly powerful example of how new media practices are as much about cultural continuity as they are about finding new forms for artistic expression and investigation.[7]

Before going further into a consideration of the relationship between audio, the archive, remix, and remediation, I need to say a little more about the ARCTICNOISE project and its engagement with Gould's *The Idea of North*. As Tarah Hogue explains in her introduction to the catalogue that accompanied the original exhibition, "The foundational relationship for ARCTICNOISE was between curators Britt Gallpen and Yasmin Nurming-Por, who invited Inutiq to respond to Gould's 1967 radio drama."[8] Rather than formulating a simple response to Gould's work, Inutiq enters into complex dialogue with it, exposing its occlusions and blindspots as well as investigating the larger political and historical contexts that generated them. Inutiq does not simply counter or contradict Gould's limited idea of the North but, along with his curatorial collaborators, also extends and enlarges it. It is through this process that he reveals Gould's inability, even failure, to account for the North in its richness and complexity.[9]

Commissioned for Canada's Centennial celebrations in 1967 and first broadcast on CBC Radio on 28 December of that year, Gould's *The Idea of North* is, quite obviously, an exercise in nation building, national commemoration, and the naturalization of settler colonial ownership of the vast expanse of territory that makes up Canada's arctic and subarctic regions. The majority of critical writing on *The Idea of North* acknowledges to some degree Gould's failure to acknowledge Inuit culture and his inability to conceive of the North as anything more than a mostly empty space that catalyzes the deepest of southern fantasies of solitude, adventure, exploration, and conquest.[10] Yet, as Mickey Vallee argues, any minimal critical recognition of the problems with Gould's work quickly gives way in most analyses to a consideration of "its aesthetic and nation-building qualities."[11] To emphasize the radical nature of Gould's radio experiment and to register the importance of the work in the consolidation of a Centennial-catalyzed quest for a Canadian national identity, critics have for the most part artificially disconnected it from both colonial history and the ongoing settler colonial domination of the North.

Gould's introduction to the piece, which he repeats in the filmed version, is oddly upfront about his relative ignorance of the North. He concedes that his ideas about it are largely the stuff of fantasy and admits that the North is a space shaped and defined by those who, by and large, have no actual experience of it: "This is Glenn Gould, and this program is called *The Idea of North*. I've long been intrigued by that incredible tapestry of tundra and taiga which constitutes the arctic and subarctic of our country. I've read about it, written about it, and even pulled up my parka once and gone there. But like all but a very few Canadians, I've had no real experience of the North. I've remained, of necessity, an outsider, and the North has remained for me a convenient place to dream about, spin tales about, and in the end, avoid."[12] Of course, Gould's remedy for this lack of exposure was not to engage in any meaningful way with Inuit or Innu culture, or with the other Indigenous cultures of the subarctic – Dene, Cree, Ojibwa, and Atikamekw – but to weave together a series of non-Indigenous voices from the South. Unlike Gould himself, the interviewees had actually gone north and confronted the very terrain and conditions about which he had only fantasied, yet ultimately they had done so in a context and from a perspective similar to his own: as a Canadian from the South. As Vallee argues, this persuasive appeal to the romance of settler colonialism, combined with Gould's compositional virtuosity in weaving together a series of voices that wrestle with the effect that the North has on those southerners who have gone there, has secured it a firm and fixed place in the Canadian national cultural imaginary: "Although *The Idea of North* enjoins the listener to surrender to romantic and ideologically mystified relations to the North, its legacy as a masterpiece of Canadian culture has left it calcified, seemingly impermeable to political criticism [...] Canadians are indeed inclined to accept *The Idea of North*, in other words, as simultaneously timeless and a product of its times – to disavow its violence as a contingency anterior to the present, so as to consolidate its powerful discursive contribution to nationalist identity and the southern relation to the North."[13] Vallee powerfully counters this critical calcification and offers a reading of *The Idea of North* that identifies its role in conveying and consolidating a national image of the North that is consistent with the state's ongoing exploitation and domination of it. Gould's work is usually celebrated for its polyphonic and contrapuntal weave of (southern) voices that express a series of hopes and fears, aspirations and anxieties, observations and insights about the North and the experience of being there. But, as Vallee argues, "there is a contrapuntal procedure in *The Idea of North*, but not between speaking voices; rather, it is between the voices active and voices silenced."[14] The speaking voices, although they may seem to be countering and contesting each other, for the most part articulate what Vallee identifies as, borrowing a phrase from Eva Mackey, a "new benevolent racism."[15] This benevolence, as Vallee explains, turns out to be little more than the latest mutation of colonial domination and neatly interlocks with state policies of multiculturalism that were emerging at the very same time, policies that imagine a compassionate colonization that saves rather than subjugates: "Disgust cast as difference delineates 'them' as being in need of saving through modernization under the guise of the welfare state. Settler-colonizers are washed (whitewashed) of their indiscretions by their own benevolent reinvention, yet it is a reinvention that exercises a more permissive power."[16]

My annexation of *The Idea of North* to the long '70s, even though it is quite clearly a Centennial project, has very much to do with the way that it inaugurates and anticipates the shift in state discourse, policy, and ideology that unfolds over the course of the next decade. This shift was signified most strongly in the language of state multiculturalism, which, although structured on ideas of equitable polyvocality, largely ended up being contrapuntal only in the way that Vallee identifies *The Idea of North* as being: the usual voices are boosted, whereas others remain mostly unheard. And just as 1971's Multiculturalism Act promised a new relationship between the dominant white settler population of Canada and its minority communities, which were growing dramatically in this period, so too was there legislation that promised a new relationship between the state and Indigenous people. For Dene scholar Glen Sean Coulthard, 1969 marks a key moment. That year's white paper, formally known as the *Statement of the Government of Canada on Indian Policy*, inaugurated what was meant to be a dramatic shift, a move from an outright policy of assimilation to one of recognition. For Coulthard, this shift was little more than one that restructured, even modernized, domination. He writes, "since 1969 we have witnessed the modus operandi of colonial power relations in Canada shift from a more or less unconcealed structure of domination to a form of colonial governance that works through the medium of state recognition and accommodation [...] [R]egardless of this shift Canadian settler-colonialism remains structurally oriented around achieving the same power effect it sought in the pre-1969 period: the dispossession of Indigenous peoples of their lands and self-determining authority."[17] The long '70s marks the period when this restructuring of dominance through the adoption and implementation of state liberalism took place. And it was this political context that formed the basis for *The Idea of North* and its subsequent critical reception and celebration.

What is particularly striking about ARCTICNOISE is that Inutiq perceives his intervention in primarily formal, sonic terms, with the political consequences deriving from them. In an interview with Kate Hennessy, Inutiq explains his fascination with Gould's use of voice, the way in which *The Idea of North* focuses on vocal textures as much as the content of the interviewees' speech: "What interested me in the work of Glenn Gould and his *Idea of North* is that even though the content is very much socio-politically charged, I believe that the work of Glenn Gould was just to simply listen to the voice as a babble. If you listen to the voice talking, it sounds like the babbling of a brook. Outside of any connotations that we give to the words, the sound of just someone talking is interesting. You give someone something to talk about and then you let them talk about it and then you record it and then you make a montage of it."[18] It may seem from this description that Inutiq is letting Gould a bit off the hook here in that he assigns the problematic political content to the interview subjects and reserves for Gould a place beyond it, assuming a vantage point from which to register only the musical properties of the voices and to hear the compositional possibilities of their orchestration. This positioning of the eccentric Gould would not be inconsistent with how he has long been seen, understood, and mythologized. Perhaps most notably, in François Girard's *Thirty-Two Short Films about Glenn Gould* (1993), there is a scene in which Gould, stopped at a roadside diner somewhere outside Toronto, begins to conduct a symphony of voices, piecing together the overheard conversations into a strikingly harmonious composition. In terms of its sound design, the scene itself echoes Gould's weave of voices in *The Idea of North*, and it very much contributes to the myth of a man who not only perceived music everywhere but, through the sheer force of his imagination, could also transform even the most cacophonous of everyday chatter into a symphonic shape. In the scene, Girard even provides a close-up of Gould's index finger moving ever so slightly, as though his powers are so great that he is not merely hearing the world differently from the rest of us but is also capable of controlling the very sounds around him.

With regard to *The Idea of North*, Inutiq explains to Hennessy, "I thought that Glenn Gould was trying to just create an aesthetic experience and that the people who were talking, they were the ones responsible for giving socio-political content."[19] Of course, the obvious counterpoint here is that Gould selected these voices and that the criteria for selection was, to say the least, limiting. But Inutiq's analysis is, I think, more interesting. For him, the task of ARCTICNOISE is to establish that there are other conversations going on, both at the time and today, in which the Inuit are participants and that these conversations are noisier and more varied and complex than Gould, in *The Idea of North*, could grasp. Despite the mythology offered in Girard's film and his work's complex contrapuntal structure, Gould's singular fascination with the idea of the North means that he does not hear those other conversations happening immediately around him. In conversation with Hennessy, Inutiq explains that ARCTICNOISE picks up on Gould's formal fascination with voice but that it also hears these other, occluded conversations:

> I wanted to reflect [Gould's focus on voice] in terms of the main piece and then using the Igloolik Isuma archives was content that was evoking socio-political identity issues and issues of climate change, issues of reconciliation between the Inuit and the Cree, which I thought was quite interesting and a way to put another kind of dialogue, a cross-cultural dialogue.

> Maybe people expect me to try to talk about colonialism or the relationship of Inuit to the Western white people. I don't know how to qualify it, but I wanted to take the discussion elsewhere

and say that the Inuit are in a conversation with the Cree as well, and we're in a conversation as well with government officials on the federal level, on the provincial level, and it's all quite contentious, and there's discussions about the climate and the climate is changing and these are all very important issues.[20]

Far from letting him off the hook, Inutiq confronts Gould's political elisions in formal, musical, and compositional terms. He draws on the Igloolik Isuma archives not simply to show the political conversations that occur beyond Gould's interviewees' speculations on what the North means and how to fix it but also in a way that attends to voice, that sees the same musicality in Inuit voices that Gould sees in the southerner's voices he selected: "I thought that ultimately it created the context to hear our voice. That was my goal, I think, to hear the voices talking about stuff, which happens to have socio-political import. But my goal was not to present the socio-political cause. My goal was to have people talking about socio-political issues, but to just experience that as an aesthetic thing."[21] As a result, Inutiq not only identifies the central problem with Gould's work but also reaches beyond an arithmetic solution that would simply add Cree or Inuit voices to the mix. Instead, he reconfigures the conversation as a whole and allows the aesthetic to do political work in revealing the importance of voice as voice and thus as a sonic element that has political force and import above, beyond, or in coordination with the speech it delivers.[22]

Equally important is the idea of noise, both auditory and optical. Inutiq's ARCTICNOISE offers a sonic experience very different from that of *The Idea of North*. Although the voices in *The Idea of North* overlap, the effect is hardly dissonant, even when the polyvocality of the piece nudges the elements toward unintelligibility. The soft tones and overall sonic texture of Gould's work conjure up an almost impossibly clichéd Canadian scene: listening to the radio at night, perhaps alone, a winter storm brewing outside, and only the disembodied voices to provide company and comfort. ARCTICNOISE is by no means a full-on sonic assault, yet both its mix of voices and languages – English, Cree, and Inuktitut – as well as its soundtrack made up of electronic sounds and beats very much distinguish it from *The Idea of North*'s altogether more polite sonic palette. Of course, the idea of noise is perspectival.

For those who speak Inuktitut or Cree or both, the experience of ARCTICNOISE is very different since more of the audio information can be received as signal. For those who do not speak these languages, the effect is humbling since it dramatizes the experience of being left outside of the conversation. But it also allows us to zero in on the materiality of voice and its musical properties, something that clearly fascinates Inutiq about Gould's work.

The soundtrack for *The Idea of North* is mostly comprised of the voices alone, blended with ambient sounds of trains and wind, until Gould introduces the final movement of Jean Sibelius's *Symphony No. 5* (1915) in its final phases, a work most famous for its evocation of the call of the whooper swan. Sibelius was inspired during the process of its composition by the sight of sixteen swans circling overhead before flying off into the sun. In *The Idea of North*, the Sibelius piece, with its swans and its sense of ascension and harmony, produces a real feeling of resolution, not simply through its appeal to nature but also precisely because the swan's call suggests a kind of contemplative solitude associated with lakes, forests, and the North more generally.[23] The loon, of course, would have been a more obvious bird for Gould to use to sum up his sense of Canada's North, and it would have placed him squarely at the forefront of the tradition of the loon-evoking and loon-sampling Canadian classical, experimental, disco, and electronic music I mapped out in chapter 1. Yet his appeal to Sibelius and the whooper swan – which is Finland's national bird and not native to North America – drives home how Gould's idea of the North is very much a romantic idea rather being derived from an on-the-ground reality.

From Noise to Signal: *ARCTICNOISE* and *Dubyadubs*

For ARCTICNOISE, Inutiq draws on his experience as a DJ and electronic musician. Although he decided to abandon the moniker in 2015, Inutiq long recorded as DJ madeskimo, releasing a series of albums online and on cassette. Inutiq's back catalogue is deep and ranges over a wide array of genres, from dub-influenced electronica and crisp, straight-up techno to chilly ambient soundscapes and electroacoustic experiments. He has long blended contemporary electronic forms with traditional

Inuit music. As Crystal Chan explains, Inutiq's "trademark sound [...] infuses the melodies of his youth with urban beats," and his early work as madeskimo prefigured the recent rise of Indigenous hip hop and electronica: "Before A Tribe Called Red popularized powwow-step, the genre mixing electronic and Indigenous dance music, Inutiq released *Developments* (2008). On the album, [Sylvia] Cloutier's [an Inuk throat singer and producer] vocals ring over the beat of the *qilauti*, an Inuit drum, patterned over dubstep beats."[24] Inutiq's sheer stylistic range is notable, but of particular significance here is his dialogue with older forms of electronic music. Some of the engagements are with fairly recent subgenres – his take on dubstep in "sealflipper" is particularly exhilarating – but others dig deeper into the history of electronic music making. Inutiq's *Dedications* (2008), in particular, seems to draw on the electronic experiments of the 1970s, from the deep Moog-like drones of the opening track "atenderheartis" to the kosmische minimalism of "insidesmile" to the loping mid-tempo beats and ambient field-recording quality of "alittlehonestydoesnthurt," which comes complete with sampled bird calls. As Inutiq notes, "Being able to sample the world around us and sample old recordings keeps us in discussion with the world and keeps us moving forward. To be able to use new sounds and old sounds [...] is an indirect way of jamming with someone."[25] This desire to engage with already existing sonic materials and to push things forward by bringing the past into the present defines much sample-based electronic music. However, it is of particular consequence for Inutiq, whose work stages multiple dialogues simultaneously – between Inuit and Canadian, analogue and digital, traditional and avant-garde, and northern and southern – and does so in an effort to trouble the relationships, even the seeming opposition, between all of these commonly paired terms. As Chan observes, "discourse about Indigenous musicians applauds the fusion of old and new," but this response is often little more than a critical cliché that refuses to recognize that Inuit culture is a living culture.[26] Innovation need not be imported into Inuit culture from elsewhere, Inutiq insists, but is integral to it: "That sense of innovation and that sense of independence comes from my Inuit culture. My will to innovate and my will to do it independently is also a reflection of my Inuit values."[27] In terms of ARCTICNOISE, Inutiq's indirect jam with

Gould results in a piece that introduces noise into the conventional accounts of the North, remixing the past as part of the process of imagining a future.[28]

The noise in ARCTICNOISE is visual as well. As Kate Hennessy, Trudi-Lynn Smith, and Tarah Hogue argue – reflecting back on the impact of the exhibition at the grunt gallery from the vantage point of having been involved in the project in different capacities virtually from its conception – the force of Inutiq's work resides in the audio-visual disruption of conventional signals, patterns, and conventions to create a situation and context where ideas of the North can be unsettled: "Noise was encountered throughout the gallery. First, it is sonic – the sound of Inuktitut and Cree language in the Igloolik Isuma films. These are entangled with electronic music that, on the night of the opening at grunt gallery, Geronimo performed in live sets. The videos themselves are marked by visual noise, glitch, and interference. Glitch is an unexpected digital malfunction [...] These videos, and the postcards shared with gallery visitors, aestheticize digital distortion as an unsettling move that defies interpretation and understanding of the context in its original form."[29] Part of the visual impact of ARCTICNOISE resides in the juxtapositions made possible by its multichannel setup, but, in addition, Inutiq digitally manipulates many of his images, producing striking compositions that emphasize the mediated status of the images themselves.[30] On the right channel feed, Inutiq overlays the archival footage of the North with intensely oversaturated reds, greens, yellows, and purples, as well as superimposing video graphics of shifting geometric shapes and patterns. There is an aesthetic dimension to these distortions that should not be ignored – many of the individual frames are strikingly beautiful and the shifting blocks and forms oddly mesmerizing – but there is a political dimension to them as well.[31] Noise becomes signal in Inutiq's work. The glitches are a way to make visible the mediated nature of all representation and, by extension, to show that the archive is never politically neutral but formed under specific historical conditions and ideological contexts. As Hennessy, Smith, and Hogue point out, ARCTICNOISE represents a "critical engagement with signal, noise, and glitch to re-present the North – as well as the archive – as an unstable, dynamic idea, instead of a static apparatus of the colonial imagination."[32] The disruption of these already existing images remediates them in the figurative sense as well: their toxic power as record and remnant of colonial conquest is contested and challenged through remix and reclamation.[33]

ARCTICNOISE builds on a sonic and visual style that Inutiq established in his earlier work. Of particular significance is *Dubyadubs*, a video piece originally produced in 2009 for an event in celebration of Quebec City's 400th anniversary and exhibited as part of *Beat Nation: Art, Hip Hop and Aboriginal Culture* at the Vancouver Art Gallery in 2012. For *Dubyadubs*, Inutiq drew on the National Film Board (NFB) archives for images of Iron Eyes Cody, the Italian American actor who was famous for impersonating an Indian, both on- and off-screen, as I discussed in chapter 2 in relation to the famed "Crying Indian" public service announcement. For *Dubyadubs*, Inutiq treated the footage digitally, introducing all kinds of glitches and artifacts. The soundtrack for the piece is an echo-laden and reverb-heavy madeskimo dub track that Inutiq initially released in 2008. The track's spacey delays and woozy rhythm have the effect of disrupting any sense of time. As a consequence, the images are set loose from their historical and ideological moorings, enabling the spectator to see and experience them anew and thereby to recognize the weirdness, even the strange wonder, in Iron Eyes Cody's impersonations. As he himself explains in the catalogue for the *Beat Nation* exhibition, Inutiq exploits the creepiness of Cody's act to think about representations of Indigeneity:

> Iron Eyes Cody was an Italian-American actor who made a career on and off the silver screen impersonating an American Indian man. One can argue he was so good a method actor that he practically epitomized what it meant to live as a First Nation. We see him in this video clip travelling across what looks like the taiga or the boreal forest as a nomad, accompanied by what we can imagine to be extended family and tribe members. The narrating written text of the silent movie, though sometimes garbled by the digital effects, points to the harsh life against the elements. Bringing the video and music together was effectuated as a sort of collage. Ultimately it presents in high contrast and in an evocative and playful way what it means to be an "Indian."[34]

Quite unexpectedly, Inutiq uses Iron Eyes Cody, a classic example of redfacing, to produce a trippy meditation on Indigenous identity and the history of Indigenous representation on-screen.[35] The playfulness of the mode and method does not exclude a critique of redfacing but subsumes it, working it into an examination of both the oddness of the practice and the weird, unexpected ways that Cody's impersonations captured aspects of Indigenous life on camera. *Dubyadubs* shows what being "an 'Indian'" meant to viewers both in terms of Cody's weird impersonation and in terms of being subjected to it. There is a sharp critical edge to Inutiq's observation here, namely that to be Indigenous is to be subject to representations such as Cody's, which are obviously deeply appropriative but strikingly uncanny as well.

Inutiq's musical selection for *Dubyadubs* is crucial. Dub, long associated with studio techniques and master producers, is a subgenre of reggae that takes an original track and distorts it, usually by stripping out the vocals and amplifying the drums and bass. Echo, delay, and reverb mess with the original reggae rhythm, slowing it down and spacing it out. The ghostly sound of dub pairs well with archival images precisely because its distorted and decelerated rhythms evoke both the melancholy of history and the utopian possibilities of a not yet fixed future. As Michael E. Veal argues in his history of the form, producers such as King Tubby and Lee "Scratch" Perry use dub to reflect on past pain and terrestrial trauma but also to envisage possible futures, both planetary and beyond. In music generally, but especially in dub, "the sensation of echo is closely associated with the cognitive function of memory and the evocation of a chronological past; at the same time, it can also evoke the vastness of outer space and hence (by association), the chronological future."[36] The ghosts of the past haunt the present but also reveal the ways that the future is yet to be determined. For the black diaspora of the 1970s – in Jamaica but also in Toronto, London, New York City, and elsewhere – dub played a very precise role. As Veal explains, dub captures "[t]he condition of simultaneously yearning for and being alienated from a cultural homeland that can never be fully experienced as home, and also from the very *history* of connection to that homeland." This characteristic, he argues, "allows us to interpret dub as a cultural sound painting of a type, vividly dramatizing the experience of diasporic exile."[37] Of course, as an Inuk, Inutiq's situation is different. Nevertheless, I would like to think that in his dub experiments there is something of an imagined affinity and affiliation with "the whole sense of loss, rupture, and repair" that Arthur Jafa identifies as being at the very heart of the genre.[38] Even though Inutiq's dub is from the North rather than the Antilles, his appeal to the genre forges a link between the displaced and the diasporic, seeing them as two facets of the experience of imperialism. The decolonial aspect of dub resides in how its manipulation of its sonic sources to produce remediations and ruptures "comes to symbolize the disruptions in cultural memory and the historical shattering of existential peace, encoded into the cultural nervous system and sublimated into musical sound."[39] Dub emerged in the 1970s and bears within its grooves and echoes the recognition that the traumas of colonialism reverberate into the present. It registers and records them but also opens up a space where the past can be reclaimed and the future imagined. With *Dubyadubs*, Inutiq, through the unlikely figure of Iron Eyes Cody, transports these decolonial impulses and energies from the past into the present and forges a political connection between arctic noise and island rhythms.[40]

"Indigenous people kicking ass on-screen": Caroline Monnet's *Mobilize*

In drawing on archive material from the National Film Board, *Dubyadubs* anticipates a set of four short works – grouped together as the *Souvenir* series – by Indigenous filmmakers commissioned by the NFB for the Aboriginal Pavilion at the Pan Am Games held in Toronto in 2015. Of the four, Mi'gmaq Jeff Barnaby's *Etlinisigu'niet (Bleed Down)* is perhaps most reminiscent of the ghostly echoes and haunted beats of Inutiq's earlier archival explorations. Soundtracked by Tanya Tagaq's "Tulugak" (2014), the film catalogues Canada's reprehensible treatment of Indigenous people, from the horrors of the residential school system to the contamination of land belonging to First Nations. Even though Barnaby's film is not processed, treated, or glitchy in the same way that Inutiq's work often is, it shares a stylistic inventiveness in the way that it makes the materiality of the film images visible. Complete with grain, flicker, and scratch, Barnaby's remediations reveal that the

NFB archives contain a record of these horrors even if they were not the focus of the films for which the footage was originally shot. Indeed, both Barnaby's film and Cree Kent Monkman's *Sisters and Brothers* zero in on images of Indigenous children sent to residential schools to reveal how any process of reconciliation must necessarily include a reckoning with these images via a resignification of what they depict and mean. Drawn from NFB films about the residential school system, such as *Northern Schooldays* (1958) and *Because They Are Different* (1964), the images were meant to show the goodness and generosity of the Canadian state in its treatment of Indigenous peoples. Remixed and recontextualized, they show the exact opposite, revealing how film was mobilized by the Canadian state to obscure what was really happening in the residential school system.[41]

Remediation does not simply reveal the actual significance of the image but can also invest it with a retroactive political power and force. There is a striking moment in Monkman's film when a young Indigenous girl stares directly into the camera. It lasts only a second and might scarcely have been notable in its original use, perhaps even ending up on the cutting room floor. But Monkman's remediation of the image in a short that parallels the mass slaughter of bison in the late nineteenth century with the deaths of over 6,000 Indigenous children in the residential school system grants it an uncanny power. Through Monkman's remediation, the image somehow evokes both the base cruelty of the residential school system and a formidable spirit of Indigenous resistance at the same time.[42] Cut to the steady drum beat of A Tribe Called Red's "The Road" (2013) and juxtaposed with images of bison thundering across the prairie landscape, the young girl stares defiantly across time and, through her gaze, holds the present accountable.

These shorts by Barnaby and Monkman, along with the third film in the *Souvenir* series, Algonquin-Métis Michelle Latimer's *Nimmikaage (She Dances for People)*, all draw primarily on black-and-white footage from the 1960s and earlier in order to document the catastrophic consequences of colonialism and the comprehensive failure of the Canadian state to fulfil its treaty obligations. The fourth film in the series, Algonquin Caroline Monnet's *Mobilize*, takes a different tack, remediating colour images from the 1960s and 1970s in a film made specifically, as Monnet herself has said, to show images of Indigenous strength and power: "What I wanted with the film was for people to be bombarded with images of Indigenous people kicking ass on-screen."[43] As Catherine Russell notes, even though "[d]eath, ruin, and loss" are "prominent tropes in archiveology" – the term she gives to contemporary forms of archival film practice – "the experiential, sensual dimensions of reanimated footage, sounds, and images can be visual, dynamic, and very much present."[44] Monnet's *Mobilize* in every way bears that out, with the 1970s images, although recognizable as 1970s images, being remarkably vibrant and energetic. Monnet's remediation of them intensifies their energy and vitality.

At the heart of Monnet's film is footage shot for Tony Ianzelo and Boyce Richardson's *Cree Hunters of Mistassini* (1974) that shows Sam Blacksmith, a master paddler and one of the hunters of the film's title, navigating his canoe across lakes and rivers of the traditional Cree hunting grounds that stretch throughout northern Quebec (see figure 5.2). This footage is exhilarating, not least because of the way that it captures Blacksmith's incredible skill and dexterity in guiding his canoe up rivers and through rapids in order to cover the expansive terrain where his family has hunted for generations. In addition to striking steadicam-like shots of Blacksmith kneeling in the stern of his canoe and using his paddle to thread his way upriver, Ianzelo and Richardson also deliver a number of shots, with the bow of the canoe in frame, that capture the harshness and the beauty of the natural landscape from Blacksmith's point of view. In the original film, Ianzelo and Richardson use these images sparingly in sequences that are, for the most part, more introspective than intense. Monnet speeds up these images of Blacksmith to match the rhythm of Tanya Tagaq's "Uja" (2014), which serves as the film's soundtrack. The result is electrifying, with the beats and breaths of Tagaq's track seeming to propel Blacksmith upriver.

Monnet structures her film as a journey from north to south, with Blacksmith's canoe serving as the vehicle that transports spectators through a landscape comprised of clips from the NFB archives. *Mobilize* shows Indigenous people as active and in motion, as dynamic cinematic agents rather than passive ethnographic subjects of the camera. Monnet uses images from *Cree Hunters of Mistassini* as well as from Bernard Gosselin's *Cesar's Bark Canoe* (1971) to show the continuity

5.2 The remediated image in Caroline Monnet's *Mobilize* (2015).

between past and present as well as the persistence of traditional practices into an era of accelerated modernization and rapid urbanization. Scenes of hunting, fishing, canoeing, and snowshoeing give way in the final third of the film to shots of Indigenous men and women in the modern city. Monnet draws on Don Owen's *High Steel* (1965) for images of Mohawk ironworkers from Kahnawake at work high atop skyscrapers under construction in early 1960s New York City. Interspersed with these shots of a heroic Indigenous masculinity are others of a young Indigenous woman in a smart, quintessentially 1960s outfit walking through Montreal. Monnet draws these images from footage shot for Michel Régnier's *Indian Memento* (1967), an NFB film commissioned by the Department of Indian and Northern Affairs to document the Indians of Canada Pavilion at Expo 67. Régnier's film is without dialogue (ideal for showing to either an English or French audience), but it does feature a loose narrative. The opening scenes show the young Indigenous woman at home with her family and feature many shots of forests, rivers, and mountains, presumably in an effort to solidify the link between Indigeneity and nature that a settler audience would expect. The film then shifts to scenes of Expo 67 itself, where we see the young woman at work as a guide at the Indian pavilion. She shows visitors through the pavilion, which features displays that seem surprisingly frank for 1967, detailing Canada's failures to honour the treaties it had signed. However, it is from the final phase of the film (and from footage shot for it but not included) that Monnet draws the bulk of her footage. It shows the young woman out and about in Montreal. Although these sequences suggest that she is new to the city, an arrival for the special event of Expo 67, they do not seem condescending. Subsequent shots show her laughing and boldly looking forward, confidently at home both in Montreal and in the modernity that it, in the late 1960s, paradigmatically represented. In the selection of these shots from Régnier's film, Monnet presents a vision of modernity that includes Indigenous subjects, using the NFB archives to cut against the grain of the majority of images that populate them, which do not necessarily show Indigenous people at home in the modern metropolis.

What primarily interests me in Monnet's use of these archival images is the way that, unlike the other filmmakers in the *Souvenir* series, she shifts their significance rather than wholly subverting them.

Cree Hunters of Mistassini is very much the product of a liberal NFB, a film that is broadly sympathetic with its Cree subjects. Beginning with a voiceover that acknowledges the Cree's fight against the hydroelectric development at James Bay and shot with what feels like great respect and admiration for the hunters whose lives it aims to document, Ianzelo and Richardson's film in many ways exemplifies the liberalism of the NFB in the period. Produced as part of the Challenge for Change program by an activist documentary strand within the NFB that focused on social issues and sought to include documentary subjects in the filmmaking process, *Cree Hunters of Mistassini* yields images that are different in tone and ideological orientation from the NFB material shot even ten to fifteen years previously on which the other films in the *Souvenir* series draw. This is not to say that the film has no limitations. There are certainly moments when it adopts a more ethnographic approach to its Cree subjects and remains silent on the ways that government intervention, from residential schools to the environmental consequences of aggressive economic development of the North, has shaped contemporary Indigenous life. That said, and perhaps because of the participatory dimension of the Challenge for Change program, it feels as though this film, as well as others from the same era that Monnet uses, provides a view of Indigenous life in the long '70s that is not characterized by pity, contempt, or condescension.[45] The material is there for Monnet to fulfil her desire to show "Indigenous people kicking ass on-screen."[46]

For both Inutiq and Monnet, the feel and texture of analogue media play a key part in formulating the relationship between the past and the present. As Crystal Chan explains, when Inutiq set up Indigene Audio, his independent label, "He returned to the cassette-tape medium of his childhood, when he made mixtape after mixtape with his boombox, because he likes how magnetic tape brings distortion, compression, and warble."[47] Whether with film or cassettes, there is an affective dimension to the analogue, one that, as I explored in chapter 4 in relation to L'Atelier's video fixations, is as tied up with lost possibilities as it is with limitations. The limits of analogue audio, the imperfections that Inutiq enumerates, tie it to a period and the pleasure of working with and within those limitations. This is not simply nostalgia but also the desire to remember and resuscitate older methods and practices. Doing so troubles, on the level of medium itself, the very same divisions – between traditional and contemporary, residual and dominant, and obsolescent and emergent – that Inutiq queries elsewhere in his work. Similarly, in reference to *Mobilize*, Monnet explains that she wanted to exploit the ambiguity of analogue, the way that the look and feel of a film pins it to a particular past at the same time that it can still feel completely contemporary: "The original footage was shot on 16mm film, and I purposely decided to only use that kind of footage. It had to be color, and it had to be film. This was important because I wanted the film to have a certain consistency. I wanted audiences to wonder if I shot the footage myself or if it was really found footage. The 16mm footage adds a level of nostalgia and warmth to the piece without being outdated."[48] What I find especially powerful about Monnet's film is that she does not concede the terrain of the past. There are, of course, plenty of reasons for Indigenous writers, filmmakers, and artists to be very suspicious of nostalgia, specifically any national nostalgia that would gloss over the betrayals and brutalities of colonization as well as ongoing inequalities and injustices. Yet, through remediation, *Mobilize* reclaims memory, even exploits medium-specific nostalgic affect as a political move, insisting on a right to these images. Monnet crafts a relationship with the NFB archives that is not merely nostalgic but also future-oriented in its image claims. As Monnet herself says, "I wanted to use the archives to speak about the future; usually archives are nostalgic but, on the contrary, I wanted to talk about the future."[49] *Mobilize* is precisely that, a film that draws on already existing audiovisual materials not simply to see the past differently through remix and remediation but also to harness the latent energies of the past in order to sketch out a dynamic future.

Crowdsourcing, Community, and Continuity: Paul Seesequasis's *Indigenous Archival Photo Project*

In its mobilization of past images to assert a presence and imagine a future, Monnet's film sits alongside a contemporary photo project that restructures the collective national understanding of the long '70s.

Willow Cree Paul Seesequasis's *The Indigenous Archival Photo Project* began online in 2015 with Seesequasis sourcing archival images of First Nations, Métis, and Inuit life and posting them on Twitter, Facebook, and Instagram. The success of the project led to an exhibition, curated by Seesequasis, of selected photographs at the Touchstones Nelson Museum of Art and History in Nelson, British Columbia, in early 2018. A book based on the project, titled *Blanket Toss under Midnight Sun* (after a 1962 photograph Seesequasis posted in June 2016) is slated for publication in 2019. Seesequasis was motivated to embark on the project after a discussion with his mother, a residential school survivor, who, as he says, "longed to hear more positive stories about the Indigenous experience, in particular the strength of families and communities in admittedly hard times."[50]

For the project, Seesequasis draws extensively on official archives, museum collections, libraries, and local historical societies across the country and internationally. He selects photos from the 1920s to the 1980s – although, as I discuss below, the images from the 1970s are particularly striking – taken by both Indigenous and non-Indigenous photographers. In most cases, the names of those pictured in the photographs that Seesequasis sources and circulates were never formally recorded. As a consequence, Seesequasis's social media feed has become a place where followers can identify those pictured and even offer memories of the people, places, and circumstances that the photographs depict. This process is deeply moving, not least in the way that it actualizes the participatory potential of social media and does so in a positive way that retains a real political edge. As with Monnet's *Mobilize*, the affective force of these images cannot be written off as mere nostalgia. They show the way that memory and feeling are fundamental political issues. As I have argued throughout *Hinterland Remixed*, memory, feeling, and even nostalgia must not be conceded to conservatives whose vision of the country or the world is a calcified fantasy of hegemonic whiteness. The power of Seesequasis's archival project resides in the way that it reclaims both the photos and the feelings that they catalyze when descendants, community members, or even the very people depicted in them see and share the remediated images. As Seesequasis explains, his online posts may initiate this process of reclamation, but ultimately it is a collective, crowdsourced effort: "As people recognized the subjects in the photographs and tried to identify dates and locations, sharing the images with their relatives in turn, the project gained its own momentum. It became an exercise in visual reclamation and digital repatriation of the photographs themselves – a return to community."[51]

Even though Seesequasis's project stretches before and beyond the 1970s, the images he selects from that decade have a special force and power. I would like to think that this effect, rather than being just an individual quirk of mine, also has something to do with the way that the simultaneous proximity and distance of the period lends images from it an uncanny resonance. Seesequasis has posted a number of photos by George Legrady, all taken in Cree communities surrounding James Bay in 1972 and 1973. Legrady himself explains that the motivation for what would become known as the *James Bay Cree Photographic Documentary* was political: "The documentary was produced in response to the political circumstances of the Cree taking legal action against the James Bay Hydro Electric Corporation, whose project consisted in creating one of North America's largest hydro-electric dam systems blocking the main rivers in the area. The flooding resulted in major ecological imbalances not to mention invasion and destruction of Indian land."[52] The project contains some photos that directly depict protest against Hydro-Quebec, yet the vast majority of the images are of everyday life, for they were meant to serve as a record of the community and to rally those of the South, in Montreal and elsewhere, to the Indigenous cause in their fight against the dam project.

In a description of the project written in the early 2000s, Legrady notes, "This photographic archive is the history of a community at a particular moment in time and my personal interaction with them. With 30 years' having gone by, the James Bay communities have changed and this material may be ready for historical reevaluation, to be annotated by the educators and cultural workers of the James Bay communities."[53] Seesequasis's remediation of these images embarks on this work. Even though he himself is not from James Bay, his posts have generated comments and reflections from many who are. They may have actually been present when Legrady visited nearly fifty years ago and may spot younger versions of themselves in the photos, or they might catch a glimpse of friends and family members now much older or even departed. Either way, the work of remediation brings the past into the present not merely as a trigger for nostalgic reminiscence but also as a timely reminder of both the continuity of Indigenous struggle against the state and the resilience of Indigenous culture in the face of assimiliation and dispossession.

Alongside the photos from Legrady, Seesequasis often draws on the work of Rosemary Gilliat Eaton, a journalist whose photos of Indigenous people and communities taken throughout the 1950s and early 1960s were, as Seesequasis says, the work of "an outside eye, but one with delicate sensitivity."[54] Seesequasis's own comments on the force and impact of Eaton's photos articulate the delicate balance inherent in his remediations. They are evidence of the happiness possible in the past but do not gloss over the strength and resilience that made these moments possible: "Indigenous and non-Indigenous viewers may see these photographs differently, but the images embody an inherent possibility of dialogue, exchange, and mutual appreciation and understanding. Eaton was taking her photos in often dark times, yet the images we see depict functioning, hard-working people and communities, reflecting the integrity of previous Indigenous generations [...] There is a resilient thread revealed in her photographs, fraying but not severed by colonialism. Eaton's subjects are not victims."[55] There is one photo in particular from Legrady's project that, for me, exemplifies this tension between the struggles of the 1970s and the strength that gave rise to Indigenous protest movements. It shows four young Cree men in Fort George, Quebec, in 1973. The majority of the photos Legrady took are in black and white, but this one is in colour. They stand together, but two men are slightly foregrounded, one with hands in pockets and the other holding a 12-gauge shotgun. The two men in the background are relaxed, one with arms crossed as he looks up at the sky, and the other smiling, his hair and hat slightly obscuring his face. It is perhaps a cliché to say that it looks like an album cover, yet it does, and it is the type of photo that could very well have complemented the liner notes for the landmark compilation *Native North America (Vol. 1): Aboriginal Folk, Rock, and Country, 1966–1985* (2014), released by Light in the Attic Records of Seattle not long before Seesequasis started his photo project online. The young men are all rocking a quintessentially 1970s look. Two are in double denim, and another has a lumberjack plaid shirt peeking out from underneath his sweater. These details ground the photo in its period and evoke a historical moment that saw the rise of an Indigenous politics fuelled by youth. It is marked by a series of stylistic signifiers connected to countercultural movements elsewhere, but these young men make them totally their own, the articulation of a politicized, even militant Cree identity that arose in relation to the Save James Bay campaign. The "Keep on Trucking" patch that the young man at the very front has sewn sideways onto the front of his jean jacket links this group to subcultural happenings in the South, but it is perhaps the two massive oil storage units in the background that serve as the most obvious symbol of the modern and modernizing North that these young Cree men both navigate and confront.

This photo by Legrady – *"Before the flood: Four young men" ~ (Cree) ~ Fort George, Quebec 1973* – struck a chord when Seesequasis posted it on Twitter in November 2016, garnering dozens of retweets and likes. Friends and family quickly identified the four men, and others reminisced more generally about the political energy of the period and the galvanizing force of the James Bay protests. This photo and its reception online are a powerful reminder that the process of remediation can be a political act in and of itself. The recirculation of this image online keeps alive the memory of past political struggles, refusing the oversimplifications of dominant historical memory and nourishing present and future political action. Furthermore, the remediation of the image as part of Seesequasis's *Indigenous Archival Photo Project* recontextualizes it as well. It becomes part of the longer and larger visual history of Indigeneity that Seesequasis is compiling through the process of remediation.[56] This is the most radical dimension of Seesequasis's project: it makes visible, as a steady stream of images on social media, the continuity and connections between Indigenous groups across North America yet never, because of the participatory dimension of the project, loses sight of the specificity of the images, their grounding in precise places and situations.

As much as the gallery installation and forthcoming book mark important extensions of Seesequasis's *Indigenous Archival Photo Project*, its manifestations online – on Twitter, Facebook, and Instagram – seem to me to be its most potent form. Fully taking advantage of the participatory dimension of social media, Seesequasis creates both a sense of community and a sense of continuity. Part of the power of the project in its online form is that it is a feed, a steady stream of images that amass and accumulate, each of which individually sparks conversations and recollections but builds on the others as well. And although Seesequasis's stream of images is very different in form from Inutiq's multiple, simultaneous projections, both use remediation to recirculate, recontextualize, and resignify the images. So, to bring this chapter to a close, I return very briefly to the sensory impact of ARCTICNOISE's three-screen simultaneity and its work with the audiovisual remains of the recent past.

Writing about John Akomfrah's *The Nine Muses* (2011) – not one of the director's multichannel works but one that, in its montage of historical materials and created tableaus, stretches the capacity of a single-screen work – Malini Guha argues that Akomfrah converts audiovisual remains into "digital and affective data." Drawing on Rey Chow, Guha notes that these remains belong to the "domain of social justice" since they are key components of any reformulation of collective memory and "the politics of collectivity and solidarity" at the same time that they are "incomplete and elusive," not fixed or frozen in a way that forecloses on possible futures.[57] In archival works such as Akomfrah's, the residues and remainders of the past are central to the political interventions of the present and to the continued possibility of better futures. Guha writes that "the political force of remains lies in their deficiency and their inability to offer up a vision of completeness. The incompleteness of remains potentially opens up a space for dialogue about the past, allowing the past to remain very much alive through reconfiguration as well as futures that have yet to be foreclosed. In addition, the power of remains resides in the kind of presences that they make possible, especially for the purposes of contestation and resistance. Remains are not just about what cannot be recovered but also about what must continue to be imagined."[58] A similar recognition of the importance of remains animates Inutiq's work, and like the use of montage in *The Nine Muses*, the multichannel format of ARCTICNOISE marks an effort to open up that space of "contestation and resistance" as a means to challenge the hegemony of voice in a way that is dynamic rather than substitutive. Inutiq's remediations, like Monnet's and Seesequasis's, illuminate the centrality of the archive to the ongoing work of decolonization. The remixing, resignification, and recirculation of already existing materials characterize an artistic practice that is also, in its very form and methods, a political one. And this work applies not only to older materials but to the more recent remains of the long '70s as well. Inutiq's remixing of Gould, Monnet's intervention into the NFB archives, and Seesequasis's recirculation of archival photos all demonstrate the ways that the past does not persist inertly inside the present but is there, like a kind of stored energy, waiting to be harnessed and unleashed.

Coda: Sorting through the Wreckage of the Twentieth Century

My emphasis throughout *Hinterland Remixed* on the residues, remainders, remixes, and remediations of the long '70s is premised on the idea that the 1970s are still with us and that it remains possible to harness the decade's energies to positive ends. Throughout the book, I have been particularly fascinated by the ways that this material has been salvaged and transmitted, the analogue containers that have transported it into the present, and the digitization protocols, whether amateur or official, that have facilitated its continued circulation. In this brief coda, I turn to the infrastructural remains of the past, those broadcast and exhibition remnants that were once essential to the transmission and circulation of sound and moving images in Canada but are now perceived as being surplus and dispensable. In the past decade, several Canadian artists and filmmakers have taken up the question of the ruins and wreckage of the recent past. In some cases, they have questioned its obsolescence, seeing life left in the analogue even as it is written off and remaindered. In other cases, they investigate seriously the question of what we are meant to do with the accumulated piles of technological waste and the decaying architecture of analogue broadcast and exhibition. Left to deteriorate, these remnants might serve as a poignant reminder of the transience of all things, but they may also pollute and poison the very ground on which they stand or have been dumped. The infrastructural ruins and technological remainders that these artists and filmmakers document do not all date to the 1970s. Nevertheless, the networks, nodes, installations, and hardware they catalogue and depict were, in many cases, operational in the long '70s and represent the technological conditions of possibility for the decade and its audiovisual world.

Mike Rollo's short films *The Broken Altar* (2013) and *Farewell Transmission* (2017) both portray, with poignancy and power, the ways that the recent past has been left to decay or slated for demolition. The earlier film visits a number of disused drive-ins on the Canadian Prairies, their screens now dirty, punctured, or peeling, and the parking spaces where spectators once sat overgrown with grasses and wildflowers. The title itself imagines these spaces in terms of abandoned rituals and ruined temples, the remains of a way of life now almost unimaginable in an era of digital projection and the gaudy chaos of the suburban multiplex. There is also a demographic story being told here of urbanization, outmigration, and rural depopulation. The emptiness and absence of these spaces stand in for wholesale changes in Canadian life. Once the terrain of cinema and community, these fields and the small towns they serviced are now full of ghosts, the spectres of Saturday nights long past.

The Broken Altar is a landscape film that captures how the flatness of the prairie and its endless horizon made it perfect for outdoor exhibition, cinema under the stars. But like the cinematic treatment of the landscape in *La Région Centrale* (1971), its depiction of the terrain has a dystopian dimension. The low-frequency buzzes and drones of the soundtrack suggest that something catastrophic or cataclysmic has happened here. The ticket huts, concession stands, and projection booths, all still intact but slowly falling apart, imply a hasty, desperate departure that has left the presence of the past uncannily preserved. In one shot, Rollo's camera slowly zooms in on a screening schedule for a drive-in near Esterhazy, Saskatchewan, weathered and worn but still tacked to a wall. The list of upcoming films speaks to that final phase of drive-in culture, with blockbusters nestled alongside sex comedies and soft porn, disaster films, and slasher movies. The double bill of *The Erotic Adventures of Young Cecily* (1974) – a film that seems to have been trafficked under that title exclusively in Manitoba and Saskatchewan – and *Secrets of Sweet Sixteen* (1973) evoke an era when euro-permissiveness travelled all the way to the Canadian Prairies. Weekends either side of this salacious double bill saw screenings of *Star Wars* (1977) and *Scream Bloody Murder* (1973), meaning that we can date the demise of this drive-in to the late 1970s. But perhaps more interesting than this forensic detail is the sheer variety of the schedule, which, like the mix of programming on SCTV, speaks to a cinematic and exhibition landscape that was as inventive as it was idiosyncratic, as daring as it was desperate. The last of the scheduled screenings that Rollo's tight focus allows us to see serves as a metacommentary on the film itself and on its study of the abandoned cinematic spaces of a motorized modernity: *The Land That Time Forgot* (1974). In the end, no specific catastrophe led to the abandonment of these spaces. Rather, they were the victims of a slow catastrophe, of the grand economic shifts that have transformed Canada and the world since the 1970s.

Rollo's *Farewell Transmission* turns its focus from exhibition to broadcast, documenting the final days and hours of the CBK-TV transmitter station in Watrous, Saskatchewan. Built in 1939, and located between Regina and Saskatoon, the station was strategically situated to deliver the CBC signal not only to the province of Saskatchewan but to the rest of the Prairies as well. As Rollo notes in a series of title cards that open the film, the chosen location was additionally important because it sits on a potash vein, meaning that the strong ground connectivity this offered ensured a robust signal. The film continues Rollo's interest in architecture and age. Whereas *The Broken Altar* captures the vernacular architecture of the drive-in as it decays and deteriorates, *Farewell Transmission* features a transmitter station distinguished, even as it is being demolished, by its elegance and form. Designed in a streamlined moderne style, the building evokes a sophistication redolent of the golden age of radio and the ambitions of the era in which it was built. The transmitter continued operation through the 1970s and up until 2007, when it was replaced with a newer installation. The building lay dormant for several years, and despite efforts to designate it a heritage site, it was demolished in 2015.

An early shot in *Farewell Transmission* of the building framed against the horizon and vast prairie sky points to the possibility of an orthodox documentary about the demolition of a building and the end of an era. But Rollo delivers something altogether more compelling and rich (see figure C.1). The soundtrack hums with ghostly signals and the images crack, blister, fizzle, and burn as if channelling the still active energies of haunted transmissions. *Farewell Transmission* is a documentation of structure and space but one that understands that there are presences there that cannot, strictly speaking, be seen. The land retains resonances of the radio broadcasts transmitted from this site, and the air remains charged by the waves that travelled through it. Rollo evokes these unseen reverberations and disturbances in his treatment of the film itself. The susceptibility of the analogue image to damage, decay, and disintegration communicates the actual frailty and fragility of systems and networks once thought permanent. The film's unsettled atmosphere suggests an unease, even an anger, with the decision to demolish the building. As much as *Farewell Transmission* is a eulogy for the analogue era, it is also a revolt against efforts to forget the past and to wholly and hastily erase its residues from the landscape. By shooting on film, and exploiting the expressive possibilities of analogue, Rollo draws on the energies of a history of Canadian 1970s experimental filmmaking – the film is reminiscent at times of Jack Chambers's *The Hart of London* (1970) both in technique and in its investigations of the psychic resonances of place – to reveal how the site, even if the building disappears, will remain haunted by the voices transmitted from there.

Amanda Dawn Christie's experimental documentary *Spectres of Shortwave* (2017) likewise investigates the connections between place and the phantom force of radio waves. Christie documents the final years of transmission from Radio Canada International's shortwave relay station on the Tantramar Marshes near Sackville, New Brunswick. Operational since the Second World War, the site broadcast Radio Canada International worldwide and also served as a relay station for a host of international broadcasters, from the Voice of America to Radio China. Part of the force of Christie's film resides in the otherworldliness of the landscape itself – the salt-water-nourished marshes providing, like Rollo's potash, enhanced ground connectivity to boost the transmitted signals – but also emerges from the strange beauty of the installation built upon it. A complex network of towers, held aloft by guylines and linked by curtain arrays, punctuates the

C.1 Demolition of CBK-TV's transmitter station in Mike Rollo's *Farewell Transmission* (2017).

flat expanse of the tidal marshes. Christie's initial plan for the film was to document the site over the course of the seasons in order to make a durational landscape film that would capture the striking juxtaposition of towers and terrain. But after hearing stories about the station from both the technicians who worked there and local residents, Christie developed *Spectres of Shortwave* into a film focused on both voice and vista.[1] The soundtrack delivers oral histories of the site, from accounts of the day-to-day and often very dangerous maintenance of the transmission towers to tales of how its radio broadcasts, intended for listeners far away, would be eerily channelled through the fridges, sinks, and radiators of those close to the site. Christie does not show her interlocutors. The film layers their voices over images of the towers, the huts that sit at their base, the transmitter station, the highway that runs alongside the site, the marshes that surround it, and, on occasion, even the insides of the homes where appliances and pipework functioned as radio receivers. As a result, *Spectres of Shortwave* combines landscape film with radio documentary, putting it in dialogue with both *La Région Centrale* (1971) and *The Idea of North* (1967), as well as with Inutiq's ARCTICNOISE (2015). But perhaps more importantly, Christie's film reveals the conjunction of people and place, the intimacy of the voices being firmly grounded in the experience of the site and the surrounding area.

Spectres of Shortwave is about the disappearance of an analogue world and the demolition of the infrastructure that made it possible. For many of those interviewed in the film, there is something to be lamented in the CBC's decision to impulsively and prematurely write off the analogue. As one of Christie's interviewees argues, the digital has its limits. Even though the Internet promises global access, its true reach falls far short. Not only are there economic obstacles to listening online, but the capability of governments to block Internet sites and broadcasts also means that analogue transmission remains the best way to ensure worldwide reach, influence, and impact. In one of the most extraordinary sequences of *Spectres of Shortwave*, Christie replays the final broadcast relayed from the Sackville site, which was transmitted on 24 June 2012 to Canada's North. The announcer, Marc Montgomery, is audibly upset about the service coming to an end and speaks out against what he sees as the short-sightedness of the decision:

It's also being said that shortwave is a technology at the end of its lifecycle or quite simply obsolete. And while there is no denying the importance of the Internet, there's also no denying that it can be and is regularly blocked by authoritarian regimes. Shortwave broadcasts, on the other hand, almost always get through to people hungry for information. Radio has also always been extremely inexpensive and highly portable, easily accessible to everyone around the world no matter what their financial situation. But now I find myself, on behalf of all of us, saying goodbye to sixty-seven years of radio, and so, for all of us, thank you so much, and goodbye.

The sense of loss and anger is palpable in Montgomery's voice as shortwave transmission is cast aside as a Cold War relic or remnant of a bygone analogue era. In its elegy to the wires and waves of analogue transmission, *Spectres of Shortwave* suggests that such a rash decision will come back to haunt us, that the reckless embrace of a digital future leaves many out and many behind. As much as the film does not shy away from the history of radio being used for political, even propagandistic, purposes, it retains a sense of radio's progressive potential and utopian possibilities.

After this moving testimony to the importance and impact of the relay station, *Spectres of Shortwave* falls silent. The mix of voices gives way to a more abstract soundscape of ambient drones, tones, buzzes, and hums, suggesting that, even after transmissions have ceased, the site still resonates with sonic energy (see figure C.2). Christie captures the melancholy of the abandoned space, the interior stripped of its fittings and the red lights atop the towers burning out one by one, never to be replaced. The demolition crew moves in, and the towers are toppled as the snap of a final guyline sends each one crashing to the ground. Fallen, they are carefully dismantled, a welder's torch cutting through metal to break them into pieces portable enough to be removed from the site. The film's final shot, of the site emptied and with only the outlines of the installation remaining, condenses into a single image the sense of loss expressed by many of those Christie interviewed. *Spectres of Shortwave* documents the demolition of this key node in the communications infrastructure of Cold War Canada

C.2 Radio Canada International transmission towers in Amanda Dawn Christie's *Spectres of Shortwave* (2017).

and in doing so preserves the history and memories of the relay station. But beyond this work of documentation, the film also communicates the uncanny aspects of the analogue, the ways that the site, even in its disappearance, remains the source of transmissions through which the past haunts the present.

Without ever losing sight of the materiality of the infrastructural remains, Rollo's and Christie's films zero in on the spectral, even hauntological, aspects of analogue systems and identify what is being lost with their destruction and demolition. To bring *Hinterland Remixed* to a close, I want to turn to the work of the Artifact Institute, which, since being founded in 2007 by Tim Dallett and Adam Kelly, has examined the processes through which, as the institute explains, "artifacts undergo changes in use, value, and meaning."[2] One aspect of their practice involves the close consideration of the afterlife of electronic equipment. An early investigation saw the Artifact Institute catalogue technology jettisoned by organizations in the sphere of the arts and cultural production. *Investigation 1: Electronic Equipment Discarded by Arts and Cultural Organizations in the Halifax Regional Municipality* (2009–14) indexed and archived the material remains of these groups.

The project included an on-site processing centre at the Art Gallery of Nova Scotia in the summer of 2009, where visitors could witness the work of the Artifact Institute as it documented the artifacts it had salvaged, assessing their potential for repurposing or redeployment. Not only does opening up the activities of the institute to public view make visible the labour involved in the process of assessing the condition, and possibly extending the life, of seemingly outmoded or obsolete technology, but it also reveals how the material remains that make the production of arts and culture possible accumulate and pile up. Neatly stacked on shelves awaiting study or carefully placed on worktables for immediate assessment, the cameras, tape recorders, computers, and other assorted hardware seem like so many dead objects from which value has been drained. A subsequent study, *Investigation 2: Electronic Equipment Not Accepted for Curbside Garbage Collection by the Halifax Regional Municipality* (2013), extended the institute's analysis of technological waste, this time turning to the remainders of arts and cultural consumption rather than production. Wes Johnston, curator of the Fieldwork Residency Project, of which the Artifact Institute's investigations formed a part, notes that this focus amounted to "a forensic audit of sorts of consumer technology," one that "prioritized the study of the artifact's flow within a larger system, at a stage where the artifact is a priori deemed obsolete by being put to curb and is considered instead for its raw materiality."[3] Combined, the two investigations provide an overview of the technological remainders of artistic and cultural production, distribution, and consumption, extrapolating from the exhausted residues something of the larger structure of the systems and networks of which they were a part and charting their consequent arc and flow.

There is clearly a performative dimension to the work of the Artifact Institute and its manifestation as an organization complete with a crisp logo and official forms to document its methodical labours. Johnston provides a compelling account of the institute's protocols when identifying and logging the consumer waste that formed the basis of *Investigation 2*: "In the course of their rounds, Artifact Institute scanned the side of the road for discarded electronics and, if any were spotted, would pull over to document the artifact(s). This involved photographing the artifact *in situ*, as well as taking down general information on the artifact such as the date and time of recovery, approximate civic address, make and model of the product, and the condition in which it was found if relevant [...] These reports accumulated in a binder that was made available to the public over the course of the project."[4] The Artifact Institute's commitment to rational processes and required paperwork makes it feel, to some degree, like an institute out of step with its times, despite the timeliness of its concern with technological waste. Even though its work involves the very contemporary process of trawling through the remains of a technological modernity, there is also something in the very identity of the institute that connects it to the bureaucratic modernism that defined the 1970s. In this way, the Artifact Institute might be understood as investigating both the technological remains of the past as well as its organizational, structural, and bureaucratic residues, assessing the ongoing viability not only of past technologies but of past structures and processes as well. The institute's various reports and investigations should not be understood as a simple parody of, or homage to, the techno-bureaucratic language and form of postwar, public service, governmental modernity but as a serious investigation into its erosion and an assessment of what might still be saved and salvaged from it.[5]

The work of the Artifact Institute shows how the 1970s still surround us, not simply in the form of their technological remains – which, alongside the ever-accumulating detritus of the decades that followed, constitute an environmental hazard that outstrips the very worst of 1970s ecological nightmares – but also in the residues of an organizational modernity committed to rational investigation and bureaucratic processes and protocols. The Artifact Institute's focus on the brute materiality of technological remainders and its sober and methodical approach to dealing with them complement the elegiac and eerie spectral studies of analogue-era infrastructure that *The Broken Altar*, *Farewell Transmission*, and *Spectres of Shortwave* provide. Together, these works and projects point to the desire, even need, to reflect on the technological remnants of the recent past and on the infrastructural remainders of the twentieth century that are all around us.

Hinterland Remixed is about the residues, remains, and wreckage of the long '70s in Canada. In some ways, it may seem as though it adopts the very vocabulary of catastrophe in which the 1970s specialized, but at its heart *Hinterland Remixed* includes the recognition that these scraps, fragments, leftovers, and remainders are not mere surplus or signs of failure but hold within them the possibility of remixing, repurposing, and redeployment. To revisit and remediate the long '70s is to enact neither a conservative retreat nor a return to the comforts of the decade but an active engagement with a past that, because of both its aspirations and its shortcomings, continues to haunt the present.

Notes

Introduction

1. For the classic formulation of Benjamin's method of "literary montage," which picks among the rags and refuse, see Benjamin, *Arcades Project*, 460.
2. Williams, *Marxism and Literature*, 128.
3. Harper, "Hauntology."
4. Derrida, *Specters of Marx*, 61–4.
5. Perhaps not surprisingly, "the past inside the present" has served as a touchstone phrase in critical accounts of hauntology. Harper uses it as the title of his 2009 blog post on the topic, and it serves as a section title for the chapter "Ghosts of Futures Pasts: Sampling, Hauntology and Mash-Ups" in Reynolds, *Retromania*.
6. Boym, *Future of Nostalgia*, xviii.
7. Fisher, *Ghosts of My Life*, 25.
8. Benjamin, "Surrealism," 210.
9. Jameson, *Marxism and Form*, 82.
10. Benjamin, "On the Concept of History," 392.
11. Williams, *Marxism and Literature*, 128.
12. Highmore, "Formations of Feelings," 146.
13. Williams, *Marxism and Literature*, 132.
14. For more on Williams's "structure of feeling" and its continued usefulness as a way to think about period and open up cultural history to the ephemeral and incidental aspects of everyday life that shape the affective and sensorial experience of it, see Engle and Wong, eds, *Feelings of Structure*.
15. Williams, *Marxism and Literature*, 134.

16 Jameson, "Periodizing the 60s," 483.
17 Snow, "*La Région Centrale*, 1969," 56.
18 Quoted in Cram, "Filmmaker Caroline Monnet."
19 Scribner, *Requiem for Communism*, 10.

Chapter One

1 Williams, *Marxism and Literature*, 128.
2 For more on *ostalgie*, the specific term given to nostalgia for East Germany, see Scribner, *Requiem for Communism*. For an article that thinks through the connections specifically between television and nostalgia in the context of Romania, see Barden, "Remembering Socialist Entertainment."
3 Hall, *Selected Political Writings*, 177.
4 Reynolds, *Retromania*, 328.
5 Ibid., 330–1.
6 In 2005, discussions began online that considered "hauntology" as a concept that could account for a group of artists exploring the relationship between past and present and the way that digital technologies are haunted by analogue ones. Reynolds and Fisher, on their sites *blissblog* and *K-Punk* respectively, inaugurated these discussions and were central to them. Two articles by Reynolds – "Spirit of Preservation" (2005) in *Frieze* and "Haunted Audio" (2006) in *The Wire* – consolidated thinking on the subject while simultaneously expressing reservations about the term itself. Nevertheless, it soon gained critical traction in music criticism and beyond. Discussion of hauntology is absorbed into Reynolds's larger consideration of the dominance of retro culture in the new millennium in *Retromania* (2011), and Fisher's writings on the subject are gathered together in *Ghosts of My Life* (2014) as well as *K-Punk* (2018). The concept soon migrated (or returned) to scholarly discourse, with articles by Jamie Sexton and David Pattie taking up the ways that, to quote Sexton, the "alternative heritage" that hauntology conjures up out of the remnants of the past generates an understanding of postwar British history that is profoundly different from the ones usually on offer. Sexton, "Weird Britain in Exile"; Pattie, "Stone Tapes." In all cases, the political dimension of hauntology is clear: in the face of a neoliberal present that refuses the need for or

possibility of meaningful political change, the past serves as a repository for revolutionary energies that, at their very minimum, preserve the recognition that a different future is possible.

7 The past few years have seen much renewed interest in the graphic design of the 1960s and 1970s as well, most notably the work of Kramer, Fritz Gottschalk, Stuart Ash, Raymond Bellemare, Rolf Harder, Georges Huel, and many others. The Canada Modern archive (http://www.canadamodern.org) provides a comprehensive visual overview of the design decade, and Greg Durrell's documentary *Design Canada* (2018) features interviews with many of the key figures in graphic design from the period.

8 Boym, *Future of Nostalgia*, 31.

9 Holdsworth, *Television, Memory and Nostalgia*, 24.

10 Ibid., 25.

11 Coupland, "32 Thoughts about 32 Short Films."

12 Through a series of projects, Coupland himself has investigated the ways that the material remnants of the Canadian 1960s and 1970s have persisted into the present. In his two-volume *Souvenir of Canada* (2002 and 2004), Coupland explores the affective force of a collection of cultural artifacts, ranging from Ookpiks to stubbies, gleaned from the period. For his installation *Canada House* (2003), Coupland placed a series of sculptures, consisting of Canadian artifacts, in a 1950s house in Vancouver designed by the Canadian Housing and Mortgage Corporation. A film by Robin Neinstein, also titled *Souvenir of Canada* (2005), documents Coupland's preparations for the *Canada House* exhibit and sees him reflect on the connections between personal and national identity. For an in-depth reading of Coupland's examination of materiality, memory, and the idea of nation, see Burke, "Nature of Things."

13 Billig, *Banal Nationalism*, 6–7.

14 The four original *Hinterland Who's Who* shorts were long thought to be lost, but a concerted effort to recover them as part of the fiftieth anniversary celebrations of the series proved fruitful. Copies of the loon spot were rediscovered in the archives of CBC Vancouver, and the beaver and moose shorts were found in the vaults of CBC Halifax. Only the gannet short remains missing. For more on the rediscovery of the loon short, see Boswell, "Hibernating or Extinct?"

15 The NFB worked with Motion Picture Centre Ltd of Toronto for the original four black-and-white spots (1963) and for the first five series of colour spots (1966–72) before seeking a production partner for the eight films in the 1973 series. Toronto's Hobel Leiterman Productions Ltd produced the 1973 spots, and the final set of four films was produced by Ottawa-based Bomi Productions Ltd.

16 NFBA, Eagles, "Television Public Service Spots," 3.

17 After a hiatus of twenty-five years, the Canadian Wildlife Service resuscitated the *Hinterland Who's Who* series in 2003. These new episodes feature a new recording of Cacavas's iconic flute melody and some of the original features of the series, yet they feel more polished and slick and do not share much of the weirdness of the ones from the 1960s and 1970s.

18 NFBA, "Narration for: BEAVER," 1.

19 For a more complete reading of the beaver and its historical role in the Canadian cultural imaginary, see Francis, *Creative Subversions*, 22–58.

20 NFBA, "Narration for: BEAVER," 1.

21 For more on the history of the wildlife film and its migration to television in the 1950s and 1960s, see Chris, *Watching Wildlife*, 28–41.

22 NFBA, Smith, "Suggested Titles," 1–2.

23 Druick, *Projecting Canada*, 101.

24 NFBA, Smith, "Suggested Titles," 1–2.

25 It seems reasonable to think that *Canadian Who's Who* would have, at this point, ceased print publication and migrated online, yet a 2018 edition was released with biographies of over 10,000 Canadians. The print edition is, of course, now accompanied by an online site that provides regular additions and updates, yet it is the 1,400-page hardcover book that is truly fascinating precisely because it feels like an anachronism, the hefty materiality of the object bringing into the present a set of ideas about politics, nation, and social capital that seem to belong properly to an earlier era.

26 Genette, *Paratexts*, 2.

27 Ibid.

28 Sconce, "'Trashing' the Academy," 372.

29 The other influential work that specifically imports Genette's concept into film studies is Jonathan Gray's *Show Sold Separately* (2010). In his focus on media, marketing, and merchandising, Gray's analysis

takes the "para-" down a path very different from the one I explore here. Nevertheless, I hope that the paratelevisual shares something of Gray's desire to open up the study of film and television to the stuff that surrounds and supplements it but should not be thought of as simply secondary and subordinate.

30 Straw, "Embedded Memories," 10.
31 Fisher, "Out and About," 195. For the field guide, see Dempsey and Millan, *Lesbian National Parks and Services*.
32 The Lesbian National Parks and Services project has, quite understandably, attracted much critical commentary and analysis. Perhaps the landmark article in this regard is Margot Francis's "The Lesbian National Parks and Services" (2000), in which she thinks through how the Banff Centre residency specifically revealed the connections between whiteness, nation, and heteronormativity: "If identity politics continually ask us who we are – performances like the LNPS stage the contradictions in answering that question, and instead invite us, as witnesses, passersby, viewers and readers to reflect on the impurity of categorization itself. In this context, the LNPS staged much more than an opportunity to examine the normative relations of gender and sex. If white supremacy works best when it is everything and nothing, hypervisible but never spoken – then the Park Ranger performance suggests the ways that whiteness is integral to symbols of Canadianness" (135). Subsequently, Catriona Sandilands's "Where the Mountain Men Meet the Lesbian Rangers" (2005) and Jennifer MacLatchy's "Lesbian Rangers on a Queer Frontier" (2015) have further extended Francis's insights, and Jennifer Fisher's "Out and About: The Performances of Shawna Dempsey and Lorri Millan" (2004) and Jayne Wark's "Queering Abjection" (2017) situate Dempsey and Millan's work more broadly in the history of performance art in Canada. My focus here is on the specific relation between the film work that forms part of the lesbian ranger universe and the *Hinterland* shorts and the way that it might serve as another way of understanding the complex interrelations that Francis's article identifies.
33 A fascination with the long '70s is evident elsewhere in Dempsey and Millan's work. Their performance piece *Tableau Vivant: Eaton's Catalogue 1976* (1998) brings to life one of the iconic Eaton's catalogue photo spreads in its interrogation of a decade when, as the performance

notes put it, "Gender was clearly defined, race was singular, and class was middle." More recently, *Transport* (2014), a site-specific performance at Winnipeg's Western Canadian Aviation Museum, saw Dempsey and Millan take on the roles of flight attendant and pilot, transporting their audience back to 1979. The program notes capture both a nostalgia for the decade and a recognition of its political limits: "This is 1979. The flight attendant is modern. She is a product of the sexual revolution and women's lib. She has a job and her own apartment. She's been to discos in big cities. Whenever she looks up into the night sky, she scans for UFOs. This is 1979, when airlines simply take hijackers where they want to go. No security checks, no searches, no air marshals. Every international pilot is issued a map of Havana's airport. It is that common. This is 1979, when everything seems possible because everything is impossible. The red button, the Cold War, nuclear war, nuclear winter ... time is ticking! Nothing inspires living like imminent death." So although I have focused here on the films associated with the LNPS project, Dempsey and Millan's work more generally marks a significant creative and critical engagement with the cultural memory of the long '70s.

34 Adams, "Artist Statement."
35 Ibid.
36 Ibid.
37 Scholars of disco have long noted the connection between disco and melancholy. In his foundational article "In Defense of Disco" (1979), while commenting on Diana Ross's albums of the time, Richard Dyer argued, "They are all-out expressions of adoration which yet have built on to them the recognition of the (inevitably) temporary quality of the experience" (106). For Dyer, "disco romanticism" is inextricable from the genre's queerness: "No wonder Ross is (was?) so important in gay male scene culture, for she both reflects what that culture takes to be an inevitable reality (that relationships don't last) and at the same time celebrates it, validates it" (106).
38 Sherburne, "'Anaconda.'" For more on Italo-disco and its connection to Montreal, see Straw, "Music from the Wrong Place."
39 Sherburne, "'Anaconda.'"
40 Evoking the call of the loon in specific sections, Schafer's *Music for Wilderness Lake* (1979), a piece for twelve trombones that was meant

to be performed around a lake in a conservation area, best exemplifies this 1970s convergence of the classical and the environmental. In his book *The Soundscape: Our Sonic Environment and the Tuning of the World* (1977), Schafer argues that sonic pollution – the noise of industrialization, urbanization, and modern life more generally – fits alongside other forms of environmental degradation as a serious problem of the present. As a result, *The Soundscape*, with its proposed soundwalks and acoustic exercises, fits alongside *Hinterland Who's Who* as an illustration of the period's desire to encourage people to pay attention to the natural world.

Chapter Two

1 Gidal, "Notes on *La Région Centrale*"; Locke, "Michael Snow's *La Région Centrale*"; Rayns, "Reflected Light."
2 Michelson, "About Snow"; Sitney, "Michael Snow's Cinema"; Elder, *Image and Identity*; Testa, "Axiomatic Cinema"; Simon, "Completely Open Space"; Wees, *Light Moving in Time*. For a representative sample of criticism of Snow's film work that concentrates largely on its formal aspects, as well as a comprehensive, annotated bibliography of Snow studies, see Shedden, ed., *Presence and Absence*.
3 Snow, "*La Région Centrale*, 1969," 53.
4 Snow, "Converging on *La Région Centrale*," 59–60.
5 Out of the antecedents that he names, Snow's chosen landscape is closest, perhaps predictably, to those of the Group of Seven, most notably the work of Lawren Harris and his arctic paintings. Yet the landscape in *La Région Centrale* feels at once more beautiful and bleak than Harris's theosophical mystifications of the North. *La Région Centrale* is only part of Snow's ongoing dialogue with the history of art, nation, and the Group of Seven. Snow's series of photographs *Plus Tard* (1977) reshoots paintings by Tom Thomson, Lawren Harris, and others, shifting the camera during long exposures to introduce movement and motion to works that had become fixed and sedimented in the Canadian cultural imagination. As Johanne Sloan argues, "if these already-seen landscapes have acquired the status of national monuments, Snow introduced temporality, movement, and immersion onto the landscape, where previously there was institutional stasis, a sense of nature as

timeless, and a singular point of view." Sloan, "Conceptual Landscape Art," 84. In this way, *Plus Tard* continues the work of *La Région Centrale* by the similar means of re-visioning landscape through camera movement.

6 Snow, "Life & Times of Michael Snow," 79.
7 Ibid.
8 Ibid. Snow referred here to Norman McLaren, a legendary animator who worked exclusively throughout his career with the National Film Board.
9 Some of the these photographs are in the Michael Snow Fonds at the Art Gallery of Ontario, and others, including the most familiar one of Snow in a parka standing alongside the camera mount, are in the collection of the National Gallery of Canada.
10 White, "Strangeloves," 77.
11 Koller, "*La Région Centrale*," 53.
12 It seems fitting that Snow edited the film at the Nova Scotia College of Art and Design, given the college's role in transforming the landscape of Canadian art in the late 1960s and throughout the 1970s. Under the auspices of Garry Neill Kennedy, the college became a key nodal point in the international art scene, central in the development of postminimal and conceptual art practices and notable for its embrace of both film and video. The college's many connections to New York also made Halifax a kind of intermediate space between Snow's Canal Street loft in Soho and the wide open emptiness of *La Région Centrale*. For more on the history of the college during this period and details of Snow's work there while editing *La Région Centrale*, see Kennedy, *Last Art College*, 140–1.
13 Snow, "Converging on *La Région Centrale*," 59.
14 For an article that takes a different approach and examines the role of horror in two classics of Canadian experimental film, Jack Chambers's *The Hart of London* (1968–70) and R. Bruce Elder's *Crack, Brutal, Grief* (2000), see Birdwise, "Where Is Fear?" Birdwise's emphasis on the complex interconnections between sensation, security, space, and place in the way that these films generate and investigate horror is exemplary of thinking about the convergences, rather than simply the disjunctions, between avant-garde and popular forms of filmmaking.
15 Frye, "Conclusion," 350.

16 Williams, *Marxism and Literature*, 128.
17 Atwood uses this precise excerpt from Frye as one of the epigraphs to *Survival*'s key chapter, "Nature the Monster." Although Atwood discusses literature rather than film, the trope she identifies as being at the heart of an astonishing array of Canadian fiction and poetry, "death by nature," also plays its part in horror film and other cinematic representations of nation: "Nature seen as dead, or alive but indifferent, or alive and actively hostile towards man is a common image in Canadian literature. The result of a dead or indifferent Nature is an isolated or 'alienated' man; the result of an actively hostile Nature is usually a dead man, and certainly a threatened one." Atwood, *Survival*, 54. Atwood ends her chapter with "An Appendix on Snow," which, even though it does not mention Michael Snow, suggests that the flakes that began to fall as Snow and his crew neared the end of the shoot, which do turn up on-screen at a few points, bind the film to a longer history of national representations as well as to snow as it swirls around in the Canadian cultural imaginary.
18 Freitag and Loiselle, "Terror of the Soul," 4.
19 For more on the tax shelter, the political controversy surrounding it, and the films produced during its existence, see Urquhart, "You Should Know Something"; and Corupe, "(Who's in the) Driver's Seat." Paul Corupe is the founder of the *Canuxploitation!* website, which is an invaluable online resource for those interested in Canada filmmaking in the 1970s, especially those films made under the tax shelter.
20 Michelson, "About Snow," 122.
21 Ibid., 123.
22 Koller, "*La Région Centrale*," 52.
23 Ibid.
24 Ibid.
25 Koller's preoccupation with connecting his experience of watching *La Région Centrale* with *Chariots of the Gods?* also situates Snow's film as being part of a culture of stoned cinema-going that flourished in the late 1960s and throughout the 1970s and, to a certain extent, bridged the divide between the popular and the experimental. Koller asked Snow, "What kind of trips do you go off on when you watch the film?" Snow conceded that the film's disorientations can be even further enhanced by drugs: "Well, there's those kinds of driftings and sensations of falling

and rising that happen, they're really great. It's good to see it high, too. I've done it on grass and hash, but I showed it in Antioch in the States and there was a guy there who was just into his second hour of psilocybin. And I talked to him the next day and Jesus, he really enjoyed it. I'd liked to do that some time, but you know, I'd have to have the proper situation." Koller, "La Région Centrale," 55. For more on stoned cinema-going, see Hoberman, "Cineaste's Guide." One further thing suggesting that *La Région Centrale* is caught up in the connections between the countercultural, the communal, and the cosmic that characterized the late 1960s and early 1970s is Snow's remark that, at one point, "I was thinking of subtitling the film 'A Rock and Grass Festival'!" Snow, "Converging on *La Région Centrale*," 60.

26 Wees, *Light Moving in Time*, 167.
27 For more on the ways that Canadian landscape art has long been predicated on the excision of Indigeneity from the frame, see Bordo, "Jack Pine."
28 Snow, "Converging on *La Région Centrale*," 59.
29 Tribbe, *No Requiem*, 207.
30 Snow, "Converging on *La Région Centrale*," 58.
31 Erickson, "Interview."
32 For more on Sinclair and how his death starkly reveals a larger "structure of indifference" toward Indigenous lives that continues to define Canada today, see McCallum and Perry, *Structures of Indifference*.
33 As Cecilia Araneda points out, surveillance footage played a key role at the inquest into Sinclair's death. The footage quashed the hospital's claim that Sinclair had never checked in when he arrived at the hospital. Even though closed-circuit television differs from Snow's camera as a kind of unblinking eye and produces a different kind of record of the event – static rather than swirling, real rather than recreated – there is nevertheless a way in which it, alongside Maddin's film, exposes the gap between what is recorded and what is recognized. Araneda, "Guy Maddin."
34 Ferguson, who "had worked on special camera-mechanism problems" with Abbeloos, recommended him to Snow as someone who would be able to help with the machinery and electronics needed to create *La Région Centrale*. For more on these preparations, see Snow, "Converging on *La Région Centrale*," 59.

35 For more on the decolonial politics of A Tribe Called Red and the way that "Electric Pow Wow" – the name of the DJ night that they host regularly in Ottawa but also a phrase that has come to name their sound more generally – draws traditional Indigenous musical forms into a present and projects them forward into a reconfigured future, see Levine, "Decolonial Bounce."

36 I will have more to say below about Boards of Canada and their connection to these themes, but I note here that *Deadly Harvest* and Mills-Cockell's soundtrack seem to serve as one of the primary influences for the Boards of Canada album *Tomorrow's Harvest* (2013), which, across its seventeen tracks, evokes a feeling of catastrophe and environmental contamination or collapse eerily similar to the feeling evoked by the film itself.

37 Koller, "*La Région Centrale*," 52.

38 Snow, "*La Région Centrale*, 1969," 56.

39 Koller, "*La Région Centrale*," 52.

40 In his recent study of avant-garde film in Canada, Stephen Broomer also notes the ways that Snow's film expresses the environmental concerns that defined its moment: "Even as it served as a culmination of the difficult aesthetics of his work, it was also a mythic declaration of cultural and ecological anxiety, an apocalyptic reckoning of Canada and of the new world itself." Broomer, *Codes for North*, 259.

41 Browne, "David Rimmer," 76.

42 Koller, "David Rimmer," 41.

43 Razutis, "David Rimmer," 65.

44 Additionally, in the title track of Joni Mitchell's debut album, *Song to a Seagull* (1968), the seagull symbolically accompanies Mitchell as she ventures from the country to the city, attracted by the allures of modernity, only to grow disenchanted with the dirt, grime, and plasticity of modern life and to flee the city in order to return to a romanticized wilderness.

45 In the fall of 1969, around the very time that Rimmer was making *Migration*, the tenth season of *The Nature of Things* began with a six-part series on pollution. The series at that time was narrated by John Livingston, who was the voice of the *Hinterland Who's Who* spots in the late 1960s and early 1970s.

46 The work that cements the centrality of the seagull as a metaphor

in 1970s culture is, of course, Richard Bach's popular nature parable *Jonathan Livingston Seagull* (1970), which was adapted into a film directed by Hall Bartlett in 1973.

47 Koller, "La Région Centrale," 55.

48 In a 1981 interview with Jonathan Rosenbaum, Snow further explained his cinematic interest in birds, indicating once again his admiration for the work of Graeme Ferguson and, in so doing, signalling a relation between his work and Ferguson's experiments with IMAX and the representation of the natural landscape: "That's one reason why I was interested in the birds, because they're a little bit more erratic, and they also make a small spot in the entire frame – like some that are very far away, and I'm following that. But you can't tell why they're going to go, so it's really interesting, trying to shoot them. Some cameramen, like this guy Graham [sic] Ferguson, tells me he keeps the other eye open when he's looking through the camera. I've tried that, I can never get it down – I always close one eye, so I'm always down to that one field, and if it goes out of the field, there's no way." Rosenbaum, "'Presents' of Michael Snow," 38.

49 Koller, "La Région Centrale," 55.

50 Baker, "Musicality of Canadian Cinema," 398.

51 Ibid.

52 Ibid.

53 Snow, "Converging on *La Région Centrale*," 60.

54 Baker, "Musicality of Canadian Cinema," 399.

55 I borrow and adapt the idea of the "poor image" from Hito Steyerl, whose definition speaks to the illicit circulation of experimental film, public service announcements, and horror films online: "The poor image is a rag or a rip; an AVI or a JPEG, a lumpen proletariat in the class society of appearances, ranked and valued according to its resolution. The poor image has been uploaded, downloaded, shared, reformatted, and reedited. It transforms quality into accessibility, exhibition value into cult value, films into clips, contemplation into distraction. The image is liberated from the vaults of cinema and archives and thrust into digital uncertainty, at the expense of its own substance." Steyerl, *Wretched of the Screen*, 32.

56 Vatnsdal, *They Came from Within*, 124.

57 For a more detailed consideration of *Rituals* that situates its importance

in the forest slasher subgenre, see Hasan, "Rituals." In addition, the *Canuxploitation!* website is an invaluable resource for the study of horror film in Canada. For more on wilderness horror, as well as related subgeneric variants such as the rural revenge film, see the *Canuxploitation!* reviews of *Rituals*, *Death Weekend* (1976), and *Trapped* (1982), listed in the bibliography by title.

58 Macfarlane, "Dam Nation."

59 For a thorough history of the James Bay hydroelectric developments and the struggles of the Eeyouch, the Eastern James Bay Cree, to confirm their rights to their traditional territory, see Desbiens, *Power from the North*; and Desbiens, "Hydroelectric Development."

60 As Kenneth White argues, this same terrain, north of Sept-Îles, is central to the story of the Cold War as well. White examines both Snow and Abbeloos's apparatus and the film itself as "an as yet unconsidered and complex case through which to understand the media cultures of the Cold War." Focusing in part on the nearby presence of Canadian Forces Station Moisie, a radar installation that formed part of Canada's – and by extension, NORAD's – monitoring system, White considers the parallels between Snow and Abbeloos's apparatus and the Cold War era's technologies of monitoring and observation, spurred by the idea that "[f]or five days in 1970, the CAM [Camera Activating Machine] and CFS Moisie spun side by side in a coterminous mission of self-regard." White, "Strangeloves," 51, 58.

61 In the way that formative years in Canada had an immense impact on later work, there is a similarity between Doig and Boards of Canada. Both remember and remediate the audiovisual ecology of 1970s and 1980s Canadian film and television in ways that emphasize its uncanny weirdness. Moreover, Doig's *Canoe Lake* (1997–98) and Boards of Canada's breakthrough album *Music Has the Right to Children* (1998) anticipate the emergence of a hauntological fascination with the 1970s in the United Kingdom in the 2000s.

62 As Johanne Sloan argues, Doig's fascination with canoes puts his work in dialogue with the Group of Seven, specifically the work of Tom Thomson. Thomson drowned in 1917 on Canoe Lake, and his overturned canoe forms a key part of the mystery that surrounds his death. As Sloan suggests, "In Doig's work, the Thomson mystery is overlaid with a cinematic *mise-en-scène* and overlaid as well with

the sociopathic drives of horror-movie villains. This layering even suggests that Jason or Freddy might have killed Tom Thomson." Sloan, "Hallucinating Landscape," 13.
63 Sloan, "Conceptual Landscape Art," 81.

Chapter Three

1 Genette, *Paratexts*, 1–2.
2 Michael Dunne provides a reading of *SCTV* that examines its self-referentiality in relationship to American pop culture of the 1970s and 1980s. He recognizes the Canadianness of the program, but obviously my reading here zeroes in much more specifically on the ways that *SCTV*'s paratelevisuality is of special significance for those with an interest in the history of Canadian television. See Dunne, *Metapop*, 29–35.
3 Although most versions of the *SCTV* opening credits feature televisions being thrown out of windows from a great height, the classic credit sequence dates to the second cycle of shows of series 4, after it moved to NBC. In referring to *SCTV*, I follow the numbering practices of the invaluable online *SCTV Guide* (http://www.sctvguide.ca), which breaks down the run into six series, with series 4 and 5 made up of five different production cycles. Each episode is also given a show number that indicates its place in the overall run of *SCTV*, which totals 135 shows. It is confusing, yes, but symptomatic of *SCTV*'s itinerant status as it migrated between many networks over the course of its run, with erratic production schedules. But, to provide an example, the classic credit sequence with the announcement "SCTV now begins its programming day" begins with series 4, cycle 2, episode 1 (show 88).
4 *SCTV* also neatly fits into a history of Canadian television comedy, much of which shares the show's interest in the workings of television itself. *Wayne and Shuster* (CBC, 1954–85), with some variation in title, both precedes and overlaps with *SCTV*'s run, but the duo's frequent parody of popular televisual forms surely influenced *SCTV*. Although none fully embrace *SCTV*'s paratelevisual format, *Four on the Floor* (CBC, 1986), *Codco* (CBC, 1987–92), *Kids in the Hall* (CBC/HBO, 1989–95), and *This Hour Has 22 Minutes* (CBC, 1993–present) all draw extensively on the legacy of *SCTV* in their attention to television and broadcast structures.

5 Williams, *Television*, 86.
6 Ibid., 5.
7 This bit was recycled in series 4, cycle 1, episode 9 (show 87) once the show migrated to NBC, but sadly, most likely due to issues of music clearance, it does not appear on Shout Factory's DVD compilation of the NBC years. This is a common problem that highlights the value of archived VHS recordings of the show and the archival limits of DVD packaging of material from the 1970s and 1980s especially. Shows such as *SCTV* tended to be quite cavalier in their use of popular music, and, as a result, their rerelease on DVD or in streaming formats is compromised by the difficult, and sometimes impossible, task of clearing these songs for use. For more on how music clearances present an obstacle to DVD reissues, see VanDerWerff, "Weird Legal Reason."
8 For an overview of the effect that the implementation of Canadian content regulations had on Canadian radio stations and Canadian music, see Henderson, "Canadian Content Regulations."
9 Hanna, "Second City or Second Country?" 53.
10 Ibid., 52.
11 The Inuk woman is legendary Inuit artist Kenojuak Ashevak. Remerowski assembled the film from NFB stock and draws here on John Feeney's documentary short *Eskimo Artist: Kenojuak* (1963).
12 Vogel is a prominent figure in Quebec jazz circles, the leader of his own big band, and a mainstay of the Montreal International Jazz Festival. He has also worked extensively as a composer and arranger for film, television, and cultural events. His work featured prominently at both Expo 67 and the 1976 Montreal Olympics. For the Olympics, Vogel not only arranged "O Canada" but, in collaboration with André Mathieu, also wrote the music for the event itself. The double-album soundtrack for the games was enormously popular in Canada, selling over 200,000 copies and going double platinum. Like Alain Clavier, whose work I discussed in chapter 2, Vogel's sonic signature is all over the Canadian 1970s and 1980s, even if most people do not know his name. For more on Vogel, see the transcript of producers Jeff Siskand and Ross Porter's *Vic Vogel: The Musical Legend* (2008), a radio documentary on his work.
13 Dating to the same era as Remerowski's version is an animated take on "O Canada" directed by Michael Mills. It uses the same Vogel arrangement as the animation swoops eastward from the Pacific Coast

to the Atlantic, touching on landmarks such as Niagara Falls, Toronto's CN Tower, and Montreal's Biosphere. It begins and ends, to refer back to chapter 2's discussion of seagulls and the 1970s, with gulls squawking and silhouetted against the sky. These versions were displaced at some point in the late 1980s by an "O Canada" that begins with a slow zoom out from a solo boy singer to reveal a children's choir all clad in "O Canada" sweatshirts bearing the official government wordmark, which, as I indicated in the introduction, dates to 1971 and is very much part of Canada's graphic modernization in the Centennial and immediately post-Centennial period. The presence of speedskater Gaetan Boucher and the Canadarm suggests that this choir version dates to the mid-1980s. Perhaps the most cinematically significant film of "O Canada" is Evelyn Lambert's animated stereoscopic film produced for the NFB in 1952, which, like Mills's later version, is an aerial view that flies over a range of Canadian landscapes.

14 Ebner, "Greg Joy Recalls."
15 Byers and VanderBurgh, "Trafficking (in) the Archive," 118. For more on the history of television scholarship in Canada and the opportunities for, and obstacles to, archival research, see Miller, "From Kine to Hi-Def." The work of VanderBurgh and Byers is invaluable to those who want to understand the state and situation of television archiving in Canada. For detailed discussions of the archive and Canadian television studies, see Byers, "Empty Archive"; Byers and VanderBurgh, "What Was Canada?"; and VanderBurgh, "(Who Knows?) What Remains."
16 There are now a number of "retro" channels on YouTube that focus on interstitial material, including Retrontario, RetroWinnipeg, and RetroQuebec. For insight into the work of these channels, see O'Mara, "Website That Chronicles."
17 Acland, "Last Days of Videotape."
18 *High Q* is from series 2, episode 9 (show 35), which aired on Global on 11 November 1978. It was repeated once the series moved to NBC, in series 4, cycle 1, episode 1 (show 79), which aired on 15 May 1981.
19 Straw, "Embedded Memories," 10.
20 Ibid.
21 Holdsworth, *Television, Memory and Nostalgia*, 112.
22 Williams, *Marxism and Literature*, 128.
23 For more on the NFB's vignette series, see Ohayon, "Canada Vignettes."

24 Both the importance of the logo and the widespread affection for it are evidenced by the success of a 2016 Kickstarter campaign to reprint the CBC's *Graphic Standards Manual* (1974) in full. For more on the campaign, and the formal recognition of Kramer's design as part of Canada's cultural heritage, see CBC Radio, "Ottawa Designer Crowdfunds Reprint."

25 Civic-TV, in David Cronenberg's *Videodrome* (1983) is, in many ways, the dark twin of SCTV. In Cronenberg's nightmare vision, Civic-TV is not a plucky SCTV-like upstart, cobbling together programming on the fly, but a desperate operation seeking something even more salaciously appealing for its audience than the softcore pornography it already broadcasts. For more on *Videodrome* and its representation of local television in the age of globalization and the VCR, see Jameson, *Geopolitical Aesthetic*, 22–35; and Benson-Allott, *Killer Tapes*, 73–4, 84–9.

26 SCTV's gentle satire of small-town life puts it squarely in a tradition of Canadian satire derived from the work of Stephen Leacock.

27 Seth here is referencing the Indian-head test pattern developed by RCA in the late 1930s. In its early years, SCTV, as part of its opening credits and as part of its paratelevisual play, also featured a fictional "Indian Head Test Pattern" with "Second City Television – Channel 109" indicated on it. For a powerful reading of the cultural significance of the Indian-head test pattern that provides a short history of the image and its use, see Tahmahkera, *Tribal Television*, 1–8.

28 Seth, *George Sprott*.

29 Straw, "Embedded Memories," 10.

30 Rifkind, "Biotopographies of Seth's *George Sprott*," 230.

31 Ibid.

32 Ibid.

Chapter Four

1 William Wees's *Recycled Images: The Art and Politics of Found Footage Films* (1993) remains the standard work on the subject. Wees's categorization of the various forms of found-footage filmmaking is helpful in understanding how the work of L'Atelier national du Manitoba participates in a longer history of cinematic experimentation.

The rescue of the tapes from a dumpster allies the group with a filmmaker such as Ken Jacobs, whose *Perfect Film* (1986) consists of unedited material found in the trash. Wees, *Recycled Images*, 5. But L'Atelier's reworking of this salvaged material links it more concretely to found-footage filmmakers such as Bruce Conner and Craig Baldwin who, as Wees puts it, share "the ability to make others' images serve their own purposes through the transformative power of montage." Ibid., 14.

2 "History is written by the losers." The additional irony here is that the film itself was almost lost to history. After a sold-out run at the Cinématheque in Winnipeg and on the eve of a scheduled screening in Toronto, the filmmakers received a cease and desist order from lawyers representing CKY, the CTV affiliate that had jettisoned the material over a year earlier. The case was resolved not in court but allegedly over clubhouse sandwiches at The Wagon Wheel, an iconic local Winnipeg restaurant, between the filmmakers and representatives of CKY. For more on how the experience of L'Atelier exemplifies the fraught relationship between Canadian copyright law and the reuse and appropriation of existing media in the arts, see Nagler, "Winnepeg Eats Itself."

3 Klein, "N.H.L."

4 In the same *New York Times* article, Guy Maddin appeals to the conventions of epic and tragedy to convey his incredulity that Winnipeg once again has its Jets: "'So improbable is their return that I'm still convinced it hasn't happened,' said the film director Guy Maddin, likening the Jets' story to 'ghostly returns in ancient texts' like Ulysses' journey in the 'Odyssey' and the shade of Hamlet's father strolling the parapet." Quoted in ibid. The framing of *Death by Popcorn* as *The Tragedy of the Winnipeg Jets* captures the way that the story of the team, the brutal economic realities of its disappearance, and the financial hopes staked on its return are somehow best expressed in the form and language of fiction.

5 For a compelling reading of the political and economic context of the Jets' departure, see Jim Silver's *Thin Ice: Money, Politics, and the Demise of an NHL Franchise* (1996). Silver lays out how the survival of the Jets could have been accomplished only with a massive injection of government funding, something that hardly seemed justified in a city renowned for its staggering level of child poverty and its more

general economic precariousness. Silver himself was involved in a social justice group in the years prior to the Jets' departure that protested against the public subsidization of professional hockey, whether in the form of further tax breaks for the club or municipal funding for the construction of a new arena. In his introduction, Silver contrasts the ascendency of the NHL as a desirable commercial product in the 1980s and 1990s with Winnipeg's long economic decline from its heyday early in the twentieth century in a manner that resonates with, if not fully anticipates, the apocalyptic tone of *Death by Popcorn*.

6 Fortuitously, the "S" of the MTS Centre sign had burned out when Maddin shot these scenes in the film, giving him the opportunity to identify the building's soullessness with the name itself. The idea of an "empty centre," however, also points to the ongoing problems of Winnipeg's downtown core, which, as a consequence of suburbanization, struggled throughout the 1990s and 2000s to retain something of the retail and urban grandeur of earlier decades.

7 Maddin, *My Winnipeg*, 83.

8 Ibid., 85.

9 Ibid., 95.

10 Paranoia and conspiracy occupy a key place in found-footage filmmaking due, at least in part, to the genre's ongoing fascination with filmic material produced during the Cold War. Such material forms part of Bruce Conner's *A Movie* (1958), which is commonly identified as a key film within the genre. But perhaps the more striking antecedent for *Death by Popcorn*'s satirical reexamination of recent history is Craig Baldwin's *Tribulations 99: Alien Anomalies in America* (1991), a found-footage film that draws on a dizzying array of material to critique US foreign policy and the country's involvement in Latin America. As Michael Zryd argues, Baldwin's film illuminates the complex relationship between found-footage film and historical representation: "Found footage filmmaking is a metahistorical form commenting on the cultural discourses and narrative patterns behind history. Whether picking through the detritus of the mass mediascape or refinding (through image processing and optical printing) the new in the familiar, the found footage artist critically investigates the history *behind* the image, discursively embedded within the history of its production, circulation, and consumption." Zryd, "Found Footage Film," 42.

As a metahistorical form, found-footage filmmaking has the capacity not only to reveal history itself as constructed but also to expose the governing ideological fantasies and powerful social anxieties that shape this construction.

11 The most significant of these studies, since it deals directly with the significance of videotape in all its analogue specificity, reproductive capability, and aesthetic opportunity is Lucas Hilderbrand's *Inherent Vice* (2009). I draw on and engage with Hilderbrand's study of videotape below. In addition to this key study specifically on videotape, there are several works that have analyzed the videocassette as a form of residual media. Articles include Will Straw's "Embedded Memories" and Kate Egan's "The Celebration of a 'Proper Product': Exploring the Residual Collectible through the 'Video Nasty,'" which appear in Charles R. Acland's edited volume *Residual Media* (2007), as well as Acland's "The Last Days of Videotape" (2009). Also important is Iain Robert Smith's "Collecting the Trash: The Cult of the Ephemeral Clip from VHS to YouTube" (2011) for the way that it situates the culture of VHS collectors and clip hunters within a larger history of cult film enthusiasts and found-footage filmmakers. In terms of a more broadly construed category of "format studies," Jonathan Sterne's *MP3: The Meaning of a Format* (2012) offers a model for thinking historically about media and format that potentially reveals all kinds of unexpected antecedents and extraordinary connections.

12 Straw, "Embedded Memories," 7.

13 Ibid.

14 For more on the connection between the audio cassette, taping practices, and cultural memory, see the bibliography for essays by Bas Jensen, Michael Bull, and Karen Bijsterveld and Annelies Jacobs published in Karen Bijsterveld and José van Dijck's edited volume *Sound Souvenirs: Audio Technologies, Memory and Cultural Practices* (2009).

15 As I have already indicated, the work of L'Atelier national du Manitoba fits neatly alongside various found-footage/archival film practices most commonly associated with the essay film. Yet the group's focus on the materiality of tape and its fascination with the historicity of the video image resonate with what Catherine Russell terms "archiveology," which she defines as "a mode of film practice that draws on archival material to produce knowledge about how history has been represented and

how representations are not false images but are actually historical in themselves and have anthropological value." Russell, *Archiveology*, 22.

16 Acland, "Last Days of Videotape."

17 This is not to devalue the importance of the programs themselves, especially when rare or "missing, believed wiped" episodes, to use the BBC's phrasing for lost programs, turn up on videocassettes taped off-air. Videocassettes that contain programming taped off-air are especially important in Canada, which does not have a national television archive that houses older programs or collects current ones. For more on the consequences of this failure to archive and on the importance of VHS in accessing the Canadian televisual past, see Byers and VanderBurgh, "What Was Canada?"

18 The August 2005 screening series, divided between the Winnipeg Cinematheque and Videopool, consisted of five separate programs: (1) LO-FI *Fantasies: VPW Cult Classics #1*, (2) *Winnipeg Babysitter: VPW Cult Classics #2*, (3) *The Self-Destructing Image: Winnipeg as Cinematic Object*, (4) *Kubasa in a Glass: Fetishized Winnipeg TV Commercials (1978–1993)*, and (5) *Au Coeur troublé de l'Amerique: Regards francophones sur l'expérience ouinnipégoise*. Barrow's contributions were compiled on the DVD *Winnipeg Babysitter* (2009) and released by the Winnipeg Film Group. As Johanne Sloan notes, Barrow fits comfortably in the conventional narrative of Winnipeg's fascination with the past, which dominates both film and the visual arts. Examining it alongside Barrow's other projector and performance work, Sloan argues that *Winnipeg Babysitter* is "yet another example of Barrow's attunement to disregarded fragments of the pop cultural past." Sloan, "Something Resembling Childhood," 375.

19 Hilderbrand, *Inherent Vice*, 15.

20 In his article on L'Atelier national du Manitoba, Solomon Nagler provides a reading that situates the group's work in relation to both Paizs and Maddin. Nagler argues that the group continues the practice of "bargain basement filmmaking" exemplified by Paizs and shares with both Paizs and Maddin a fascination with form and material: "L'Atelier's obsession with partially ruined visual materials can also be seen as a mannerism inherited from previous generations of prairie auteurs. Degraded celluloid that looks discovered rather than created and beaten Beta tapes that have lost most of their magnetic resonance

are yet another means of expressing the ironic historicism of the prairie postmodern." Nagler, "Winnipeg Eats Itself."

21 For more on the institutional and regulatory factors that led to the rich fertility of Winnipeg cable access television in the 1980s and 1990s, see Allison Gillmor's article on Barrow's compilation DVD *Winnipeg Babysitter* (2009). As she explains, unlike the CTV material that the members of L'Atelier salvaged from a dumpster, the public access material had already been destroyed: "Original tapes of the shows were junked shortly after Shaw acquired local cable provider Videon in 2001, so Barrow's footage – which he has been hunting down for almost three years – was scavenged through informal channels, mostly from the private archives of show hosts or the stashes of packrat fans." Gillmor, "Channeling Mayhem."

22 In an article published in an edited volume dedicated to the history and ongoing significance of the Summit Series, Kashmere further glosses the glitch, identifying it as "a metaphor for nearly imperceptible visible evidence" and representative of a national desire not to see what actually occurred. Kashmere, "Lessons from *Valery's Ankle*," 249.

23 For more on Egoyan's *Gross Misconduct*, its exploration of masculinity and violence, and its place in the history of Canadian films about hockey, see Beaty, "Not Playing, Working."

24 I do not know of a comprehensive history of home-taping practices and the culture of VHS, but in the absence of such a study, YouTube might serve as evidence that VCRs were used extensively to tape both music videos and sports events. Many of the clips on the site bear the traces of the material's broadcast origin and such digital remediations constitute evidentiary traces of a whole set of material practices of taping that existed in the 1980s and 1990s.

25 The history of the *Rock'em Sock'em* series neatly recapitulates the rise and fall of VHS. Volumes 1–9 (1989–97) were released only on VHS, with the first DVD release coinciding with the tenth anniversary of the series in 1998. Volumes 10–18 (1998–2006) were released in both formats, with the VHS release being discontinued with volume 19 in 2007. Since 2007 the series has been available only on DVD.

26 The sections of Kashmere's *Valery's Ankle* that focus on the increase in fighting in the 1970s and its continued commercial exploitation in the contemporary game also engage in a dialogue with the *Rock'em Sock'em*

series, albeit in a more pointedly critical manner than in *Death by Popcorn*.
27 L'Atelier national du Manitoba, "Seven Pillars."
28 "Our struggle is a struggle of freedom and independence. Our country, the true homeland of our Manitoba, is Quebec, not Canada." L'Atelier national du Manitoba, "Horizontalist Manifesto."
29 Quoted in Brown, "Conversation."
30 "Winnipeg's dream."
31 See especially Mary Agnes Welch's report on the 2008 election debates. She writes that Steen was "by all accounts and appearances a lovely and honourable gentleman" but concludes that he was "radically out of his depth, muzzled by his party and unfamiliar with the issues." Welch, "Don't Give Up Hope," A6. Such an assessment points to the political capital that Steen brought to the election as someone associated with the Jets, even twelve years after the team's dissolution, and the care with which the criticism is worded, braced as it is for angry letters to the editor and ferocious online comments from Jets fans and Steen supporters, points to the perceived hazards of challenging the team's legacy in any way.
32 Bangs, *Psychotic Reactions*, 112–13.
33 Although the 7-Eleven incident does not play a part in *Death by Popcorn*, it is the subject of two key post-L'Atelier films by its members. The Burton Cycle, which includes Walter Forsberg's *Fahrenheit 7-Eleven* (2011) and Matthew Rankin's *Negativipeg* (2011), investigates the incident through interviews and re-enactments. For more on Burton Cummings, the role he plays in Winnipeg's civic imaginary, and these later works by Forsberg and Rankin, see Burke, "Stand Tall."
34 Quoted in Janisse, "Ecstatic Professional."

Chapter Five

1 Williams, *Marxism and Literature*, 128.
2 For more on the concept of remediation and its use in media studies, see Bolter and Grusin, *Remediation*, 19.
3 For more on the inclusion of a waiting room area in the Trinty Square Video iteration that featured a single-channel video that remixed archival footage of Gould, see Nurming-Por, "Please Wait."

4 Chang, "Reclaiming the North."
5 *Tshiuetin* (2016), a short documentary by Caroline Monnet, whose extraordinary archive-footage film *Mobilize* (2015) I examine later in this chapter, stands in interesting comparison to the television version of Gould's *The Idea of North*. *Tshiuetin* captures life on board an Innu-owned train that travels between Sept-Isles and Schefferville, Quebec, close to where Michael Snow shot *La Région Centrale* (1971). In its mix of interviews and ambient sounds of the train and shots of the terrain, *Tshiuetin* is reminiscent of Gould's work but of course focuses on Innu voices since they make up the majority of the train's ridership.
6 Igloliorte, Nagam, and Taunton, "Introduction," 11.
7 My close focus here on techniques of remediation and the afterlife of the long '70s in ARCTICNOISE does include some consideration of Inutiq's relationship to the longer history of Inuit art and other forms of contemporary Inuit artistic practice, yet I recognize that any such investigation would be a full-length book in and of itself. The work of Heather Igloliorte is indispensable for anyone coming to grips with the richness and depth of Inuit artistic production, both historical and contemporary, and its complex relationship with government and gallery alike. Igloliorte's "Arctic Culture/Global Indigeneity" (2014) is of particular importance for the way that it maps out the long relationship between the Inuit and the Canadian state with an eye to the role that Inuit art has played in this relationship.
8 Hogue, "Introduction," 13.
9 Although I will be writing here of ARCTICNOISE as Inutiq's project, one of the most fascinating things about it is the extent to which it is clearly a product of an extraordinary collaboration between the artist, the curators who initiated the project (Britt Gallpen and Yasmin Nurming-Por), the gallery that hosted the original exhibition (Vancouver's grunt gallery), and a host of other academic partners and community institutions. For a compelling account of the fuller context of ARCTICNOISE and the series of events and dialogue that surrounded its exhibition, see Hogue, "Introduction."
10 Two works in particular signal the importance that they assign to Gould's work in their very titles: Peter Davidson's *The Idea of North* (2005) and Sherrill Grace's *Canada and the Idea of North* (2007). Although each registers the self-acknowledged shortcomings of Gould's

vision of the North, both works reproduce the centrality of southern voices in their reckoning with the history of representations of the North despite efforts to include Inuit voices. For a critical piece that takes up the innovations and limitations of Gould's work from the vantage point of sound studies, see Scott, "The Idea (of an Idea)."

11 Vallee, "Glenn Gould's *The Idea of North*," 28.
12 For the full transcription of the prologue to *The Idea of North* as well as his introduction to the series, see Gould, "Prologue from 'The Idea of North'"; and Gould, "'The Idea of North': An Introduction."
13 Vallee, "Glenn Gould's *The Idea of North*," 28.
14 Ibid. For a reading of how Inutiq "extends and renews forms of the contrapuntal" that draws extensively on Edward Said's argument that the imperial archive must be read contrapuntally, see Hart, "Reading Contrapuntally."
15 Vallee, "Glenn Gould's *The Idea of North*," 28.
16 Ibid.
17 Coulthard, *Red Skin, White Masks*, 25.
18 Inutiq, with Hennessy, "Interview," 34.
19 Ibid.
20 Ibid.
21 Ibid.
22 Inutiq's ARCTICNOISE is not the only recent work to revisit and remediate Gould's *The Idea of North*. Black Canadian violinist Andrew Forde performed, along with his band The Ghost Tapes, a reinterpreted and remixed version of Gould's piece in February 2018 as part of Black History Month celebrations in Toronto. By collaborating with rapper Shad as well as Cree-Dene singer IsKwé, Forde wanted to open up Gould's piece in order to include the voices left out of the 1967 idea of Canada's North: "We're going to hear what it meant to be, what it means to identify as a black Canadian, as an Indigenous person, as a young person, even [...] There's a lot of different narratives that we've now opened up the conversation to." Nathoo, "Violinist Andrew Forde."
23 For a bracing account of Sibelius and the swans, see Ross, *Rest Is Noise*, 171–93.
24 Chan, "Sonic Transmissions," 27.
25 Ibid., 30.
26 Ibid.

27 Ibid., 30–1.
28 Inutiq's releases on Indigene Audio point to an interest in various forms of retrofuturism and in the dormant possibilities of the past. As Chan notes, adopting various recording aliases allows Inutiq "to avoid the discomfort of the spotlight" and to explore alternative ideas about what is and what could be. Most notably, Inutiq explained to Chan, recording as Private Getaway facilitates explorations "into a fresh and exciting virtual getaway of our future pasts." Ibid., 30.
29 Hennessy, Smith, and Hogue, "ARCTICNOISE and Broadcasting Futures," 220.
30 As cheyanne turions explains, Inutiq's North is not fixed or frozen. For the installations in Toronto and Saskatoon, Inutiq programmed the multichannel installation so that the individual components would be out of phase with one another; the "videos loop dis-synchronously, meaning that each visit to the show yields a new relationship between images." turions, "Being Local," 52. In this way, Inutiq refuses to assume a position of absolute authority: "The randomized combination of audio and video further disrupts Inutiq himself as an authorial Inuit voice. As such, the work represents the creation of a subjective, unstable experience of the North, a refusal of singular meaning and understanding." Hennessy, Smith, and Hogue, "ARCTICNOISE and Broadcasting Futures," 221.
31 Inutiq's investigations into the past continue with his installation for *In Search of Expo 67* (2017), a major show held at Montreal's Musée d'art contemporain and curated by Leslie Johnstone and Monika Kin Gagnon. Inutiq's multimedia installation for this show, *Ensemble/Encore, Together/Again, Katimakainnarivugut*, was centred on one of Expo 67's iconic buildings: the inverted pyramid named Katimavik, which in Inuktitut means "meeting place." For the video component of the work, Inutiq remixed film of Expo 67 drawn from the Prelinger Archives, and for the audio, he developed a new composition that references Otto Joachim's original four-channel electroacoustic sound installation for the pavilion. As Inutiq himself explains, in addition to thinking about the concept of a "meeting place," the installation explores the proximity and distance of the recent past. With it, he says, "I am also exploring the space and time that distance us from and also bring us closer to the 1967 Montreal World's Fair." Inutiq's examination of Expo 67 is caught

up with ideas of modernity and its failures, the ways that the event in general and the Katimavik pavilion in particular represented "a pinnacle of the possibilities of futurism and the potentiality of the nation state as an agent of newfangled corporate and technological breakthroughs." Inutiq, "In Search of Expo 67," 15. The long '70s represent the comedown from this pinnacle, the process of recognition of the limits of technology and of state and corporate ideologies.

32 Hennessy, Smith, and Hogue, "ARCTICNOISE and Broadcasting Futures," 215.

33 Inutiq's audiovisual remixes and remediations exist alongside those of other Indigenous DJs and new media artists, including, most notably, Haudenosaunee Jackson 2bears. Sampling, particularly the critical and cathartic dimension of finding and flipping audio fragments, is key to 2bears's work. As he explains, the chance Salvation Army discovery of a vinyl copy of the nursery rhyme "Ten Little Indians" led him to develop a remix technique and performance practice grounded in exploiting and exorcising the hauntological dimensions of old recordings: "As with my remix of 'Ten Little Indians,' I began sampling different media fragments and layering them together with hip hop breaks – scratching, looping, and cutting them together to create live audio/video montages. What I wanted was to perform a live audio/video narrative that would speak of resistance; to tell a live cinema story that would shore up against all the occidental simulations of our people in the mediascape and the colonial appropriations, constructions, and misrepresentations of First Nations identity." 2bears, "My Post-Indian Technological Autobiography," 23.

34 Quoted in Ritter, *Beat Nation*, 32.

35 For more on redface and its long history in Hollywood and beyond, see Raheja, *Reservation Reelism*, 102–44. For a more specific critique of redface as it relates to contemporary practices of remediation, see Brady and Kelly, *We Interrupt This Program*, 80–108.

36 Veal, *Dub*, 198.

37 Ibid., 199.

38 Quoted in ibid., 205.

39 Ibid.

40 Although I am primarily imagining a dialogue here between Canada's North and dub's spiritual home in Jamaica, I want to emphasize Toronto's key role in the dub universe and how the Canadian 1970s

included the impact of a dub diaspora. For more on the history of dub in Toronto, particularly the dub scene there in the 1970s and early 1980s, see Walker, *Dubwise*, esp. the chapter "One-Dub Drops the Maple Leaf: The Story of Reggae in Canada," 155–76. Essential too is *Jamaica to Toronto: Soul, Funk & Reggae 1967–74* (2006), an album compiled by DJ and Canadian music historian Kevin "Sipreano" Howes and released by the Seattle-based label Light in the Attic Records.

41 Barnaby's feature film *Rhymes for Young Ghouls* (2014) is set on the fictional Red Crow Mi'gMaq Reserve in 1976 and follows its young protagonist, Aila (Kawennahere Devery Jacobs), as she grows up in the shadow of her mother's suicide with her father in jail. The film is by no means a conventional Canadian social realist drama. Instead, Barnaby draws extensively on 1970s film tropes, especially horror, to present the nearby residential school as a house of terrors. For a powerful reading of *Rhymes for Young Ghouls* in relationship to 1970s rape revenge horror, see Smith, "Trespassed Lands, Transgressed Bodies."

42 For more on Monkman's complex remediations in his paintings, videos, and gallery installations, see Brady and Kelly, *We Interrupt This Program*, 89–97.

43 Quoted in Cram, "Filmmaker Caroline Monnet."

44 Russell, *Archiveology*, 16.

45 For more on the radical innovations of the Challenge for Change films, see Waugh, Baker, and Winton, eds, *Challenge for Change*. In that volume, Michelle Stewart addresses the question of voice directly, noting that although *Cree Hunters of Mistassini* was not shot by one of the Indian Film Crews that were in operation at the NFB at that time, the voices of its Cree subjects do come through in those "moments of dialogue with the camera" and in their participation in the process of shooting and editing. Stewart, "*Cree Hunters of Mistassini*," 185. Zoë Druick also provides a detailed reading of the film, with special attention to the way that it handles the James Bay hydroelectric development. Druick, *Projecting Canada*, 153–7.

46 Quoted in Cram, "Filmmaker Caroline Monnet."

47 Chan, "Sonic Transmissions," 30.

48 Quoted in Pregot, "Quick Chat from Sundance."

49 David, "A Different Kind of Souvenir."

50 Quoted in Ngangura, "Meet the Indigenous Writer."

51 Seesequasis, "How Crowdsourcing." Seesequasis's project exists alongside Library and Archives Canada's Project Naming initiative, which has been ongoing since 2002. Although the formal archival efforts of Library and Archives Canada have succeeded in identifying the people and places in many of its collection of nearly 10,000 photos, the feel of this initiative is somehow totally different from Seesequasis's effort, which in its online informality and sense of personal investment and passion falls into a different category of project. For more on Project Naming, its relationship with archive-driven projects elsewhere, and the concept of "visual repatriation," see Smith, "From Nunavut to Micronesia"; and Payne, "Lessons with Leah."
52 Legrady, *James Bay Cree*.
53 Ibid.
54 Seesequasis, "How Crowdsourcing."
55 Ibid.
56 In its interrogation of the photographic archive, national cultural memory, and the elisions and exclusions that structure it, Seesequasis's project shares something with Jacqueline Hoàng Nguyễn's *The Making of an Archive*, an ongoing project initiated at Toronto's Gendai Gallery in 2014 and expanded at Vancouver's grunt gallery in 2018. As curator Vanessa Kwan explains, "*The Making of an Archive* addresses a specific lack in state-run archives in Canada. While researching at the Canadian Broadcasting Corporation, the National Film Board, and the Library and Archives Canada, Nguyễn found they had precious little in their holdings under the search heading of 'multiculturalism' that reflected the lived experience of immigrants in this country. *The Making of an Archive* is a grassroots attempt to provide a more representative photographic record [...] It is a simple premise at the base: collect and preserve the photo albums and ephemera from immigrants and their families who identify as persons of colour (POC), and in the process offer a service to an intergenerational donor base: digitized copies of precious family archives." Kwan, "Looking Up," 12. Even though Seesequasis draws on already existing official collections of various sorts for his photos whereas Nguyễn draws on donations, the projects share the capacity to transform the meaning and significance of a photograph through their archivization or remediation. As Gabrielle Moser argues in relation to Nguyễn's project, drawing on Tina Campt,

the possibility of recontextualizing the photograph in a way that makes it mean something else "insists on the sovereignty of the photograph as a continuously unfolding event – one in which the viewer and archival researcher can intervene." Moser, "Porous Sounds," 73. For more on *The Making of an Archive*, see Nguyễn, Kwan, and Pon, eds, *Making of an Archive*.
57 Guha, "Beyond the Archive."
58 Ibid.

Coda

1 Kenins, "This New Brunswick Town."
2 Artifact Institute, *Study 1*.
3 Johnston, "Technological Regionalisms," 249, 254.
4 Ibid., 255.
5 For a more detailed account of the Artifact Institute's working methods as well as an analysis of how its investigations into the relationships between objects and organizations constitute an intervention into the very processes that produce and constitute them, see Johnston, "Technological Regionalisms," 254–60.

Bibliography

Archival Sources

National Film Board Archives (NFBA), Montreal
Eagles, Darrell. "Television Public Service Spots Good Business for any Renewable Resource Agency." 1968.
"Narration for: BEAVER." 1963.
Smith, Dave. "Suggested Titles – Canadian Wildlife Series." 1963.

Secondary Sources

Acland, Charles R. "The Last Days of Videotape." *Flow TV* 11, no. 2 (2009). http://flowtv.org/2009/11/the-last-days-of-videotapecharles-r-acland-concordia-university.
– ed. *Residual Media*. Minneapolis: University of Minnesota Press, 2007.
Adams, K.C. "Artist Statement." *Perception*. http://urbanshaman.org/perception/statement.
Araneda, Cecilia. "Guy Maddin and the Language of Early Cinema." *WNDX: Festival of the Moving Image*, 2011. http://platformgallery.org/wp-content/uploads/2016/08/2011_maddin.pdf.
Artifact Institute. *Study 1: Participants in the Institutions by Artists Convention, Report 1*. Halifax and Montreal: Artifact Institute, 2012.
Atwood, Margaret. *Survival: A Thematic Guide to Canadian Literature*. Toronto: House of Anansi, 1972.
Baker, Michael Brendan. "The Musicality of Canadian Cinema." In *The Oxford Handbook of Canadian Cinema*, ed. Janine Marchessault and Will Straw, 391–407. Oxford: Oxford University Press, 2019.
Bangs, Lester. *Psychotic Reactions and Carburetor Dung*. Ed. Greil Marcus. New York: Vintage, 1988.

Barden, Alice. "Remembering Socialist Entertainment: Romanian Television, Gestures and Intimacy." *European Journal of Cultural Studies* 20, no. 3 (2017): 341–58.

Beaty, Bart. "Not Playing, Working: Class, Masculinity, and Nation in the Canadian Hockey Film." In *Working on Screen: Representations of the Working Class in Canadian Cinema*, ed. Malek Khouri and Darrell Varga, 113–33. Toronto: University of Toronto Press, 2006.

Benjamin, Walter. *The Arcades Project*. Trans. Howard Eiland and Kevin McLaughlin. Cambridge, MA: Belknap Press of Harvard University Press, 1999.

– "Left-Wing Melancholy." In *Walter Benjamin: Selected Writings, Volume 2, Part 2, 1931–1934*, ed. Michael W. Jennings, Howard Eiland, and Gary Smith, 423–7. Cambridge, MA: Belknap Press of Harvard University Press, 1999.

– "On the Concept of History." In *Walter Benjamin: Selected Writings, Volume 4, 1938–1940*, ed. Howard Eiland and Michael W. Jennings, 389–400. Cambridge, MA: Belknap Press of Harvard University Press, 2003.

– "Surrealism: The Last Snapshot of the European Intelligentsia." In *Walter Benjamin: Selected Writings, Volume 2, Part 1, 1927–1930*, ed. Michael W. Jennings, Howard Eiland, and Gary Smith, 207–24. Cambridge, MA: Belknap Press of Harvard University Press, 1999.

Benson-Allott, Caetlin. *Killer Tapes and Shattered Screens: Video Spectatorship from VHS to File Sharing*. Berkeley and Los Angeles: University of California Press, 2013.

Bijsterveld, Karin, and José van Dijck, eds. *Sound Souvenirs: Audio Technologies, Memory and Cultural Practices*. Amsterdam: Amsterdam University Press, 2009.

Bijsterveld, Karin, and Annelies Jacob. "Storing Sound Souvenirs: The Multi-Sited Domestication of the Tape Recorder." In *Sound Souvenirs: Audio Technologies, Memory and Cultural Practices*, ed. Karin Bijsterveld and José van Dijck, 25–42. Amsterdam: Amsterdam University Press, 2009.

Billig, Michael. *Banal Nationalism*. London: Sage, 1995.

Birdwise, Scott. "Where Is Fear? Space, Place, and the Sense of Horror in Canadian Avant-Garde Film." In *The Canadian Horror Film: Terror of the Soul*, ed. Gina Freitag and André Loiselle, 185–205. Toronto: University of Toronto Press, 2015.

Bolter, Jay David, and Richard Grusin. *Remediation: Understanding New Media*. Cambridge, MA: MIT Press, 1998.

Bordo, Jonathan. "Jack Pine – Wilderness Sublime or the Erasure of Aboriginal Presence from the Landscape." *Journal of Canadian Studies* 27, no. 4 (1992–93): 98–128.

Boswell, Randy. "Hibernating or Extinct? Original Black-and-White Hinterland Who's Who TV Spots Missing on 50th Anniversary." *National Post*, 9 July 2013. http://news.nationalpost.com/2013/07/09/hibernating-or-extinct-original-black-and-white-hinterland-whos-who-tv-spots-missing-on-50th-anniversary.

Boym, Svetlana. *The Future of Nostalgia*. New York: Basic Books, 2001.

Brady, Miranda J., and John M.H. Kelly. *We Interrupt This Program: Indigenous Media Tactics in Canadian Culture*. Vancouver: UBC Press, 2017.

Broomer, Stephen. *Codes for North: Foundations of the Canadian Avant-Garde Film*. Toronto: Canadian Filmmakers Distribution Centre, 2017.

Brown, Todd. "A Conversation with Winnipeg Film Maker Matthew Rankin." Interview conducted by Kier-La Janisse. *Screen Anarchy*, 15 April 2009. https://screenanarchy.com/2009/04/a-conversation-with-winnipeg-film-maker-matthew-rankin.html.

Brown, Wendy. "Resisting Left Melancholy." *boundary 2*, 26, no. 3 (1999): 19–27.

Browne, Colin. "David Rimmer: Re-Fusing the Contradictions." In *Reading David Rimmer: Commentary on the Films, 1967–2014*, ed. Mike Hoolboom and Brett Kashmere, 76–7. Toronto: Canadian Filmmakers Distribution Centre, 2014.

Bull, Michael. "The Auditory Nostalgia of iPod Culture." In *Sound Souvenirs: Audio Technologies, Memory and Cultural Practices*, ed. Karin Bijsterveld and José van Dijck, 83–93. Amsterdam: Amsterdam University Press, 2009.

Burke, Andrew. "The Nature of Things: Coupland, Cinema, and the Canadian Sixties and Seventies." In *Double-Takes: Intersections between Canadian Literature and Film*, ed. David Jarraway, 259–75. Ottawa: University of Ottawa Press, 2013.

– "Stand Tall: Winnipeg Cinema and the Civic Imaginary." In *The Oxford Handbook of Canadian Cinema*, ed. Janine Marchessault and Will Straw, 269–84. Oxford: Oxford University Press, 2019.

Byers, Michele. "The Empty Archive: Canadian Television and the Erasure of History." *Flow TV* 6, no. 3 (2007). http://flowtv.org/2007/06/the-empty-archive-canadian-television-and-the-erasure-of-history.

Byers, Michele, and Jennifer VanderBurgh. "Trafficking (in) the Archive: Canada, Copyright, and the Study of Television." *ESC: English Studies in Canada* 36, no. 1 (2010): 109–26.

– "What Was Canada? Locating the Language of an Empty National Archive." *Critical Studies in Television* 5, no. 2 (2010): 105–17.

CBC Radio. "Ottawa Designer Crowdfunds Reprint of 1974 CBC 'Graphic Standards Manual.'" *As It Happens*, 9 August 2016.

Chan, Crystal. "The Sonic Transmissions of Geronimo Inutiq." *Musicworks*, no. 129 (Winter 2017): 22–31. https://www.musicworks.ca/sonic-transmissions-geronimo-inutiq.

Chang, Weiyi. "Reclaiming the North." *Luma Quarterly* 1, no. 2 (2015). https://lumaquarterly.com/issues/2015/002-fall/reclaiming-the-north.

Chris, Cynthia. *Watching Wildlife*. Minneapolis: University of Minnesota Press, 2006.

Corupe, Paul. "(Who's in the) Driver's Seat: The Canadian Brute Unleashed in *Death Weekend*." In *The Canadian Horror Film: Terror of the Soul*, ed. Gina Freitag and André Loiselle, 91–107. Toronto: University of Toronto Press, 2015.

Coulthard, Glen Sean. *Red Skin, White Masks: Rejecting the Colonial Politics of Recognition*. Minneapolis: University of Minnesota Press, 2014.

Coupland, Douglas. *Souvenir of Canada*. 2 volumes. Vancouver: Douglas and McIntyre, 2002 and 2004.

– "32 Thoughts about 32 Short Films." *New York Times*, 1 May 1994. http://coupland.tripod.com/nyt3.html.

Cram, Stephanie. "Filmmaker Caroline Monnet Aims to Show Indigenous People 'Kicking Ass On-Screen.'" *CBC News*, 28 May 2016. https://www.cbc.ca/news/indigenous/filmmaker-wants-to-show-indigenous-people-kicking-ass-1.3604261.

David, Jennifer. "A Different Kind of Souvenir." *National Gallery of Canada*, 6 February 2018. https://www.gallery.ca/magazine/in-the-spotlight/a-different-kind-of-souvenir.

Davidson, Peter. *The Idea of North*. London: Reaktion, 2005.

"Death Weekend." In *Canuxploitation! Your Complete Guide to Canadian B-Film*. http://www.canuxploitation.com/review/deathweekend.html.

Dempsey, Shawna, and Lorri Millan. *Lesbian National Parks and Services Field Guide to North America: Flora, Fauna and Survival Skills*. Toronto: Pedlar, 2002.
– *Tableau Vivant: Eaton's Catalogue 1976*. 1998. http://www.shawnadempseyandlorrimillan.net.
– *Transport*. 2014. http://www.shawnadempseyandlorrimillan.net.
Derrida, Jacques. *Specters of Marx: The State of the Debt, the Work of Mourning, and the New International*. Trans. Peggy Kamuf. New York and London: Routledge, 1994.
Desbiens, Caroline. "Hydroelectric Development in Eeyou-James Bay." NICHE: *Network in Canadian History and Environment*, 19 September 2016. http://niche-canada.org/2016/09/19/dam-nation-hydroelectric-development-in-eeyou-istche-baie-james.
– *Power from the North: Territory, Identity, and the Culture of Hydroelectricity in Quebec*. Vancouver: UBC Press, 2013.
Druick, Zoë. *Projecting Canada: Government Policy and Documentary Film at the National Film Board*. Montreal and Kingston: McGill-Queen's University Press, 2007.
Dunne, Michael. *Metapop: Self-Referentiality in Contemporary American Popular Culture*. Jackson: University Press of Mississippi, 2010.
Dyer, Richard. "In Defense of Disco 1979." *New Formations* 58, no. 1 (2006): 101–8.
Ebner, David. "Greg Joy Recalls Moment in the Sun." *Globe and Mail*, 7 August 2012.
Egan, Jennifer. "The Celebration of a 'Proper Product': Exploring the Residual Collectible through the 'Video Nasty.'" In *Residual Media*, ed. Charles R. Acland. 200–21. Minneapolis: University of Minnesota Press, 2007.
Elder, Bruce. *Image and Identity: Reflections on Canadian Film and Culture*. Waterloo, ON: Wilfrid Laurier University Press, 1989.
Engle, Karen, and Yoke-Sum Wong, eds. *Feelings of Structure: Explorations in Affect*. Montreal and Kingston: McGill-Queen's University Press, 2018.
Erickson, Steve. "Interview: Guy Maddin and Evan Johnson on *The Forbidden Room*." *Slant*, 4 October 2015. https://www.slantmagazine.com/film/interview-guy-maddin-and-evan-johnson.
Fisher, Jennifer. "Out and About: The Performances of Shawna Dempsey and Lorri Millan." In *Caught in the Act: An Anthology of Performance Art by Canadian Women*, ed. Tanya Mars and Joanna Householder, 189–97. Toronto: YYZ Books, 2004.

Fisher, Mark. *Ghosts of My Life: Writings on Depression, Hauntology and Lost Futures*. Winchester, UK: Zero Books, 2014.
– *K-Punk: The Collected and Unpublished Writings of Mark Fisher (2004–2016)*. London: Repeater, 2018.
Francis, Margot. *Creative Subversions: Whiteness, Indigeneity, and the National Imaginary*. Vancouver: UBC Press, 2011.
– "The Lesbian National Parks and Services: Reading Sex, Race, and the Nation in Artistic Performance." *Canadian Woman Studies* 20, no. 2 (2000): 131–6.
Freitag, Gina, and André Loiselle. "Terror of the Soul: An Introduction." In *The Canadian Horror Film: Terror of the Soul*, ed. Gina Freitag and André Loiselle, 3–17. Toronto: University of Toronto Press, 2015.
Frye, Northrop. "Conclusion to the First Edition of *Literary History of Canada*." 1965. Reprinted in *Northrop Frye on Canada*, ed. Jean O'Grady and David Staines, 339–72. Toronto: University of Toronto Press, 2003.
Genette, Gérard. *Paratexts: Thresholds of Interpretation*. Trans. Jane E. Lewin. Cambridge, UK: Cambridge University Press, 1997.
Gidal, Peter. "Notes on *La Région Centrale*." In *Structural Film Anthology*, ed. Peter Gidal, 52–5. London: British Film Institute, 1976.
Gillmor, Alison. "Channelling Mayhem." *CBC News*, 12 April 2006. https://www.cbc.ca/news/entertainment/channelling-mayhem-1.628907.
Gould, Glenn. "'The Idea of North': An Introduction." In *The Glenn Gould Reader*, ed. Tim Page, 391–3. New York: Random House, 1984.
– "Prologue from 'The Idea of North.'" In *The Glenn Gould Reader*, ed. Tim Page, 389–90. New York: Random House, 1984.
Grace, Sherrill. *Canada and the Idea of North*. Montreal and Kingston: McGill-Queen's University Press, 2007.
Gray, Jonathan. *Show Sold Separately: Promos, Spoilers, and Other Media Paratexts*. New York: NYU Press, 2010.
Guha, Malini. "Beyond the Archive: The Work of Remembrance in John Akomfrah's *The Nine Muses*." *Screening the Past*, no. 43 (April 2018). http://www.screeningthepast.com/2018/02/beyond-the-archive-the-work-of-remembrance-in-john-akomfrahs-the-nine-muses.
Hall, Stuart. *Selected Political Writings: The Great Moving Right Show and Other Essays*. Ed. Sally Davison, David Featherstone, Michael Rustin, and Bill Schwarz. Durham, NC: Duke University Press, 2017.
Hanna, Erin. "Second City or Second Country? The Question of Canadian

Identity in SCTV's Transcultural Text." *Cineaction* 78 (2009): 52–9.

Harper, Adam. "Hauntology: The Past Inside the Present." *Rouge's Foam*, 27 October 2009. http://rougesfoam.blogspot.com/2009/10/hauntology-past-inside-present.html.

Hart, Sydney. "Reading Contrapuntally: Geronimo Inutiq's ARCTICNOISE." *esse arts + opinions*, no. 86 (Winter 2016): 62–7.

Hasan, Mark R. "*Rituals*: Creating the Forest Slasher in the Canadian Tax Shelter Era." In *The Canadian Horror Film: Terror of the Soul*, ed. Gina Freitag and André Loiselle, 108–31. Toronto: University of Toronto Press, 2015.

Henderson, Scott. "Canadian Content Regulations and the Formation of a National Scene." *Popular Music* 27, no. 2 (2008): 307–15.

Hennessy, Kate, Trudi Lynn Smith, and Tarah Hogue. "ARCTICNOISE and Broadcasting Futures: Geronimo Inutiq Remixes the Igloolik Isuma Archive." *Cultural Anthropology* 33, no. 2 (2018): 213–23.

Highmore, Ben. "Formations of Feelings, Constellations of Things." *Cultural Studies Review* 22, no. 1 (2016): 144–67.

Hilderbrand, Lucas. *Inherent Vice: Bootleg Histories of Videotape and Copyright*. Durham, NC: Duke University Press, 2009.

Hoberman, J. "The Cineaste's Guide to Watching Movies While Stoned." *The Nation*, 30 October 2013. https://www.thenation.com/article/cineastes-guide-watching-movies-while-stoned.

Hogue, Tarah. "Introduction." In *ARCTICNOISE: Geronimo Inutiq*, ed. Tarah Hogue, 12–14. Vancouver: grunt gallery, 2016.

Holdsworth, Amy. *Television, Memory and Nostalgia*. London: Palgrave, 2011.

Igloliorte, Heather. "Arctic Culture/Global Indigeneity." In *Negotiations in a Vacant Lot: Studying the Visual in Canada*, ed. Lynda Jessup, Erin Morton, and Kirsty Robertson, 150–70. Montreal and Kingston: McGill-Queen's University Press, 2014.

Igloliorte, Heather, Julie Nagam, and Carla Taunton. "Introduction – Transmissions: The Future Possibilities of Indigenous Digital and New Media Art." In Heather Igloliorte, Julie Nagam, and Carla Taunton, eds, *Indigenous Art: New Media and the Digital*, special issue of *Public* 27, no. 54 (2016): 5–13.

– "In Search of Expo 67." *Inuit Art Quarterly* 30, no. 3 (2017): 15.

Inutiq, Geronimo, with Kate Hennessy. "Interview." In *ARCTICNOISE: Geronimo Inutiq*, ed. Tarah Hogue, 24–35. Vancouver: grunt gallery, 2016.

Jameson, Fredric. *The Geopolitical Aesthetic: Cinema and Space in the World System*. Bloomington: Indiana University Press; London: British Film Institute, 1992.
– *Marxism and Form: Twentieth-Century Dialectical Theories of Literature*. Princeton, NJ: Princeton University Press, 1971.
– "Periodizing the 60s." 1984. Reprinted in *The Ideologies of Theory*, 483–533. London: Verso, 2008.
Janisse, Kier-La. "An Ecstatic Professional: The Weird World of Winnipeg Character Actor Robert Vilar." *Spectacular Optical*, 1 March 2012. http://www.spectacularoptical.ca/2012/03/an-ecstatic-professional.
Jansen, Bas. "Tape Cassettes and Former Selves: How Mix Tapes Mediate Memories." In *Sound Souvenirs: Audio Technologies, Memory and Cultural Practices*, ed. Karin Bijsterveld and José van Dijck, 43–54. Amsterdam: Amsterdam University Press, 2009.
Johnston, Wes. "Technological Regionalisms: The Fieldwork Residency Project." In *Urban Encounters: Art and the Public*, ed. Martha Radice and Alexandrine Boudreault-Fournier, 249–68. Montreal and Kingston: McGill-Queen's University Press, 2017.
Kashmere, Brett. "Lessons from *Valery's Ankle*." In *Coming Down the Mountain: Rethinking the 1972 Summit Series*, ed. Brian Kennedy, 239–56. Hamilton, ON: Wolsak and Wynn, 2014.
Kenins, Laura. "This New Brunswick Town Was Literally Haunted by the Radio." *CBC Arts*, 22 September 2016. http://www.cbc.ca/arts/this-new-brunswick-town-was-literally-haunted-by-the-radio-1.3768831.
Kennedy, Garry Neill. *The Last Art College: Nova Scotia College of Art and Design, 1968–1978*. Cambridge, MA: MIT Press, 2012.
Klein, Jeff Z. "N.H.L.: Giddy Winnipeg Reclaims Its Long-Lost Prairie Companion." *New York Times*, 8 October 2011. http://www.nytimes.com/2011/10/09/sports/hockey/nhl-giddy-winnipeg-reclaims-its-long-lost-prairie-companion.html.
Koller, George Csaba. "David Rimmer: Honesty of Vision." In *Reading David Rimmer: Commentary on the Films, 1967–2014*, ed. Mike Hoolboom and Brett Kashmere, 40–4. Toronto: Canadian Filmmakers Distribution Centre, 2014.
– "*La Région Centrale*: Interview with Michael Snow." *Cinema Canada*, no. 4 (October-November 1972): 50–5. http://cinemacanada.athabascau.ca/index.php/cinema/article/view/115/190.

Kwan, Vanessa. "Looking Up: An Introduction." In *The Making of an Archive*, ed. Jacqueline Hoàng Nguyễn, Vanessa Kwan, and Dan Pon, 11–16. Vancouver: grunt gallery, 2018.

L'Atelier national du Manitoba. "The Horizontalist Manifesto." INCITE: *Journal of Experimental Media*, no. 1 (2008–09). http://www.incite-online.net/manitoba.html.

– "The Seven Pillars of Winnipeg: Atelier Aide-Mémoire on the Cinematic Form of the Winnipeg Jets." Annotated by Matthew Rankin. *BlackFlash* 23, no. 3 (2006): 26. https://cineflyer.wordpress.com/2011/03/31/l%E2%80%99atelier-national-du-manitobas-lists-manifestos.

Legrady, George. *James Bay Cree Photographic Documentary, 1972–73*. https://www.mat.ucsb.edu/g.legrady/glWeb/Projects/jb/james_bay.html.

Levine, Gabriel. "Remixing Return: A Tribe Called Red's Decolonial Bounce." TOPIA: *Canadian Journal of Cultural Studies* 35 (Spring 2016): 27–46.

Locke, John W. "Michael Snow's *La Région Centrale*." *Artforum* 12, no. 3 (1973): 66–71, no. 4 (1973): 66–72.

Loft, Steven, and Kerry Swanson, eds. *Coded Territories: Tracing Indigenous Pathways in New Media Art*. Calgary: University of Calgary Press, 2014.

Macfarlane, Daniel. "Dam Nation: Hydroelectric Developments in Canada." NICHE: *Network in Canadian History and Environment*, 12 September 2016. http://niche-canada.org/2016/09/12/dam-nation-hydroelectric-developments-in-canada.

MacLatchy, Jennifer. "Lesbian Rangers on a Queer Frontier." *Canadian Literature* 224 (Spring 2015): 156–63, 169.

Maddin, Guy. *My Winnipeg*. Toronto: Coach House, 2009.

McCallum, Mary Jane Logan, and Adele Perry. *Structures of Indifference: An Indigenous Life and Death in a Canadian City*. Winnipeg: University of Manitoba Press, 2018.

Michelson, Annette. "About Snow." *October* 8 (Spring 1979): 111–25.

Miller, Mary Jane. "From Kine to Hi-Def: A Personal View of Television Studies in Canada." In *Canadian Television: Text and Context*, ed. Marian Bredin, Scott Henderson, and Sarah A. Matheson, 21–37. Waterloo, ON: Wilfrid Laurier University Press, 2012.

Moser, Gabrielle. "Porous Sounds: Frequencies of Refusal in Diasporic Family Photographs." In *The Making of an Archive*, ed. Jacqueline Hoàng Nguyễn, Vanessa Kwan, and Dan Pon, 69–90. Vancouver: grunt gallery, 2018.

Nagler, Solomon. "Winnipeg Eats Itself: L'Atelier national du Manitoba's Scheme for Sovereignty." INCITE: *Journal of Experimental Media*, no. 1 (2008–09). http://www.incite-online.net/nagler.html.

Nathoo, Zulekha. "Violinist Andrew Forde Brings Glenn Gould to Contemporary Audience." *CBC News*, 3 February 2018. https://www.cbc.ca/news/entertainment/andrew-forde-glenn-gould-1.4518170.

Ngangura, Tari. "Meet the Indigenous Writer Using Photos to Tell His People's History over Twitter." *Vice*, 9 January 2017. https://www.vice.com/en_ca/article/kbwmba/meet-the-indigenous-writer-using-photos-to-tell-his-peoples-history-over-twitter.

Nguyễn, Jacqueline Hoàng, Vanessa Kwan, and Dan Pon, eds. *The Making of an Archive*. Vancouver: grunt gallery, 2018.

Nurming-Por, Yasmin. "Please Wait." In ARCTICNOISE: *Geronimo Inutiq*, ed. Tarah Hogue, 44–8. Vancouver: grunt gallery, 2016.

Ohayon, Albert. "Canada Vignettes: Essential Canadiana, Eh!" *NFB Blog*, 16 November 2011. https://blog.nfb.ca/blog/2011/11/16/canada-vignettes-essential-canadiana-eh.

O'Mara, Matthew. "The Website That Chronicles Ontario's Broadcasting History – One VHS Tape at a Time." *TVO*, 23 March 2017. https://www.tvo.org/article/current-affairs/-the-website-that-chronicles-ontarios-broadcasting-history--one-vhs-tape-at-a-time.

Pattie, David. "Stone Tapes: Ghost Box, Nostalgia and Post-War England." In *The Oxford Handbook of Music and Virtuality*, ed. Sheila Whiteley and Shara Rambarran, 392–408. Oxford: Oxford University Press, 2016.

Payne, Carol. "Lessons with Leah: Re-Reading the Photographic Archive of Nation in the National Film Board of Canada's Still Photography Division." *Visual Studies* 21, no. 1 (2006): 4–22.

Pregot, Kristine. "Quick Chat from Sundance: 'Mobilize' Director Caroline Monnet." *postPerspective*, 3 February 2016. https://postperspective.com/quick-chat-from-sundance-mobilize-director-caroline-monnet.

Raheja, Michelle H. *Reservation Reelism: Redfacing, Visual Sovereignty, and Representations of Native Americans in Film*. Lincoln: University of Nebraska Press, 2010.

Rayns, Tony. "Reflected Light." *Sight and Sound* 43, no. 1 (1973–74): 16–19.

Razutis, Al. "David Rimmer: A Critical Analysis." In *Reading David Rimmer: Commentary on the Films, 1967–2014*, ed. Mike Hoolboom and Brett Kashmere, 63–71. Toronto: Canadian Filmmakers Distribution Centre, 2014.

Reynolds, Simon. "Haunted Audio." *The Wire*, November 2006. http://reynoldsretro.blogspot.com/2012/05.
– *Retromania: Pop Culture's Addiction to Its Own Past*. London: Faber, 2011.
– "Spirit of Preservation." *Frieze*, 13 October 2005. https://frieze.com/article/spirit-preservation.
Rifkind, Candida. "The Biotopographies of Seth's *George Sprott (1894–1975)*." In *Material Cultures in Canada*, ed. Thomas Allen and Jennifer Blair, 225–46. Waterloo, ON: Wilfrid Laurier University Press, 2015.
Ritter, Kathleen. *Beat Nation: Art, Hip Hop and Aboriginal Culture*. Vancouver: Vancouver Art Gallery and grunt gallery, 2012.
"Rituals." In *Canuxploitation! Your Complete Guide to Canadian B-Film*. http://www.canuxploitation.com/review/rituals.html.
Rosenbaum, Jonathan. "The 'Presents' of Michael Snow." *Film Comment* 17, no. 3 (1981): 35–8. https://www.jonathanrosenbaum.net/1981/05/the-presents-of-michael-snow.
Ross, Alex. *The Rest Is Noise: Listening to the Twentieth Century*. New York: Vintage, 2008.
Russell, Catherine. *Archiveology: Walter Benjamin and Archival Film Practices*. Durham, NC: Duke University Press, 2018.
Sandilands, Catriona. "Where the Mountain Men Meet the Lesbian Rangers: Gender, Nation, and Nature in the Rocky Mountain National Parks." In *This Elusive Land: Women and the Canadian Environment*, ed. Melody Hessing, Rebecca Raglon, and Catriona Sandilands, 142–62. Vancouver: UBC Press, 2005.
Schafer, R. Murray. *The Soundscape: Our Sonic Environment and the Tuning of the World*. Toronto: McClelland and Stewart, 1977.
Sconce, Jeffrey. "'Trashing' the Academy: Taste, Excess, and an Emerging Politics of Cinematic Style." *Screen* 36, no. 4 (1995): 371–93.
Scott, Cam. "The Idea (of an Idea) of North (Of the North): Glenn Gould's Piece at 50." *Sounding Out!*, 5 February 2018. https://soundstudiesblog.com/2018/02/05/the-idea-of-an-idea-of-north-of-the-north-glenn-goulds-cbc-radio-piece-at-50.
Scribner, Charity. *Requiem for Communism*. Cambridge, MA: MIT Press, 2003.
Seesequasis, Paul. "How Crowdsourcing Is Helping Communities Reclaim Their Stories." *The Walrus*, 4 May 2018. https://thewalrus.ca/how-crowdsourcing-is-helping-communities-reclaim-their-stories.
Seth. *George Sprott, 1894–1975*. Montreal: Drawn & Quarterly, 2009.

Sexton, Jamie. "Weird Britain in Exile: Ghost Box, Hauntology, and Alternative Heritage." *Popular Music and Society* 35, no. 4 (2012): 561–84.

Shedden, Jim, ed. *Presence and Absence: The Films of Michael Snow, 1956–1991*. Toronto: Art Gallery of Ontario and Knopf Canada, 1995.

Sherburne, Philip. "'Anaconda,' 'Pacific State,' 'Sueño Latino,' and the Story of a Sample That Keeps Coming Back." *Pitchfork*, 8 September 2014. https://pitchfork.com/thepitch/474-anaconda-pacific-state-sueno-latino-and-the-story-of-a-sample-that-keeps-coming-back.

Silver, Jim. *Thin Ice: Money, Politics, and the Demise of an NHL Franchise*. Winnipeg: Fernwood, 1996.

Simon, Bill. "A Completely Open Space: Michael Snow's *La Région Centrale*." *Millennium Film Journal* 4, no. 5 (1979): 93–100.

Siskand, Jeff, and Ross Porter, producers. *Vic Vogel: The Musical Legend*. Canadian Jazz Archive Online, 27 April 2008. http://www.canadianjazzarchive.org/en/documentaries/vic-vogel-the-musical-legend.html.

Sitney, P. Adams. "Michael Snow's Cinema: *Wavelength*, ↔, *The Central Region*." In *The Essential Cinema*, ed. P. Adams Sitney, 219–29. New York: Anthology Film Archives and NYU Press, 1975.

Sloan, Johanne. "Hallucinating Landscape, Canadian-Style." In *Peter Doig*, 10–14. Vancouver: Belkin Art Gallery, 2001.

– "Conceptual Landscape Art: Joyce Wieland and Michael Snow." In *Beyond Wilderness: The Group of Seven, Canadian Identity, and Contemporary Art*, ed. John O'Brian and Peter White, 73–84. Montreal and Kingston: McGill-Queen's University Press, 2007.

– "Something Resembling Childhood: Artworks by Jack Chambers, Daniel Barrow, and Rodney Graham." In *Depicting Canada's Children*, ed. Loren Lerner, 365–85. Waterloo, ON: Wilfrid Laurier University Press, 2009.

Smith, Ariel. "Trespassed Lands, Transgressed Bodies: Horror, Rage, Rape, and Vengeance within Indigenous Cinema." *Bitch Flicks*, 24 April 2014. http://www.btchflcks.com/2014/04/trespassed-lands-transgressed-bodies-horror-rage-rape-and-vengeance-within-indigenous-cinema.html.

Smith, David A. "From Nunavut to Micronesia: Feedback and Description, Visual Repatriation and Online Photographs of Indigenous Peoples." *Partnership: The Canadian Journal of Library and Information Practice and Research* 3, no. 1 (2008): 1–19. https://journal.lib.uoguelph.ca/index.php/perj/article/view/330/848.

Smith, Iain Robert. "Collecting the Trash: The Cult of the Ephemeral Clip from VHS to YouTube." *Flow TV* 14, no. 8 (2011). http://flowtv.org/2011/09/collecting-the-trash.

Snow, Michael. "Converging on *La Région Centrale*: Michael Snow in Conversation with Charlotte Townsend, 1971." In *The Collected Writings of Michael Snow*, 57–60. Waterloo, ON: Wilfrid Laurier University Press, 1994.

– "*La Région Centrale*, 1969." In *The Collected Writings of Michael Snow*, 53–56. Waterloo, ON: Wilfrid Laurier University Press, 1994.

– "The Life & Times of Michael Snow, 1971." Interview by Joe Medjuck. In *The Collected Writings of Michael Snow*, 68–80. Waterloo, ON: Wilfrid Laurier University Press, 1994.

Sterne, Jonathan. *MP3: The Meaning of a Format*. Durham, NC: Duke University Press, 2012.

Stewart, Michelle. "*Cree Hunters of Mistassini*: Challenge for Change and Aboriginal Rights." In *Challenge for Change: Activist Documentary at the National Film Board of Canada*, ed. Thomas Waugh, Michael Brendan Baker, and Ezra Winton, 180–9. Montreal and Kingston: McGill-Queen's University Press, 2010.

Steyerl, Hito. *The Wretched of the Screen*. Berlin: Sternberg, 2012.

Straw, Will. "Embedded Memories." In *Residual Media*, ed. Charles R. Acland, 3–15. Minneapolis: University of Minnesota Press, 2007.

– "Music from the Wrong Place: On the Italianicity of Quebec Disco." *Criticism* 50, no. 1 (2008): 113–32.

Tahmahkera, Dustin. *Tribal Television: Viewing Native People in Sitcoms*. Chapel Hill: University of North Carolina Press, 2014.

Testa, Bart. "An Axiomatic Cinema: Michael Snow's Films." In *Presence and Absence: The Films of Michael Snow, 1956–1991*, ed. Jim Shedden, 26–83. Toronto: Art Gallery of Ontario and Knopf Canada, 1995.

"Trapped." In *Canuxploitation! Your Complete Guide to Canadian B-Film*. http://www.canuxploitation.com/review/trapped.html.

Tribbe, Matthew D. *No Requiem for the Space Age: The Apollo Moon Landings and American Culture*. Oxford: Oxford University Press, 2014.

turions, cheyanne. "Being Local." In *ARCTICNOISE: Geronimo Inutiq*, ed. Tarah Hogue, 50–4. Vancouver: grunt gallery, 2016.

2bears, Jackson. "My Post-Indian Technological Autobiography." In *Coded Territories: Tracing Indigenous Pathways in New Media Art*, ed. Steven Loft and Kerry Swanson, 1–29. Calgary: University of Calgary Press, 2014.

Urquhart, Peter. "You Should Know Something – *Anything* – about This Movie. You Paid for It." *Canadian Journal of Film Studies* 12, no. 2 (2003): 64–80.

Vallee, Mickey. "Glenn Gould's *The Idea of North*: The Cultural Politics of Benevolent Domination." TOPIA: *Canadian Journal of Cultural Studies* 32 (Fall 2014): 21–41.

VanderBurgh, Jennifer. "(Who Knows?) What Remains to Be Seen: Archives, Access, and Other Practical Problems for the Study of Canadian 'National' Television." In *Canadian Television: Text and Context*, ed. Marian Bredin, Scott Henderson, and Sarah A. Matheson, 39–57. Waterloo, ON: Wilfrid Laurier University Press, 2012.

VanDerWerff, Todd. "The Weird Legal Reason Many of Your Favorite Shows Aren't on DVD." *Vox*, 26 March 2015. https://www.vox.com/2014/11/3/7145231/shows-not-on-dvd-music-rights-wonder-years-wkrp.

Vatnsdal, Caelum. *They Came from Within: A History of Canadian Horror Cinema*. 2nd ed. Winnipeg: Arbeiter Ring, 2014.

Veal, Michael E. *Dub: Soundscapes and Shattered Songs in Jamaica Reggae*. Middletown, CT: Wesleyan University Press, 2007.

von Däniken, Erich. *Chariots of the Gods? Unsolved Mysteries of the Past*. New York: Putnam, 1968.

Walker, Klive. *Dubwise: Reasoning from the Reggae Underground*. Toronto: Isomniac, 2005.

Wark, Jayne. "Queering Abjection: A Lesbian, Feminist, and Canadian Perspective." In *Desire Change: Contemporary Feminist Art in Canada*, ed. Heather Davis, 96–117. Montreal and Kingston: McGill-Queen's University Press; Winnipeg: Mentoring Artists for Women's Art, 2017.

Waugh, Thomas, Michael Brendan Baker, and Ezra Winton, eds. *Challenge for Change: Activist Documentary at the National Film Board of Canada*. Montreal and Kingston: McGill-Queen's University Press, 2010.

Wees, William C. *Light Moving in Time: Studies in the Visual Aesthetics of Avant-Garde Film*. Berkeley: University of California Press, 1992.

– *Recycled Images: The Art and Politics of Found Footage Films*. New York: Anthology Film Archive, 1993.

Welch, Mary Agnes. "Don't Give Up Hope ... Yet." *Winnipeg Free Press*, 12 October 2008, A6.

White, Michael. "Strangeloves: From/De la région centrale, Air Defense Radar Station Moisie, and Media Cultures of the Cold War." *Gray Room*, no. 58 (2015): 50–83. http://www.greyroom.org/issues/58/53/strangeloves-from-de-la-rgion-centrale-air-defense-radar-station-moisie-and-media-cultures-of-the-cold-war.

Williams, Raymond. *Marxism and Literature*. Oxford: Oxford University Press, 1977.

– *Television: Technology and Cultural Form*. London: Fontana, 1974.

Zryd, Michael. "Found Footage Film as Discursive Metahistory: Craig Baldwin's Tribulation 99." *Moving Image* 3, no. 2 (2003): 40–61.

Index

Figures are indicated by page numbers in italics.

Abba (band), 49–50
Abbeloos, Pierre, 54–5, 196n34
Acland, Charles, 36, 98–9, 123, 206n11
Adams, K.C.: *Perception* (2014), 44, 46–7
Akomfrah, John: *The Nine Muses* (2011), 174; *The Unfinished Conversation* (2012), 149, 151; *Vertigo Sea* (2016), 149, 151
Alexander, Andrew, 107
Allard, Charles, 107
American Indian Movement, 67
Amisk (Obomsawin, 1977), 82
analogue media: affective dimension of, 5–7, 168–9; hauntology and, 7; impacts from loss of, 181–2, 184. *See also* infrastructure, technological; video
Andersen, Thom: *Los Angeles Plays Itself* (2003), 113
Araneda, Cecilia, 196n33
archive: comparison to cultural memory, 96; political use of, 160–1, 174–5. *See also* remediation
archiveology, 165, 206n15

ARCTICNOISE (Inutiq, 2015): collaborative aspect of, 152, 210n9; comparison to Akomfrah's work, 149, 151, 174; description of, 148–9; engagement with *The Idea of North* (Gould, 1967), 147, 152, 155–8; inclusion of other voices, 156–7; Indigenous new media art and, 151–2; introduction, 17, 146–7; 1970s periodization and, 11; noise in, 157–61; remediation as political act, 174–5; and *Spectres of Shortwave* (Christie, 2017), 181; subjectivity of North within, 212n30; three-channel form, 149, *150*, 151; visual noise, 160–1. *See also The Idea of North* (Gould, 1967); Inutiq, Geronimo
Artifact Institute, 19, 184–6, 216n5
Ashevak, Kenojuak, 201n11
Atanarjuat: The Fast Runner (Kunuk, 2001), 148
Atwood, Margaret: *Survival*, 59–60, 195n17

Austin Powers in Goldmember (Roach, 2002), 103

Bach, Richard: *Jonathan Livingston Seagull* (1970), 197n46
Baker, Michael Brendan, 76, 78–9
Baldwin, Craig, 203n1; *Tribulations 99* (1991), 205n10
banal nationalism, 28
Bangs, Lester, 139
Barnaby, Jeff, 147; *Etlinisigu'niet (Bleed Down)* (2015), 163–4; *Rhymes for Young Ghouls* (2014), 214n41
Barrow, Daniel, 123–4, 207n18, 208n21
Baruchel, Jay: *Goon: The Last of the Enforcers* (2017), 128
Because They Are Different (NFB, 1964), 164
Bell, Brett: *Sign-Off* (2010), 95–6, 97
Benjamin, Walter, 4, 19; "Left-Wing Melancholy" (1931), 8–9
Bettman, Gary, 118, 120
Billig, Michael, 28
birds, 74, 75–6, 198n48. See also loon; seagull
Birdwise, Scott, 194n14
Blackburn, Maurice, 76
Blacksmith, Sam, 165
Boards of Canada (band), 5–7, 25, 79, 197n36, 199n61; *Geogaddi* (2002), 6–7; *Music Has the Right to Children* (1998), 6, 79, 199n61; "Music Is Math" (2002), 6–7; "Ready Let's Go" (2002), 6; *Tomorrow's Harvest* (2013), 197n36
Bomi Productions Ltd, 190n15

Bond, Timothy: *Deadly Harvest* (1977), 70–1, 76, 197n36
Borges, Jorge Luis, 37
Bourdon, Luc: *La part du diable* (2017), 13
Boym, Svetlana, 8, 26
Breakfast (Table-Top Dolly) (Snow, 1972–76), 75
The Brian Sinclair Story (Maddin, 2010), 68–9, 196nn32–3
Brittain, Donald: *Paperland: The Bureaucrat Observed* (1979), 35–6
The Broken Altar (Rollo, 2013), 18, 177–8
Broomer, Stephen, 197n40
Brown, Wendy: "Resisting Left Melancholy," 8
Browne, Colin, 74
The Burton Cycle, 209n33
Byers, Michele, 96, 98, 202n15

Cacavas, John, 26
Campt, Tina, 215n56
Canada and the Idea of North (Grace, 2007), 210n10
Canada Modern archive, 189n7
Canadian Film Development Corporation (CFDC), 55, 60–1
Canadian Radio and Television Commission (CRTC), 92, 126
Canadian Who's Who (reference publication), 35, 190n25
Canadian Wildlife Service, 14, 21, 23, 29–30, 190n17. See also *Hinterland Who's Who* (1963–78)
Canuxploitation! (website), 195n19, 198n57

Carle, Gilles: *Percé on the Rocks* (1964), 95
Carter, Peter: *Rituals* (1977), 80–1, 84
CBC: decision to stop using analogue, 181; end of sign-off protocols, 90; "exploding pizza" logo, 26, 38–9, 106–7, 203n24; *Graphic Standards Manual* (1974), 26, 203n24
Cesar's Bark Canoe (Gosselin, 1971), 165, 167
A Chairy Tale (McLaren, 1956), 106
Chambers, Jack: *The Hart of London* (1970), 179, 194n14
Chan, Crystal, 159, 168, 212n28
Chang, Weiyi, 149
Chow, Rey, 174
Christie, Amanda Dawn: *Spectres of Shortwave* (2017), 18–19, 179, 181–2, *183*, 184
Churchill Falls Generating Station (Labrador), 81
CKY, 204n2
Clark, Bob, 55
Clark, Joe, 50
Clarke, Bobby, 127–8
Clavier, Alain, 76, 78–9
Cloutier, Sylvia, 159
Codco (CBC, 1987–92), 200n4
Cody, Iron Eyes, 66, 161–2, 163
Cold War, 199n60, 205n10
colonialism. *See* settler colonialism
comedy, television, 200n4. *See also* *SCTV* (1976–84)
Concept Sound Studio, 76
Conner, Bruce, 203n1; *A Movie* (1958), 95–6, 205n10
contrapuntal, 154, 211n14
Corupe, Paul, 195n19
Coulthard, Glen Sean, 154–5
Coupland, Douglas, 28, 189n12
Crack, Brutal, Grief (Elder, 2000), 194n14
C.R.A.Z.Y. (Vallée, 2005), 13
Cree Hunters of Mistassini (Richardson and Ianzelo, 1974), 82, 165, 168, 214n45
Cronenberg, David, 55; *Videodrome* (1983), 203n25
"Crying Indian" ad ("Keep America Beautiful"), 66, 72, 83
cultural memory: analogue media and, 5–7, 168–9; comparison to archival storage, 96; contestation of, 13–14; hauntology and "the past inside the present," 5–8, 24–6, 28, 187n5, 188n6; heterogenous experience of, 13; nature of recalling, 78–9; nostalgia and, 8–9, 26, 169, 170; paratelevisual material as, 90–1, 95; reclamation of, 170–1; television and, 27; video and, 103, 116–17, 122–3, 126–8; wilderness dread, 59–61, 80–1, 195n17
Cummings, Burton, *138*, 139–40, 209n33
Cunningham, Sean S. *Friday the 13th* (1980), 83

Dallett, Tim, 19, 184. *See also* Artifact Institute
Davidson, Peter: *The Idea of North* (2005), 210n10

Deadly Harvest (Bond, 1977), 70–1, 76, 197n36

Death by Popcorn (L'Atelier national du Manitoba, 2005): aesthetic dimension of analogue video, *125*, *126*, *128*; on Burton Cummings, *138*, 139–40; categorization issues, 115–16; comparison between Quebec and Manitoba in, 132–4; comparison to *SCTV*, 124; critical analysis of Winnipeg and Jets, 116, 121–2, 129–31, 133–7, 139–41, 143; on Dale Hawerchuk, 130–1; demonization of Gretzky, 120–1; *Don Cherry's Rock'em Sock'em Hockey* franchise and, 131–2; on emotional impact of loss of Jets, 135–7; as found-footage filmmaking, 116, 203n1; introduction, 16, 114–17; legal action against, 204n2; 1970s periodization and, 11; opening montage and collective anxiety and resentment, 117–20; origins of, 115, 123–4; on Selanne, 133–4; on self-loathing of Jets fans and Winnipeggers, 141, *142*, 143; on Steen, 137; title, 140–1, 143; video culture and, 116–17, 124, 131–2, 143, 145; on "Winnipeg White Out" tradition, 140. *See also* L'Atelier national du Manitoba

Dempsey, Shawna: *Lesbian National Parks and Services* (with Millan, 1997–present), 41–4, *45*, 191n32; *Tableau Vivant: Eaton's Catalogue 1976* (with Millan, 1998), 191n33; *Transport* (with Millan, 2014), 191n33

Derrida, Jacques, 7, 25

Design Canada (Durrell, 2018), 189n7

Devitt, Mark, 131–2

disco, 49–50, 192n37

Doig, Peter, 83, 199nn61–2

Don Cherry's Rock'em Sock'em Hockey franchise, 131–2, 208nn25–6

Don Messer's Jubilee (CBC, 1967–69), 111

Dowse, Michael: *Goon* (2011), 128

drive-in theatres: *The Broken Altar* (Rollo, 2013) on, 18, 177–8

drugs, 195n25

Druick, Zoë, 34, 214n45

dub, 162–3, 213n40

Dubyadubs (Inutiq, 2009), 161–3

Dunne, Michael, 200n2

Durrell, Greg: *Design Canada* (2018), 189n7

Dyer, Richard, 192n37

Eagles, Darrell, 29–30

Earth Day, 66, 72

Eastern Bloc, 19, 24

Eaton, Rosemary Gilliat, 172

echo, 162

Edmonton Oilers, 118, 121, 130, 133, 140–1

Egan, Kate, 206n11

Egoyan, Atom: *Gross Misconduct* (1993), 128

808 State (band): "Pacific 202" (1989), 51

Elder, R. Bruce, 54; *Crack, Brutal, Grief* (2000), 194n14

electronic music: dub, 162–3, 213n40; hauntology and, 7–8, 25; by Inutiq, 158–9; loon call in, 51
E-MU Emulator II (sampling keyboard), 51
Ensemble/Encore, Together/Again, Katimakainnarivugut (Inutiq, 2017), 212n31
environment: association with Indigenous peoples, 66; mediation by television, 22; remediation and, 147–8; wilderness dread, 59–61, 80–1, 195n17
environmental disaster genre, 64–5, 70–1, 76
Environment Canada: biodiversity public service announcement, 46–7
Eoin, Marcus, 5. See also Boards of Canada (band)
Eskimo Artist: Kenojuak (Feeney, 1963), 201n11
Etlinisigu'niet (Bleed Down) (Barnaby, 2015), 163–4

Face-Off (McCowan, 1971), 113
Fahrenheit 7-Eleven (Forsberg, 2011), 209n33
Famous Players, 55
Farewell Transmission (Rollo, 2017), 18, 177–9, 180
Feeney, John: Eskimo Artist: Kenojuak (1963), 201n11
Ferguson, Graeme, 196n34, 198n48; North of Superior (1971), 69
film, 103. See also video

Fisher, Jennifer, 41, 191n32
Fisher, Mark, 7–8, 25, 188n6
Flight Stop (Snow, 1979), 75–6
Flooding Job's Garden (Richardson, 1991), 82
Foldès, Peter: Metadata (1971), 76
Forde, Andrew, 211n22
Forsberg, Walter, 115; Fahrenheit 7-Eleven (2011), 209n33
found-footage filmmaking, 116, 203n1, 205n10. See also Death by Popcorn (L'Atelier national du Manitoba, 2005)
Four on the Floor (CBC, 1986), 200n4
Francis, Margot, 191n32
Freitag, Gina, 59–60
Friday the 13th (Cunningham, 1980), 83
The Friendly Giant (WHA-TV, 1953–58; CBC, 1958–85), 111–12
Frye, Northrop, 59–61

Gallant, Patsy: "From New York to L.A." (1976), 50
Gallpen, Britt, 152, 210n9
Garbage Hill (L'Atelier national du Manitoba, 2005), 124
Gaynor, Gloria: "I Will Survive" (1978), 49
Genette, Gérard, 37, 87, 190n29
George Sprott, 1894–1975 (Seth, 2006), 110–12, 203n27
Ghost Box (record label), 25
Gidal, Peter, 53
Gillmor, Allison, 208n21
Girard, François: Thirty-Two Short Films about Glenn Gould (1993), 155–6

Goon (Dowse, 2011), 128
Goon: The Last of the Enforcers (Baruchel, 2017), 128
Gosselin, Bernard: *Cesar's Bark Canoe* (1971), 165, 167
Gould, Glenn: fascination with voice, 155–6; *Solitude Trilogy* (1967–77), 146–7. See also *The Idea of North* (Gould, 1967)
Goussard, Bernard, 55
Grace, Sherrill: *Canada and the Idea of North* (2007), 210n10
graphic design, 26, 189n7
Graphic Standards Manual (CBC, 1974), 26, 203n24
Gray, Jonathan: *Show Sold Separately* (2010), 190n29
Gretzky, Wayne, 118, 120–1, 130–1
Gross Misconduct (Egoyan, 1993), 128–9
Group of Seven, 54, 193n5, 199n62
The Guess Who (band), 139
Guha, Malini, 174

Hall, Stuart, 24–5
Hanna, Erin, 92
Harper, Adam, 6, 187n5
The Hart of London (Chambers, 1970), 179, 194n14
hauntology, 7–8, 24–6, 28, 187n5, 188n6
Hawerchuk, Dale, 129–31
Henderson, Paul, 127
Hennessy, Kate, 155–6, 160
Highmore, Ben, 10
high school quiz show, 100, 102
High Steel (Owen, 1965), 167

Hilderbrand, Lucas, 123–4, 206n11
Hill, George Roy: *Slap Shot* (1977), 128
hinterland horror genre, 15, 65
Hinterland Who's Who (1963–78): affective tone, 33–4; beaver episode, 32–4; continued cultural residue, 23–4, 36, 52; formal consistency and defining characteristics, 30–2, 31; hauntology and nostalgia of, 24, 26–8; homemade parodies of, 47–8; introduction, 11, 14–15, 21–2, 28–9, 51–2; and *Lesbian National Parks and Services* (Dempsey and Millan, 1997–present), 41–4, 45, 191n32; loon calls in, 48–9, 50; and *Migration* (Rimmer, 1969), 74–5; on modernization, 30; and *The Nature of Things* (CBC, 1960–present), 197n45; and *Paperland: The Bureaucrat Observed* (Brittain, 1979), 35–6; and *Perception* (Adams, 2014), 44, 46–7; political message in, 33–5; production details, 29–30, 190n15; rediscovery of original shorts, 189n14; remediation of, 40–1; SCTV parody of, 38–40; sense of impending danger, 39–40, 50; and "So Lonely" (Soccio, 1979), 49–51; stylistic and tonal oddness, 22–3; theme tune as mnemonic cue, 26–8; *This Hour Has 22 Minutes* (CBC, 1993–present) parodies of, 40–1; title, 34–5; 2003 relaunch, 190n17; woodchuck episode, 39–40

Hobel Leiterman Productions Ltd, 190n15
hockey: films on, 127–9; video culture and, 131–2. See also *Death by Popcorn* (L'Atelier national du Manitoba, 2005)
Hogue, Tarah, 152, 160
Holdsworth, Amy, 27, 104
horror: eerie calm, 83–4; hinterland horror genre, 15, 65; influence on Doig, 83; *La Région Centrale* (Snow, 1971) and, 15, 58–9, 81; wilderness dread, 59–61, 80–1, 195n17
hydroelectricity, 81–3
Hydro-Lévesque (Rankin, 2007), 134–5

Ianzelo, Tony: *Cree Hunters of Mistassini* (with Richardson, 1974), 82, 165, 168, 214n45; *Our Land Is Our Life* (with Richardson, 1974), 82
The Idea of North (Davidson, 2005), 210n10
The Idea of North (Gould, 1967): Andrew Forde's musical remediation, 211n22; ARCTICNOISE's (Inutiq, 2015) engagement with, 147, 152, 155–8; comparison to *Tshiuetin* (Monnet, 2016), 210n5; contemporary influences of, 210n10; contrapuntal in, 154; fascination with voice, 155–6; introduction, 146–7; narrative conceit of, 149; nation building and settler colonialism aspects, 152–4, 158; political context, 154–5; soundtrack, 158; and *Spectres of Shortwave* (Christie, 2017), 181. See also ARCTICNOISE (Inutiq, 2015)
Igloliorte, Heather, 210n7; *Indigenous Art* (with Nagam and Taunton, 2016), 151–2
Igloolik Isuma, 148, 156–7
Indian-head test pattern, 203n27
Indian Memento (Régnier, 1967), 167
Indigene Audio (record label), 168, 212n28
Indigenous Archival Photo Project (Seesequasis, 2015–present): comparison to *The Making of an Archive* (Nguyễn, 2014–present), 215n56; comparison to Project Naming initiative (Library and Archives Canada, 2002–present), 215n51; introduction, 17–18, 169–70; online manifestations, 173–4; as reclamation of memory, 170–1; remediation as political act, 171–3, 175
Indigenous Art (Igloliorte, Nagam, and Taunton, 2016), 151–2
Indigenous peoples: and environmental and planetary issues, 66–7; as haunting hinterland horror films, 65; Inutiq on Indigenous identity and representation, 161–2; as invisible yet resurgent, 68–70; James Bay and Northern Quebec Agreement (1975), 82; in

La Région Centrale (Snow, 1971), 65–9; as living cultures, 159; new media art, 151–2; 1970s cultural memory and, 13; remediation by, 147–8, 163–4; residential schools, 163–4; restructuring of dominance over, 154–5. See also ARCTICNOISE (Inutiq, 2015); Barnaby, Jeff; *Indigenous Archival Photo Project* (Seesequasis, 2015–present); Inutiq, Geronimo; *Mobilize* (Monnet, 2015); Monkman, Kent; Monnet, Caroline
infrastructure, technological: Artifact Institute on, 184–6; *The Broken Altar* (Rollo, 2013) and, 177–8; *Farewell Transmission* (Rollo, 2017) and, 178–9; introduction, 176–7; *Spectres of Shortwave* (Christie, 2017) and, 179, 181–2, *183*, 184
Innu, 65, 210n5
In Search of Expo 67 (Musée d'art contemporain, Montreal, 2017), 212n31
Inuit and Inuit art, 151, 159, 210n7
Inutiq, Geronimo: DJ career, 158–9; *Dedications* (2008), 159; *Developments* (2008), 159; dub and, 162–3; *Dubyadubs* (2009), 161–3; *Ensemble/ Encore, Together/Again, Katimakainnarivugut* (2017), 212n31; Indigene Audio (record label), 168, 212n28; use of analogue media, 168–9; on voice in *The Idea of North* (Gould, 1967), 155–7. See also ARCTICNOISE (Inutiq, 2015)
Investigation 1 (Artifact Institute, 2009–14), 184
Investigation 2 (Artifact Institute, 2013), 184–5
Isaacson, Magnus: *Power* (1996), 82
ITV, 87, 107

Jacobs, Ken: *Perfect Film* (1986), 203n1
Jafa, Arthur, 163
James Bay and Northern Quebec Agreement (1975), 82
James Bay Cree Photographic Documentary (Legrady, 1972–73), 171–2
Jameson, Fredric, 9, 12
Janisse, Kier-La, 141
Jefferies, Richard: *After London, or Wild England* (1885), 64
Johnston, Wes, 184–5
Joy, Greg, 94

Kashmere, Brett: *Valery's Ankle* (2006), 127–8, 208n22, 208n26
Katz, Sam, 117
"Keep America Beautiful" ("Crying Indian" ad), 66, 72, 83
Kelly, Adam, 19, 184. See also Artifact Institute
Kharlamov, Valery, 127
Kids in the Hall (CBC/HBO, 1989–95), 200n4
Kiersch, Fritz, 94
King, Stephen: "Children of the Corn" (1977), 94

Koller, George Csaba, 62, 71, 75, 195n25
Kramer, Burton, 26, 38–9, 106
Kubasa in a Glass (L'Atelier national du Manitoba, 2006), 124
Kubrick, Stanley: *2001: A Space Odyssey* (1968), 62–3
Kunuk, Zacharias: *Atanarjuat: The Fast Runner* (2001), 148
Kwan, Vanessa, 215n56

Lambert, Evelyn, 201n13
landscape cinema. See *La Région Centrale* (Snow, 1971)
La part du diable (Bourdon, 2017), 13
L'Apocalypse des Animaux (Rossif, 1970), 75
La Région Centrale (Snow, 1971): Atwood on, 195n17; camera apparatus, 54, 56, 57, 65, 68–9, 72, 196n34, 199n60; Cold War and, 199n60; editing process and decisions, 56, 58, 61, 194n12; eerie calm of, 83–4; as environmental disaster film, 64–5, 70–2, 74, 76, 197n40; as experimental science fiction, 61–5; funding, 55; Group of Seven and, 54, 193n5; horror and, 15, 58–9, 81; hydro installations as haunting landscape, 81–3; on Indigenous land and colonialism, 65–9; inspiration for, 54–5; introduction, 4, 15, 53–4, 60–1, 84; location depicted in, 54–5, 73; lunar and space exploration aspects, 61–4; meteorological conditions and, 56, 70–1; 1970s periodization and, 11; and Parks Canada shorts and public service announcements, 78; as product of 1960s and 1970s, 60; shooting schedule, 55–6; soundtrack, 63, 71; and *Spectres of Shortwave* (Christie, 2017), 181; time capsule aspect, 71–2; title, 67–8, 195n25; viewing while high, 195n25; on YouTube, 79–80
L'Atelier national du Manitoba: archiveology and, 206n15; fascination with Burton Cummings, 139; *Garbage Hill* (2005), 124; "The Horizontalist Manifesto" (2005), 133, 209n28; *Kubasa in a Glass* (2006), 124; members, 115; Nagler on, 207n20; origins, 115, 123–4. See also *Death by Popcorn* (L'Atelier national du Manitoba, 2005)
Latimer, Michelle: *Nimmikaage (She Dances for People)* (2015), 164
Leacock, Stephen, 203n26
Legrady, George: "Before the flood: Four young men" (1973), 172–3; *James Bay Cree Photographic Documentary* (1972–73), 171–2
lens flare, 84
Lesbian National Parks and Services (Dempsey and Millan, 1997–present), 41–4, 45, 191n32
Les Dales Hawerchuk (band), 131
Library and Archives Canada: Project Naming initiative (2002–present), 215n51

Life on Mars (BBC, 2006–07), 104
Livingston, John, 197n45
Locke, John W., 53
Loft, Steven: *Coded Territories* (with Swanson, 2014), 151
Loiselle, André, 59–60
loon, 28, 48–51, 158, 192n40. *See also* birds
Los Angeles Plays Itself (Andersen, 2003), 113

Macfarlane, Daniel, 81
Mackey, Eva, 154
MacLatchy, Jennifer, 191n32
Maddin, Guy: *The Brian Sinclair Story* (2010), 68–9, 196nn32–3; comparison to L'Atelier national du Manitoba, 207n20; on *La Région Centrale*'s camera apparatus, 68–9; *My Winnipeg* (2008), 119–20, 130, 205n6; on Winnipeg Jets, 204n4; Winnipeg's film culture and, 126
The Making of an Archive (Nguyễn, 2014–present), 215n56
Manitoba, 132–5
Maryniuk, Mike, 115
The Mary Tyler Moore Show (CBS, 1970–77), 86
Math with Marty (Winnipeg TV show), 124
McCowan, George: *Face-Off* (1971), 113
McLaren, Norman, 55, 194n8; *A Chairy Tale* (1956), 106
melancholy: and disco, 49–50, 192n37
memory. *See* cultural memory
Metadata (Foldès, 1971), 76

metonymy, 27–8, 105
Michelson, Annette, 53, 61
Migration (Rimmer, 1969), 74–5
Millan, Lorri: *Lesbian National Parks and Services* (with Dempsey, 1997–present), 41–4, 45, 191n32; *Tableau Vivant: Eaton's Catalogue 1976* (with Dempsey, 1998), 191n33; *Transport* (with Dempsey, 2014), 191n33
Mills, Michael, 201n13
Mills-Cockell, John, 71, 197n36
Mitchell, Joni: "Big Yellow Taxi" (1970), 72; *Song to a Seagull* (1968), 197n44
mnemonic, 23–4, 27–8, 38, 105
Mobilize (Monnet, 2015): introduction, 17; remediation for showcasing Indigenous peoples, 164–5, 166, 167–8, 169; use of analogue media, 169
modernity, 30, 64, 167
Monkman, Kent, 147; *Sisters and Brothers* (2015), 164
Monnet, Caroline, 147; *Tshiuetin* (2016), 210n5. *See also Mobilize* (Monnet, 2015)
Montgomery, Marc, 181–2
Montreal Olympic Games (1976), 93–4, 201n12
Monty Python's Flying Circus (BBC 1969–74), 88–9
Morris, Robert: *Observatory* (1971), 60
Moser, Gabrielle, 215n56
Motion Picture Centre Ltd, 29, 190n15
A Movie (Conner, 1958), 95–6, 205n10
Mr. Dressup (CBC, 1967–96), 112

Mulroney, Brian, 26
Multiculturalism Act (1971), 154
Mutual of Omaha's Wild Kingdom (1963–88), 34
My Winnipeg (Maddin, 2008), 119–20, 130, 205n6

Nagam, Julie: *Indigenous Art* (with Igloliorte and Taunton, 2016), 151–2
Nagler, Solomon, 207n20
National Film Board (NFB): government realism of, 34; *Hinterland Who's Who* (1963–78) and, 14, 21, 29, 190n15; as inspiration for Boards of Canada (band), 6; shorts and public service announcements for Parks Canada, 61, 76, 77, 78–80, 83–4; *Souvenir* series (2015), 163–4
Native North America (Vol. 1) (Light in the Attic Records, 2014), 172
nature. *See* environment
The Nature of Things (CBC, 1960–present), 75, 197n45
Negativipeg (Rankin, 2011), 209n33
Nguyễn, Jacqueline Hoàng: *The Making of an Archive* (2014–present), 215n56
Nimmikaage (She Dances for People) (Latimer, 2015), 164
The Nine Muses (Akomfrah, 2011), 174
1967, 3
1970s: approach to, 3–4, 14, 19–20, 176, 186; hauntology and "the past inside the present," 5–8, 24–6, 28, 95; heterogenous associations within, 12; national, regional, and minority experiences, 13–14; nostalgia, 8–9; periodization and structure of feeling, 10–12, 24, 40, 49, 59, 84, 106, 146; residue of, 3–4, 116, 186; textual dimension of works from, 5. *See also* analogue media; cultural memory; infrastructure, technological; paratelevisual; remediation; video; *specific works*
Nineteen Eighty-Four (Radford, 1984), 117, 137
No Blade of Grass (Wilde, 1970), 72, 74
noise, 157–61
Northern Schooldays (NFB, 1958), 164
North of Superior (Ferguson, 1971), 69
nostalgia, 8–9, 26, 169–70
Nova Scotia College of Art and Design, 56, 194n12
Nurming-Por, Yasmin, 152, 210n9

Obomsawin, Alanis: *Amisk* (1977), 82
Observatory (Morris, 1971), 60
"O Canada" (national anthem): Lambert's animated take on, 201n13; Mills's animated take on, 201n13; for Montreal Olympics (1976), 93–4, 201n12; in SCTV sketch, 91–2; in *Sign-Off* (Bell, 2010), 95–6
O Canada #1: National Anthem: "With Glowing Hearts" (Remerowski, 1979), 93–6, 201n11
Olympic Games (Montreal, 1976), 93–4, 201n12

Our Land Is Our Life (Richardson and Ianzelo, 1974), 82
Owen, Don: *High Steel* (1965), 167

Paizs, John, 126, 207n20
Paperland: The Bureaucrat Observed (Brittain, 1979), 35–6
paracinematic, 37–8
paratelevisual: as cultural memory, 90–1, 95; Gray and, 190n29; introduction, 16, 37–8; metatelevisual play, 88–9; preservation by SCTV, 86–7, 95, 99, 104–5; video archive of, 98–9, 123
paratextual, 37
Parks Canada: shorts and public service announcements, 61, 76, 77, 78–80, 83–4
Pattie, David, 188n6
Pearlman, Judith, 146
Percé on the Rocks (Carle, 1964), 95
Perception (Adams, 2014), 44, 46–7
Perfect Film (Jacobs, 1986), 203n1
periodization, 10–12
Plus Tard (Snow, 1977), 193n5
poor image, 79–80, 198n55
Power (Isaacson, 1996), 82
Presents (Snow, 1982), 75
Project Naming initiative (Library and Archives Canada, 2002–present), 215n51
public service announcements, 29, 36–7, 47

Quebec, 13, 82, 132–5
quiz show: high school, 100, 102

racism, 13, 154. See also *Perception* (Adams, 2014); settler colonialism
Radford, Michael: *Nineteen Eighty-Four* (1984), 117, 137
radio: *Spectres of Shortwave* (Christie, 2017) on, 18–19, 179, 181–2, *183*, 184
Rankin, Matthew, 115, 131–2, 141, 143; *Hydro-Lévesque* (2007), 134–5; *Negativipeg* (2011), 209n33
Rayns, Tony, 53
Reach for the Top (CBC, 1965–85), 100, 102
redfacing, 161–2
Régnier, Michel: *Indian Memento* (1967), 167
Reitman, Ivan, 55
remediation: definitions, 147–8; extension of cultural shadow by, 40–1, 146; by Indigenous peoples, 147–8; in *Mobilize* (Monnet, 2015) to showcase Indigenous peoples, 164–5, *166*, 167–9; as political act, 173–5; in *Souvenir* series (NFB, 2015) to reveal colonial injustices, 163–4. See also ARCTICNOISE (Inutiq, 2015)
Remerowski, Ted: *O Canada #1: National Anthem: "With Glowing Hearts"* (1979), 93–6, 201n11
residential schools, 163–4
residual media, 36
Reynolds, Simon, 7, 25, 188n6
Rhymes for Young Ghouls (Barnaby, 2014), 214n41
Richardson, Boyce: *Cree Hunters of*

Mistassini (with Ianzelo, 1974), 82, 165, 168, 214n45; *Flooding Job's Garden* (1991), 82; *Our Land Is Our Life* (with Ianzelo, 1974), 82
Rifkind, Candida, 111–12
Rilla, Wolf: *Village of the Damned* (1960), 94
Rimmer, David: *Migration* (1969), 74–5
Rituals (Carter, 1977), 80–1, 84
Roach, Jay: *Austin Powers in Goldmember* (2002), 103
Rob What? (Vermette, 2015), 141
Rollo, Mike: *The Broken Altar* (2013), 18, 177–8; *Farewell Transmission* (2017), 18, 177–9, *180*
Rosenbaum, Jonathan, 198n48
Rossif, Frédéric: *L'Apocalypse des Animaux* (1970), 75
Russell, Catherine, 165, 206n15

Said, Edward, 211n14
Sainte-Marie, Buffy, 69; "Moonshot" (1972), 66–7
Sandilands, Catriona, 191n32
Sandison, Michael, 5. *See also* Boards of Canada (band)
Saturday Night Live (NBC, 1975–present), 85, 89
Schafer, R. Murray, 51, 192n40; *Music for Wilderness Lake* (1979), 192n40; *The Soundscape* (1977), 192n40
science fiction: and *La Région Centrale* (Snow, 1971), 61–5
Sconce, Jeffrey, 37
Scribner, Charity: *Requiem for Communism* (2003), 19

SCTV (1976–84): ad parodies, 109–10; as archive of disappearing television forms, 99–100, 102–7; *Benny Hill Street Blues* sketch, 114; comparison to *Death by Popcorn* (L'Atelier national du Manitoba, 2005), 124; contemporary access to, 96, 98, 201n7; critique of CRTC policy, 92; Dunne on, 200n2; episode numbering practices, 200n3; filming on location as record of place, 112–13; *High Q* high school quiz show parody, 100, *101*, 102, 202n18; *Hinterland Who's Who* parody, 38–40; as history of televisual flow, 88–93, 95, 98–9, 105–7; Indian-head test pattern parody, 203n27; introduction, 4, 11, 15–16, 85–8; as juxtaposition of British and American influences, 113–14; K-Tel parodies, 105; lack of geographic specificity, 113–14; Melonville-focused shows, 108–9; national anthem parody, 91–3; opening credit sequence, 88, 200n3; other Canadian television comedy and, 200n4; paratelevisual preservation, 86–7, 95, 99, 104–5; production locations, 107; as record of local place, 107–10, 203n26; satiric approach of, 38; sitcom format, 86; "The Great White North" segments, 92; "Walter Cronkite's Brain" episode, 99

seagull, 74–5, 197n44, 197n46. *See also* birds
The Second City (theatre), 86, 107
Seesequasis, Paul, 147. See also *Indigenous Archival Photo Project* (Seesequasis, 2015–present)
Séguin, Sylvain, 131–2, 143, *144*
Selanne, Teemu, 129, 133–4, 136
sentimentality, 47
Seth: *George Sprott, 1894–1975* (2006), 110–12, 203n27
settler colonialism: dub and, 162–3; as haunting presence in 1970s film, 65; in *The Idea of North* (Gould, 1967), 152–4, 158; perpetuation by cultural memory, 13
Sexton, Jamie, 188n6
Shelley, Mary: *The Last Man* (1826), 64
Shenkarow, Barry, 143
Sherburne, Philip, 51
Shout Factory, 98
Sibelius, Jean: *Symphony No. 5* (1915), 158
Sign-Off (Bell, 2010), 95–6, 97
sign-on/sign-off television, 90–1, 93
Silent Running (Trumbull, 1972), 71
Silver, Jim, 204n5
Simon, Bill, 54
Sisters and Brothers (Monkman, 2015), 164
Sitney, P. Adams, 54
Slap Shot (Hill, 1977), 128
Sloan, Johanne, 84, 193n5, 199n62, 207n18
Smith, Iain Robert, 206n11
Smith, Trudi-Lynn, 160
Smithson, Robert: *Spiral Jetty* (1970), 60

Snow, Michael: on birds, 75–6, 198n48; *Breakfast (Table-Top Dolly)* (1972–76), 75; *Flight Stop* (1979), 75–6; *Plus Tard* (1977), 193n5; *Presents* (1982), 75. See also *La Région Centrale* (Snow, 1971); SCTV (1976–84)
Soccio, Gino: "Dancer" (1979), 49; "So Lonely" (1979), 49–51
Solaris (Tarkovsky, 1972), 63
Solitude Trilogy (Gould, 1967–77), 146–7. See also *The Idea of North* (Gould, 1967)
"So Lonely" (Soccio, 1979), 49–51
sonic pollution, 192n40
Souvenir series (NFB, 2015), 163
Spectres of Shortwave (Christie, 2017), 18–19, 179, 181–2, *183*, 184
Spiral Jetty (Smithson, 1970), 60
Stanton, Andrew: WALL-E (2008), 65
Steen, Thomas, 129, 137, 139, 209n31
Sterne, Jonathan, 206n11
Stewart, Michelle, 214n45
Steyerl, Hito, 198n55
Straw, Will: "Embedded Memories" (2007), 41, 103, 122–3, 206n11
structure of feeling, 4, 10–11, 24, 105
Sueño Latino: "Sueño Latino" (1989), 51
Summit Series (1972), 127–8, 208n22
Survival (Winnipeg TV show, 1982–87), 135–6
Swanson, Kerry: *Coded Territories* (with Loft, 2014), 151

Tableau Vivant: Eaton's Catalogue 1976 (Dempsey and Millan, 1998), 191n33

Tagaq, Tanya: "Tulugak" (2014), 163; "Uja" (2014), 165
Tarkovsky, Andrei: *Solaris* (1972), 63
Taunton, Carla: *Indigenous Art* (with Igloliorte and Nagam, 2016), 151–2
technology. *See* analogue media; infrastructure, technological; video
television: cultural memory and, 27; formal sign-on and sign-off, 90–1, 93; nature mediated by, 22; planned flow, 89–90; public service announcements, 29, 36–7, 47; video archive of, 96, 98, 123, 207n17; Williams on, 89. *See also* paratelevisual; video
Testa, Bart, 54
Thatcherism, 24
That Was the Week That Was (BBC, 1962–63), 88
Thirty-Two Short Films about Glenn Gould (Girard, 1993), 155–6
This Hour Has Seven Days (CBC, 1964–66), 88
This Hour Has 22 Minutes (CBC, 1993–present), 40–1, 200n4
Thomson, Tom, 199n62
time capsules, 71–2, 87
The Tommy Hunter Show (CBC, 1965–92), 111
transmitter stations: *Farewell Transmission* (Rollo, 2017) on, 18, 178–9, *180*
Transport (Dempsey and Millan, 2014), 191n33
Trebek, Alex, 100

Tribbe, Matthew D., 67
A Tribe Called Red: "The Road" (2013), 164; "We Are the Halluci Nation" music video (2016), 69–70
Tribulations 99 (Baldwin, 1991), 205n10
Trudeau, Justin, 25–6
Trudeau, Pierre Elliott, 26, 50
True-Life Adventures (Disney, c. 1948–60), 33–4
Trumbull, Douglas: *Silent Running* (1972), 71
Tshiuetin (Monnet, 2016), 210n5
turions, cheyanne, 212n30
2bears, Jackson, 213n33
2001: A Space Odyssey (Kubrick, 1968), 62–3

The Unfinished Conversation (Akomfrah, 2012), 149, 151
United Kingdom, 24–5, 51, 199n61
University Challenge (ITV, 1962–87; BBC2, 1997–present), 102

Valery's Ankle (Kashmere, 2006), 127–8, 208n22, 208n26
Vallée, Jean-Marc: *C.R.A.Z.Y.* (2005), 13
Vallee, Mickey, 152–4
VanderBurgh, Jennifer, 96, 98, 202n15
Vatnsdal, Caelum, 80
Veal, Michael E., 162
Vermette, Rhayne: *Rob What?* (2015), 141
vernacular moving image library, 123
Vertigo Sea (Akomfrah, 2016), 149, 151

video: aesthetic dimension of, 5, 122, 126–8; cultural memory and, 103, 116–17, 122–3, 126–8; in music and sports cultures, 131, 208n24; as television archive, 96, 98, 123, 207n17; video era, 122–4
Videodrome (Cronenberg, 1983), 203n25
Vilar, Rob, 141, *142*
Village of the Damned (Rilla, 1960), 94
Vogel, Vic, 201n12; "O Canada" arrangement, 93–4
von Däniken, Erich: *Chariots of the Gods?* (1968), 62
Voyager 1 and *Voyager 2* spacecrafts, 72

WALL-E (Stanton, 2008), 65
Wark, Jayne, 191n32
Wayne and Shuster (CBC, 1954–85), 200n4
Weakerthans: *Left and Leaving* (2000), 136–7
Wees, William C., 54, 63, 203n1
Welch, Mary Agnes, 209n31
Werren, Phil, 75
White, Kenneth, 56, 199n60
Who's Who (reference publication), 35
Wieland, Joyce, 55–6, 68
Wilde, Cornel: *No Blade of Grass* (1970), 72, 74
Wild Kingdom (NBC, 1963–71), 75
wildlife films, 33–4. See also *Hinterland Who's Who* (1963–78)
Williams, Raymond, 4, 10–11, 89, 105
Winnipeg, 126, 136, 205n6. See also *Death by Popcorn* (L'Atelier national du Manitoba, 2005)
Winnipeg Babysitter (Winnipeg Film Group, 2009), 207n18, 208n21
Winnipeg Film Group, 126, 207n18
Winnipeg Jets, 117–20, 130, 204nn4–5. See also *Death by Popcorn* (L'Atelier national du Manitoba, 2005)
WKRP in Cincinnati (CBS, 1978–82), 86

Young, Neil, 15
YouTube: *Hinterland Who's Who* parodies on, 47–8; as repository for old television clips, 23, 96, 98, 123; "retro" channels, 26, 202n16; VHS culture and, 208n24
YouTube: *La Région Centrale* (Snow, 1971) on, 79–80

Zryd, Michael, 205n10